Introduction to Computer Game Programming with DirectX 8.0

D1567616

Ian Parberry, Ph.D.

Wordware Publishing, Inc.

Library of Congress Cataloging-in-Publication Data

Parberry, Ian
    Introduction to computer game programming with directX 8.0 / by Ian Parberry.
      p. cm.
    Includes index.
    ISBN 1-55622-810-4 (pbk.)
    1. Computer games--Programming.   2. DirectX.   I. Title.

    QA76.76.C672 P35   2001
    794.8'167768--dc21   2001017801
                                             CIP

ISBN 1-55622-810-4
10 9 8 7 6 5 4 3
0101

All inquiries for volume purchases of this book should be addressed to Wordware Publishing, Inc., at the above
address. Telephone inquiries may be made by calling:

(972) 423-0090

Contents

Contents

Contents

Foreword

So, you want to be a game programmer? But how do you get that first gig?

First, you will need a concise and relevant resume listing, along with education and experience, any (repeat any) and all computer skills that are not from the Land That Time Forgot. Next, code samples are an absolute must; approximately three pages of very clean, well-commented code. Finally, you'll need a game demo. Game companies want to know that not only can you cut code, but that you have a passion for games. So dedicated are you to the making of games, that you would program your own game just out of sheer love for the industry. It doesn't matter if the game is a pixelated mess; just show that you made the effort and you have the passion. This goes a long way. Ask around. You'll find that most folks in this biz are not here for the money.

It is essential that you know the right tools for the job, but even more important that you learn those tools by doing a real-world application. To get a programming job in this burgeoning industry, you'll need to know the most common programming tools utilized by the industry. Enter DirectX. Enter *Introduction to Computer Game Programming with DirectX 8.0* by Dr. Ian Parberry.

There are plenty of programming courses out there, but rare is the one that actually prepares budding software engineers for what it takes to land a job in the gaming industry. Dr. Parberry's smart and innovative program at the University of North Texas is that rare course. Wisely teaming computer science students with computer graphic art students to create a real game demo, Dr. Parberry's unique program provides the skills necessary for a future job.

Now, Dr. Parberry brings his teaching style and expertise out of the classroom and directly to you. If you are serious about doing all that you can to gain entrance into the wonderful world of game programming, then Ian Parberry's *Introduction to Computer Game Programming with DirectX 8.0* is a must read.

Melanie Cambron, Game Recruiting Goddess
Virtual Search
www.vsearch.com

Preface

I am constantly amazed by the politeness of students in Texas. Not one of the students in my game programming classes has ever, in seven years, asked me the obvious question, which is "Who are you, and what makes you think that you know anything about game programming?" with its equally obvious corollary, "If you're so good, why aren't you out in the game industry earning the Big Bucks?" The answers to those questions apply to you, the reader, too. Why should you buy a book on game programming from just anybody?

Before I answer, let me digress and tell you how I got into game programming. In 1993 I was going through what in academic circles passes for a midlife crisis. In the business world, the recognized panacea for men who go through midlife crises usually involves a red sports car and a young trophy wife. In academia we rarely have enough money or panache for the red sports car and the trophy wife, but we have coping strategies of our own.

Part of the typical midlife crisis involves questioning who we are and what we are doing in life. The academic midlife crisis sometimes involves questioning the validity of the typical academic lifestyle, which for a computer scientist like myself involves doing research, publishing the results of that research in scientific journals, and getting grants from federal funding agencies to do more research. Oh, and we teach too.

I had a lot of experience doing all of the above. But that "Oh, and we teach too" attitude was beginning to bother me. And the rising pace of the computer industry, the way it was beginning to transform the economy and *everything* about modern life was beginning to bother me. Actually, it was more the fact that computer science as taught at universities just *didn't get it*, and our students *knew* that it didn't get it. We were beginning to see entering college the crest of what was once called the *Nintendo generation*, the generation of kids for whom computers were a normal fixture of everyday life, as much as a microwave oven or a CD player was to the previous generation. This generation thinks nothing of reformatting their hard drive and installing a new operating system, a process that is *still* beyond the reach of many Ph.D.-bearing professors of computer science. And yet computer science in college was—and mostly still is—being taught much the way it was taught in the 1970s. The excuse that most academics give is that we are teaching "fundamentals," and leaving the cutting-edge aspects of computer science to on-the-job training. "Give them a firm foundation of fundamentals," they say, "and the students will be able to learn the tools they need to get a job."

During my midlife crisis, I underwent what is euphemistically called a *paradigm shift*. I changed from being a card-carrying theoretician who always quoted the party line on college education, to holding the following belief. While I agree that students need a firm grasp of the fundamentals of computer science, I believe that it is *now no longer enough*. The tools of the trade that they will be using on the job have become too large, too sophisticated, and there are just too many of them to leave it all to "on-the-job training" (making it Somebody Else's Problem) after college. Students have the right to training in fundamentals, and to have those fundamentals illustrated on at least one real-world application using the exact same tools and techniques that they will be using in their first job, weeks or days after they graduate.

This poses a challenge for academia. The tools that programmers use change too quickly. Academics don't like to change what they teach, and for good reason. State legislators seem to believe that the average academic is basically lazy, so we are allowed very little time for the preparation of new material. Developing new classes takes time. Computer science professors are typically burned by this already—they must revamp most of their classes every few years. The prospect of doing this *every semester* is frightening.

Nonetheless, I was coming to the conclusion that *some* of us need to do it. We owe it to our students. I was (and still am) under no illusion that I can change academia by talking and writing papers about the phenomenon. Instead, I chose to lead by example—I would just go ahead and do it. After all, I have tenure, and the concept of *academic freedom*, the freedom of a professor to develop his or her own vision of education, is strong at the University of North Texas.

The question was, what area of computer science should I apply my grandiose scheme to? There are just too many areas to choose from. It should be something new and different, something that captures the imagination of students, territory that is largely untrodden by academic feet. One evening, with these kinds of thoughts on my mind I walked by the General Access Computer Lab on my way out of the building and noticed that the usual group of students playing games was absent. Instead, there was a sign on the wall saying something like "The Playing of Games in the General Access Lab is Banned." This kind of "Dilbert Decision" is one that always annoys me—a rule made by administrators to make their lives easy. The desired result is to make sure that students don't play games when other students are waiting in line for computers to finish their homework assignments, but it is so much easier to ban games altogether than to constantly have to confront students who either by accident or design continue playing into busy periods.

This dislike of arbitrary rules and a general feeling of restlessness drove me to talk to some of these students who seemed addicted to games. After a few minutes' conversation, I quickly learned that, more than playing games, these students wanted to *write their own games*. The problem was, in 1993 there was almost no published material on game programming—almost no books, and no information on the fledgling World Wide Web. That was a *"Eureka!"* moment for me. I had found my niche. With hubris typical of a theoretician, I signed up to teach an experimental course on game programming, with the idea that the students would help me research the area and we would learn together. The course was a wild success, and the rest, as they say, is history. The class became more formal, got its own course code, and now my game laboratory is recognized as one of the premier places in the country to learn game programming.

Since then, I have written and published several games and trained hundreds of students in game programming, the very best of whom have gone on to become successful game programmers in major corporations. I have over 16 years of experience as a professor, and seven years of experience in teaching game programming. I know how to teach a class, and I know how to structure a book so that people can actually learn from it. That's who I am, and what makes me think I can write a book on game programming.

As for making Big Bucks, I am doing OK without becoming a full-time member of the computer game industry. The salary for a full professor of computer science at the University of North Texas is pretty good for a non-flagship state university —my salary for the 2000-2001 academic year is within 8% of the national average for my rank. Still, with the money I make writing games and other cool Windows apps in the three-month summer break, I make a salary that is every bit as good as most of my colleagues in industry. And it would take a great deal of money to replace the *buzz* I get from what I do.

Acknowledgments

I would like to take this opportunity to thank the talented team of people who worked on this book with me. Although I wrote the text and the code, I had a *lot* of help.

I owe a great debt to Keith Smiley, who designed and created the incredible artwork in *Ned's Turkey Farm*. Good artwork can make the difference between a lame game and a cool one, and Keith's artwork is *excellent*. I would also like to thank Steve Wilson and his wife, Mikayla, for the voice-overs that you will hear once you get to Demo 8 (Chapter 10). Steve also acted as sound engineer on that project, a service he has performed for me on many occasions. (No, they don't normally sound like that.)

My thanks goes to Paul Bleisch, a graphics developer who has worked with graphics hardware vendors and game development companies, for checking the manuscript of this book for technical accuracy. His diligence saved me from several *faux pas* and improved the quality of my material substantially. Thanks also to Virginia Holt, a technical writer who read the manuscript for pedagogical soundness. Her suggestions helped make the manuscript a lot more readable than it otherwise would have been.

I am very grateful to Melanie Cambron, the Game Recruiting Goddess from Virtual Search, for writing the foreword to this book. I have been fortunate to have Melanie as a regular guest speaker in my game programming class at the University of North Texas for several years. For some reason, my students will accept what she says about getting a job in the game industry more readily than they will accept what I say. (Go figure.)

I also need to thank a select group of administrators at the University of North Texas: chancellor Dr. Albert Hurley; former provost Blaine Brownell; the former and current dean of the College of Arts and Sciences, Nora Bell and Warren Burggren, respectively; and the former and current chair of the Computer Sciences Department, Paul Fisher and Tom Jacob, respectively. Their support has enabled me to establish and operate my game laboratory and my game programming classes in the face of vocal opposition from many of my colleagues, some of which continues today. Although my activities have generated more than their fair share of controversy, I am privileged to work in an institution of higher education whose administrators are visionary and tolerant of intellectual diversity, and are more protective of academic freedom than many of its faculty. Without the time and facilities to develop my laboratory and my courses, this book would never have been written.

Finally, I should thank generations of my students for poking and prodding at my code until it was halfway decent enough to publish.

To everybody, thank you.

Introduction to Computer Game Programming with DirectX 8.0

Chapter 1

Here's what you'll learn:

- What this book is all about

- What background knowledge you need

- What DirectX is all about

- How to take best advantage of this book

- How to install the stuff on the CD

- How to set up the Visual C++ 6.0 compiler so you can begin

Read This First

Have I got your attention yet? "Read this First" reminds me of the purchase of my first home computer in the 1980s. It came with no less than seven documents that said "Read This First" in big bold letters at the top of the page and they all threatened dire consequences if I failed to do the things listed on that particular piece of paper *first*. I did my best to follow the instructions, but bad things happened anyway. I suspect that bad things would have happened no matter *what I did*.

Such is *not* the case for this book. Browsing this chapter will, however, help you to get started on the right foot.

Does This Look Familiar?

This book is a short, inexpensive version of the author's book *Learn Computer Game Programming with DirectX 7.0*. If you already own that book, then *don't* buy this one. The difference between that book and this is that:

- This book does not contain Chapters 13-15.
- This book does not have the code listings at the end of each chapter. Instead, they are included in a pdf supplement on the companion CD.
- This book has three new appendices. (Owners of *Learn Computer Game Programming with DirectX 7.0* can, if they wish, get them online from http://larc.csci.unt.edu/book/updates.html.)
- This book includes the recently released DirectX 8.0 SDK on the CD instead of the DirectX 7.0a SDK.

Are You Reading This in the Bookstore?

Are you reading this while standing in the bookstore trying to decide whether to buy this book? If you are, then this section is written just for you. Sit on the floor for a few minutes while I explain what it's all about and how purchasing this book can help you get your start in the computer game industry. If you are in one of those wonderful bookstores that have plush chairs and actually *encourage* you to sit and browse through the books, you may as well make yourself comfortable instead of skulking in the aisles getting in the way of other customers. A cup of coffee might go down well too. My writing style is highly caffeinated. Just don't spill any on the pages.

I assume that you picked up this book and opened it because you are an aspiring game programmer and the title looked appealing, not because you are male and "Melanie Cambron, Game Recruiting Goddess" sounded attractive. Well, maybe a little of both. Let me tell you right now that she is intelligent and very good at what she does, which is find employees for game companies. If you haven't read her foreword already, I recommend that you do it *right now*. It contains sensible advice about getting started in the game industry, *and* a picture of Melanie. Have you done it yet? Good. Now that we've satisfied our curiosity, let's take a more serious look at what this book has to offer.

First, let me tell you what this book is *not*.

Most DirectX books fall into two categories. Some attempt an encyclopedic coverage of the DirectX API, describing all of the possible permutations of all of the awesome and confusing choices of parameters of almost every DirectX function. You can spot those books by their huge tables listing functions and parameters—tables that often look as if they were cut-and-pasted directly from the DirectX documentation. This book is *not* like that. It assumes that you are smart enough to look up parameters yourself using the DirectX online help.

The second category of DirectX books gives you a monolithic game engine, essentially a wrapper for the DirectX API, that you can use to make a game of your own. They plunk this huge piece of code "thunk" on the table, and then explain how to go about making it work for *you*. It is usually a piece of code that attempts to be all things to all people, and even though it contains more than you need to know to get started, it may not end up being exactly what you need. This book is *not* like that. It assumes that you want to write your own code from the ground up, not customize somebody else's engine.

There is nothing wrong with either of these approaches. I have both kinds of books on my bookshelf. The approach that I take in this book, however, is different. It is the product of seven years of teaching game programming to students of computer science at the University of North Texas. Typically, those students are smart enough to read the documentation that comes with the DirectX SDK, and smart enough to experiment with the code samples. The problem is, all that information is fragmentary and overwhelming in its complexity. There's just so much information that it's hard to know where to begin.

That's where my class comes in. I teach using a series of game demos for a side-scroller called *Ned's Turkey Farm*. Each demo adds a new feature or set of features onto the previous one, much as a real game is developed. Thus, the class is as much about the *process* of coding a game as it is about DirectX.

This book is designed to give you a taste of the same experience without having to come to Texas. Admittedly, you lose out on the other things that my class would give you—including the experience of hanging out in my lab and the opportunity to work on a game demo in a group with other programming and art students, but there's not much I can do about that. I will go through the code function by function, line by line, explaining what I am doing and why I am doing it. There's nothing cut-and-pasted from the DirectX documentation, and I won't ever assume that you are a dummy or an idiot. If this sounds good to you, then go ahead and buy this book.

What You Need to Know

There are a few things that you need to know before using this book. First, you need to be a competent C++ programmer. If you know C but not C++ yet, you will need to brush up on a few C++ tricks, including the following:

- Classes, with private and public member variables and functions
- Derived classes, protected members
- Function overloading
- Virtual functions
- The operators `new` and `delete`
- Call-by-reference parameters
- Default values for parameters in functions
- Conditional assignment using the `?` operator

You should be familiar with elementary data structures such as arrays, lists, structures, and pointers. You also need to be familiar with at least one C++ compiler under Windows. The code in this book was developed under Visual C++ 5.0 and 6.0, and I'll be giving instructions for how to compile *Ned's Turkey Farm* using Visual C++ 6.0 later in this chapter.

You don't need to learn Windows API programming to be able to use this book. I will give you enough insight into it to get started. However, it wouldn't hurt to get more information about it from other sources.

DirectX: Who, What, Where, When, How, and Why?

Before we get down to business, let's take a quick look at the who, what, where, when, how, and why of DirectX.

The Who

Who developed DirectX? Microsoft, of course. And who is using it? Almost every company in the business of producing PC games.

The What

What is this thing called DirectX? DirectX is what Microsoft calls an API, an *application programming interface*. It consists of a collection of libraries that you compile into your game. Developers use what is called the DirectX SDK, another acronym which stands for *software developer's kit*. DirectX is an API that allows the programmer direct access to the computer's hardware instead of going through the many layers of slow and clunky Windows API. It consists of many parts. We will be using two of them in this book: DirectDraw (which allows direct access to the graphics hardware) and DirectSound (which allows direct access to the sound hardware). Also of interest to the game developer but beyond the scope of this book are DirectInput (which allows direct access to the input hardware) and DirectPlay (which allows direct access to the networking hardware).

The Where

Where do you get it? Microsoft has always distributed the DirectX SDK free of charge so that game developers will be encouraged to use it. Sometimes it can be downloaded from the Microsoft web page, although they have been known to discontinue downloading when traffic gets too high. If you don't have access to a fast connection to the Internet, you can purchase a CD from their web site for about the price of the media and shipping. Fortunately for you, the DirectX 8.0 SDK is included on the CD at the end of this book.

The When

When was it created? The DirectX SDK has a long history, but the most powerful thing about it is that it is constantly updated and improved. The updates often come out several times per year, so odds are that version 8.0 of the SDK will be out of date by the time you read this. However, the two parts of DirectX that we need for this book, DirectDraw and DirectSound, are relatively stable. I don't expect them to change much in the next few years. To forestall any fears that you may have about compiling the code from this book under later versions of DirectX, I will maintain a web site containing updates and supplements to this book,

including exactly this type of information, at
`http://larc.csci.unt.edu/book2/updates.html`.

The How

How do you use DirectX? Well, that's a large enough subject for a book—or several of them. Funny about that. Read on, MacDuff. (And damn'd be him that first cries, "Hold, enough!")

The Why

Why use DirectX? Because it's important to know about it if you want a job in the game industry, since it's the API that most game companies use. There are other graphics APIs in use, such as Glide and OpenGL, but DirectX is currently the most popular.

Why develop games for Windows? Because it is a large market, and one that is cheap and easy to get into. The Mac and Linux markets are smaller, and the console market usually requires proprietary and expensive hardware and software—and DirectX is now moving into consoles too.

How to Use This Book

Each chapter of this book describes the code to a game demo that was built out of the code from the previous chapter. Here's how to get the most out of this experience. Every chapter begins with a section called "Experiment with Demo xx." It invites you to play with the demo for that chapter, and directs you to experiment with and observe the relevant features. You can go to the `Experiment` folder in the *Ned's Turkey Farm* software installed from the CD and run the demo by double-clicking on the appropriate icon, for example, `Demo00.exe` for Demo 0.

At the end of each chapter you will find a section that lists the code files for the chapter's demo, describing which files are reused from the previous demo, which files have been updated, and which files are new. Pay close attention to the list of required library files. If you don't list these in the list of library files that the compiler keeps for your project, you will get linker errors when you try to compile. See the later section titled "The Linker Settings" for instructions on how to do this with Visual C++ 6.0.

The `pdf` supplement on the CD contains a series of code listings for the new and modified files in each chapter (although a long file may not be listed if the changes involve only a few lines of code). The body of the chapter will proceed methodically through the code, describing the changes and the new code in detail. The descriptions in the chapter will proceed in a logical order, whereas the file listings in the `pdf` supplement are in alphabetical order so that you can navigate amongst them more easily (in the one departure from strict alphabetical ordering, each header file has been printed before the corresponding code file to aid comprehension).

Code that has changed or been added since the previous demo will be high-lighted in the `pdf` supplement in red. It is important that you refer to the code listings frequently as you read through the chapter text so that you can see the changes *in the context of the existing code*. I suggest that you do this by reading this book in front of your computer while referring to the code listings in the `pdf` sup-plement. (See the section titled "Using the Companion CD" for instructions on how to install the CD contents and how to access the `pdf` supplement.)

Using the Companion CD

When you install *Ned's Turkey Farm* from the companion CD, it will by default cre-ate a folder named `Ned's Turkey Farm` on the root of your primary drive. You may, during the setup process, direct it to install *Ned's Turkey Farm* into a different folder. However, we will assume in the rest of this chapter that you used the default location. Inside the `Ned's Turkey Farm` folder you will find the follow-ing folders, as depicted in Figure 1.1.

- `Demo00` to `Demo10`: Each of these folders contains one of the demos described in this book. It consists of the complete code, header, image, and sound files for the demo. Each demo corresponds to a chapter. Demo 0 is described in Chapter 2, Demo 1 is described in Chapter 3, etc. Demos 4a and 4b are described in Appendixes B and C.

- `Experiment`: This folder contains the executables for Demos 0 through 10 and a copy of all of the image and sound files. This is where you should come to experiment with each of the demos to see what it does (you are asked to do this at the start of each chapter).

- `Pdf`: This folder contains the code listings supplement to this book in Adobe `pdf` file format. To view it, open the `Pdf` folder and double-click on `index.html`. This will open the index file using your default web browser. There, you will find instructions on how to obtain a free `pdf` file viewer from the web, links to the code listings for each of the chapters in `pdf` format, and some useful web links for more information relating to this book.

- `Sound Test`: This folder contains some extra sound samples that will be used to illustrate some of the sound quality issues discussed in Chapter 10.

The *Ned's Turkey Farm* setup program will also place some new entries into your Start menu. To access them, click on the Start button, then select Programs, then Ned's Turkey Farm (see Figure 1.2). You will then see the following options.

- Code: Selecting this will pop up a submenu with 13 items, named Demo 00 through Demo 10. Selecting Demo 00, for example, will open an Explorer window on the C:\Ned's Turkey Farm\Demo00 folder so that you can browse the Demo 0 code files.

- Code Listings: Selecting this will open the pdf supplement containing the code listings from each chapter.

- Demos: Selecting this will pop up a submenu with 13 items, named Demo 00 through Demo 10. Selecting Demo 00, for example, will run Demo 0.

- Sound Test: Selecting this will open an Explorer window on the C:\Ned's Turkey Farm\Sound Test folder, which is used in Chapter 10.

- Uninstall: Selecting this will open a maintenance window that will allow you to install or uninstall selected components of *Ned's Turkey Farm*, to reinstall it, or to uninstall it completely. You can also uninstall *Ned's Turkey Farm* using the Add/Remove Programs control in the Control Panel.

Figure 1.1
Folders installed from the companion CD

Figure 1.2
The Start menu items for Ned's Turkey Farm

Installing Ned's Turkey Farm

If Autorun is enabled on your computer, simply inserting the CD from this book into your CD-ROM drive will start the *Ned's Turkey Farm* setup. Otherwise, open the CD-ROM drive with the Explorer and double-click on the `Setup.exe` icon. Simply follow the instructions that appear. During the installation, you will be asked to choose from three different setup types.

- Typical: This setup type will install everything, as shown in Figure 1.1.

- Compact: This setup type will install only the executables and media files. In the `C:\Ned's Turkey Farm` folder you will get only the `Experiment` and `Sound Test` folders shown in Figure 1.1, but neither the code files nor the `pdf` supplement. Use this setup type if you plan to run the demos and the sound test in later chapters but do not wish to either compile the code, nor use the `pdf` supplement.

- Custom: This setup type will let you pick exactly which components you want installed. You can install all of the code, or just a few demos. You can also choose whether or not to install the executables and the `pdf` supplement. If you change your mind later, you can adjust your installation by selecting Uninstall from the Start menu.

Installing the DirectX 8.0 SDK

The last dialog box of the *Ned's Turkey Farm* setup has a check box for installing the DirectX 8.0 SDK (see Figure 1.3). Clicking on the Finish button with that check box checked will begin the installation of the DirectX 8.0 SDK. Should you choose not to install it at this time, you can install it later by opening the `Dx8sdk` folder on the CD-ROM and double-clicking on the `Setup.exe` icon.

Figure 1.3
Installing the DirectX 8.0 SDK from the Ned's Turkey Farm setup

The rest of this chapter assumes that the DirectX 8.0 SDK has been installed to the default location `C:\mssdk`. If Microsoft changes this default location in later versions of the SDK or you chose to install it in a different location, then you'll just have to wing it.

Some important folders that you'll want to explore after installing the DirectX 8.0 SDK include:

◉ `C:\mssdk\doc\DirectX8` contains the help file `directx8_c.chm`. To view this, you will need Internet Explorer 5.0 or higher. I use this so often that I have a shortcut to it on my desktop. You should use it rather than the help file that comes with your compiler because it contains more up-to-date information.

◉ `C:\mssdk\samples\Multimedia` contains some sample DirectX programs.

Setting up Visual C++ 6.0

Although I assume that you are familiar with using the Visual C++ 6.0 compiler, let me take a few moments to describe how to set it up for use with the code for *Ned's Turkey Farm*. If you are using a different compiler, the details of the setup process will be different, but the issues will be the same. Setup for Visual C++ 5.0 is almost identical, but the exact sequence of dialog boxes will be slightly different. You may also see slightly different menus and dialog boxes depending on which edition of Visual C++ 6.0 you have installed.

Setting the Include and Library Directories

When you install Visual C++ it will come with an old version of the header and library files for DirectX. Naturally, you will want to use the latest version of DirectX, not the one that shipped with your compiler. The following description assumes that you have installed the latest version of the DirectX SDK, which at the time of writing is 8.0. If you haven't already done so, refer to the previous section for instructions on installing the SDK from the CD that comes with this book. I do recommend, however, that you use the latest version of the SDK that you can find. Information about updates can be found on a web page maintained by the author at `http://larc.csci.unt.edu/book2/updates.html`.

The first thing that you will need to do is to add the folders from the new SDK to the list of folders from which the compiler gets headers and library files. Select Options from the Tools menu of Visual C++ 6.0, as shown in Figure 1.4. This will display the Options dialog box, from which you should select the Directories tab. Select Include Files from the drop-down menu at upper right. Enter the new folder `c:\mssdk\include` in the large pane and make sure that it is listed *before* the default folders as shown in Figure 1.5. Then, select Library Files from the drop-down menu and enter `c:\mssdk\lib` in the large pane as shown in Figure 1.6. Click on OK when you are finished.

Figure 1.4
Selecting
Options
from the
Tools menu

Figure 1.5
Setting the
Include
directory
for the
DirectX 8.0
SDK

Figure 1.6
Setting the
Library
directory
for the
DirectX 8.0
SDK

Creating a Project

The next thing you need to do if you want to modify the code for any of the demo versions of *Ned's Turkey Farm* using Visual C++ 6.0 is create a project. Start by selecting New from the File menu (see Figure 1.7).

Select the Projects tab from the New dialog box that pops up (see Figure 1.8). Select Win32 Application from the large pane on the left. Type a name for the project in the upper of the two edit boxes on the right—we'll use "Demo 0" for this example. Select a location for the project in the edit box beneath it. We will use C:\Ned's Turkey Farm\Demo00, which is the default installation location for the CD that came with this book. (If you opted to have the software installed in a different location, you will just have to browse for it.) Be careful though—Visual C++ thinks it is smarter than you are, and while you are not looking it may try to make the location C:\Ned's Turkey Farm\Demo00\Demo00. You should double-check that the location is correct before hitting the OK button.

Figure 1.7 Selecting New from the File menu

Figure 1.8
Filling out
the New
Projects tab

After clicking OK on the New dialog box, you will see a dialog box with the title
Win32 Application—Step 1 of 1. (Nice job, Microsoft.) You should select the radio
button for an empty project as shown in Figure 1.9, and then click on the Finish
button.

Figure 1.9
Specifying
an empty
project

Next, you will see the New Project Information dialog box (Figure 1.10), in which you should click OK. Now you have a new project with nothing in it.

Figure 1.10
The New
Project
Information
dialog box

Your next step is to add the Demo 0 files to the project. Select Add To Project, then Files from the Project menu as shown in Figure 1.11. You will see the Insert Files into Project dialog box. Select all of the code and header files by clicking on the icons with the left mouse button while holding down the Ctrl key. Once they are all highlighted, as shown in Figure 1.12, click on OK to add them to the project. Now, you are *almost* ready to roll. (If you don't see the code files as depicted in Figure 1.12, it probably means that, as I tried to warn you, Visual C++ 6.0 sneakily created the project in C:\Ned's Turkey Farm\Demo00\Demo00. You can either scrap the project and begin again, or copy the code files down from the folder above.)

Figure 1.11
Adding files
from the
Project menu

Figure 1.12
Selecting
files to
insert into
the project

The Linker Settings

In each chapter there is a section that lists the library files that must be used by the compiler in compiling the corresponding demo. Failure to notify the compiler of this will result in linker errors. Here's how to add `ddraw.lib`, the library file for DirectDraw, to the default libraries for your project. Start by selecting Settings from the Project menu as shown in Figure 1.13.

Figure 1.13
Selecting
Settings
from the
Project
menu

Next, you will see the Project Settings dialog box. Type `ddraw.lib` in the pane for Object/library modules on the Link tab, as shown in Figure 1.14. (Be sure that the pull-down menu has the General Category selected.) Click on the OK button when this is done. Now you are ready to roll.

Figure 1.14
Inserting
ddraw.lib
under the
Link tab

Online Resources

For additional online information about this book, including updates and corrections, browse:

    http://larc.csci.unt.edu/book2

For online information about the author, browse:

    http://www.cs.unt.edu/~ian

For information about game programming at the University of North Texas, including the author's game programming class on which this book is based, browse:

    http://larc.csci.unt.edu

For information about other current and future game programming books by the same author, browse:

    http://larc.csci.unt.edu/books.html

If you have any comments, suggestions, or questions about this book, the author will be happy to receive email at ian@cs.unt.edu.

Chapter 2

Here's what you'll learn:

- What's involved in choosing a screen format
- How to write your first Windows API program
- How to implement WinMain and the message pump
- How to handle Windows messages with a window procedure
- How to set up DirectDraw and create a primary surface
- How to set screen resolution
- How to read in and display a background image
- How to exit the program correctly

Displaying the Background

In Demo 0, we learn how to read in an image created by an artist and display it on the screen. Of course, there are many different image file formats, such as gif, jpeg, tiff, bmp, postscript, etc. We are going to use bmp format, for a simple reason: It is native to the Windows API, meaning that the API is set up to make reading bmp files very easy for you. Well… relatively easy compared to the other options.

Demo 0 does something that at first glance looks very simple. It reads in a bmp file called `Bckgnd.bmp` from disk and displays it on the screen. Then it just sits there until you hit the Escape key (Esc) to exit. The Escape key is the programmer's friend. It is a good idea to make sure that wherever you are in your program—in the middle of a game, in the third level of a series of nested menus, or wherever—you can exit the game by repeatedly hitting the Escape key. You will be running your program thousands of times during development, testing, and debugging, and even a seemingly innocent series of keystrokes and mouse moves can become irritating over time. There is something satisfying about being able to exit your program by closing your eyes and mashing on the Escape key repeatedly to get out safely after your code failed again—for the hundredth time—while debugging, especially at 4 a.m.

There's a lot going on in such a seemingly simple program. It registers a default display window with the operating system, creates the window, initializes DirectDraw, sets the screen resolution to 640x480x8, reads in an image from a file, converts it to an internal format, loads the image to video memory where it will be displayed on your screen, then waits patiently for you to hit the Escape key. When you do, it shuts down DirectDraw, cleans up, resets the display resolution to whatever it was before you ran the program, and shuts down gracefully.

Experiment with Demo 0

Take a moment now to run Demo 0.

- You should see the picture shown in Figure 2.1. Notice that it is displayed in 640x480 resolution, no matter what resolution your desktop is set to by default.
- Hit the Escape key to exit the program. Notice that your desktop is set back to the original resolution.
- Double-click on `Bckgnd.bmp` to fire up the default paint program on your computer (usually Microsoft Paint) to verify to yourself that when you ran Demo 0 you were seeing the image that is stored in that file.

Figure 2.1
Screen shot of
Demo 0

Choosing the Screen Format

Before you even begin coding, you should choose the screen format for your game, specifically, the screen resolution and the number of colors (called the *color depth*). Ideally, your game should run in a number of different formats—high-resolution, high-color formats for people with expensive computers and graphics cards, and low-resolution, low-color formats for people with the bargain basement PCs that you get almost for free when you sign up with an Internet service provider. This is a very important point—there are more people with low-end PCs than high-end ones, and their money is the same color as everybody else's (green). I know that you probably want to make the coolest game possible, and that means you will want to use the latest hardware and display devices to make it look as cool as possible—and there is nothing wrong with that. I am just suggesting that you have some low-power settings for everybody else. Although they have cheap computers, they will have paid as much for your game as people with high-end computers, and so they have a right to expect your game to run. Sure, it may not look as cool, but it ought to look as cool as everything else that they run on their computer, assuming you have done your job correctly.

Here are some of your choices for screen resolution, from low end to high end:

- 640x480, meaning 640 pixels wide, 480 pixels high
- 800x600
- 1024x768
- 1280x960

Here are some of your choices for color depth, from low end to high end:

- 8-bit color, in which each pixel is stored as an 8-bit index into a color table (called a *palette*) of 256 potentially (though not necessarily) distinct 24-bit color values
- 16-bit color, in which each pixel is stored as a 16-bit color value (65,536 colors)
- 24-bit color, in which each pixel is stored as a 24-bit color value (16,777,216 colors)
- 32-bit color, which is really 24-bit color with an unused 8-bit field (actually, it is used in 3D programming for the alpha value, but that is out of the scope of this book)

Although I am not much of an artist, I will say this: For your average picture, 16-bit color is dramatically better than 8-bit color, while 24-bit color is a little better. This is for an *average* picture—I have seen 8-bit color pictures that look every bit as good as a 16-bit color version, and I have seen 24-bit color pictures that are dramatically better than 16-bit color. It depends on the individual picture and, of course, the quality of your artist and his or her art tools.

I have chosen the lowest acceptable screen format for the code demos in this book, 640x480, 8-bit color. Why? Because it saves on disk space, and because 8-bit color is arguably the hardest to program for. The Windows API has some wonderful functions for loading images and displaying them on the user's screen. They will automatically stretch or shrink the image and remap the colors to fit the user's screen resolution and color depth. You would find that converting the code demos in this book to 24-bit color, for example, would be a breeze using these functions. You might even be tempted to let them take care of everything, converting your artwork to 8-bit color if the player has his or her desktop set to 8-bit color. Why not—it is a breeze to the programmer.

Unfortunately, there are two serious drawbacks to doing this. The first is that the Windows API is heartbreakingly slow at remapping colors. This speed problem is particularly bad on a slow machine, and you can be pretty sure that the user who has his desktop set at 256 colors is doing it because he has an old computer with a low-end graphics card and a slow processor. The second problem is that the Windows API is notoriously bad at producing a 256-color image. If left alone to map your 24-bit color file into an 8-bit color image, it will do a commendable job—for a machine. However, to the human eye it will often look terrible. What do you expect? It is only a machine—it knows nothing about art, aesthetics, or even what you wanted it to look like. Worse still, it will have a hankering to meddle with your palette even if you provide your images in 8-bit format. What I will do in this chapter is explain how to deal with 8-bit artwork while telling Windows to keep its hairy hands away from your palette.

I have also chosen to go full screen, that is, to take over the Windows desktop completely. You may also want to run your game inside a normal Windows window if it is appropriate for your style of game. That is more complicated, since it means cooperating with Windows, and we will not be covering that in this book.

It is a good idea to decide on what screen resolutions and color depths you are going to be using *before* you start coding. Make sure your artists have some input into this and understand what is at stake here. You can do some conversions on-the-fly in your code, but it is a good idea to have several versions of the artwork shipped with your program—at least a version in 8-bit color and a version in 24-bit color (Note: there is no 16-bit bmp file format). You might want to consider having a low-resolution and a high-resolution version of the artwork too, since the tools available to the artist will most likely be more sophisticated than the code that you will write, and artists typically will have a better eye for color and detail than you do. To simplify things in this book, we will stick with the one screen resolution and color depth.

Getting Started

We begin by looking at the code in the Demo00 folder. The main source code file is Main.cpp. This file begins with some system includes. The first two includes get us access to the Windows API functions that we need for this program. The third include is the header file for DirectDraw, Ddraw.h.

```
#include <windows.h>
#include <windowsx.h>
#include <ddraw.h>
```

If you forget to include Ddraw.h, the compiler will complain that the DirectDraw functions used in your project have not been declared.

Next, we have a system define that gets us the smallest, fastest version of the API:

```
#define WIN32_LEAN_AND_MEAN
```

Now we are ready for some global declarations. First, there are some DirectDraw things that we will skip over now and come back to later.

```
LPDIRECTDRAW lpDirectDrawObject; //direct draw object
LPDIRECTDRAWSURFACE lpPrimary; //primary surface
LPDIRECTDRAWPALETTE lpPrimaryPalette; //its palette
```

The next declaration is a Boolean variable that we will ensure is set to TRUE whenever our game is the active application (as opposed to it being minimized on the Windows taskbar, for example):

```
BOOL ActiveApp; //is this application active?
```

Finally, the last declaration is our bmp file reader class CBmpFileReader, which we will meet later in Bmp.cpp and Bmp.h. Its job is to read in an image from a bmp file and hold it in memory until it is delivered to DirectDraw to be drawn on the screen.

```
CBmpFileReader background; //background image
```

Next, we have prototypes for two very important functions, WinMain, and the window procedure WindowProc:

```
int WINAPI WinMain(HINSTANCE hInstance,
    HINSTANCE hPrevInstance,LPSTR lpCmdLine,int nCmdShow);
long CALLBACK WindowProc(HWND hwnd,UINT message,
    WPARAM wParam,LPARAM lParam);
```

WinMain is the Windows equivalent of the function main that you may be used to if you are familiar with old-style text processing. This is the operating system's main entry point into your program, that is, where it starts execution when the user runs it. We are interested in only two of WinMain's parameters. The first parameter, hInstance, gives us an instance handle, which is an operating system bookkeeping thing we will need to pass on to other Windows API functions. The last parameter, nCmdShow, will be nonzero if Windows thinks that the window associated with our program should be visible to the user.

The *window procedure* is the operating system's second entry point into your program. Windows is a *message passing* operating system. This means that the operating system will communicate with your program by passing it messages. These messages contain useful information such as user keystrokes, mouse motion, that your program has been minimized, etc. It passes this information to your program by calling your window procedure. I have called it WindowProc in this code, but you are free (within the normal C++ function naming rules) to call it what you like. The first parameter in the window procedure is hwnd, a handle to the window that is to receive the message. This is useful in programs that open several windows on the desktop. For example, it helps you decide which of your windows received a mouse click, but it is less useful to us because we will open only one window that will cover the whole screen. The second parameter, `mes-sage`, tells us what message is being delivered, and the last two parameters, `wParam` and `lParam`, convey any parameters that the message has. For example, if the message is a mouse move message, then `lParam` will contain the new mouse cursor screen coordinates.

WinMain

Skip over the functions in `Demo0.cpp` until you come to `WinMain`. `WinMain`'s job is to open a window on the desktop, but before it can do that it must register the window with the operating system and maintain a message pump to deal with Windows messages. It has these local variables:

```
MSG msg; //current message
HWND hwnd; //handle to fullscreen window
```

Local variable `msg` is used to store the current Windows message in the message pump. The next local variable, `hwnd`, is used to store a handle to the display window, which the operating system will provide us when we create the window. The window handle can be passed to various Windows API functions to perform useful operations on the display window.

The first thing we do is create a default window for our game, which we have wrapped up in the function `CreateDefaultWindow`, found in `Ddsetup.cpp`. We pass it a name for our application and the instance handle for our program, which is given to us by the operating system as parameter `hInstance` to `WinMain`. It returns a window handle, which we store in `hwnd`.

```
hwnd=CreateDefaultWindow("directX Demo 0",hInstance);
```

The call to `CreateDefaultWindow` actually returns a handle to the created window only if it was successful. If it fails, it returns `NULL`. In the unlikely event of this happening, we should bail out of `WinMain`.

```
if(!hwnd)return FALSE;
```

Having created a window, we can go ahead and do some initialization. The next three function calls use the window handle `hwnd` returned by `CreateDefault-Window`. We show the window and draw it.

```
ShowWindow(hwnd,nCmdShow); UpdateWindow(hwnd);
```

Next, we set up the input devices, specifically the keyboard and the mouse, using Windows API function calls. We allow keyboard input.

```
SetFocus(hwnd); //allow input from keyboard
```

We hide the mouse cursor:

```
ShowCursor(FALSE); //hide the cursor
```

Setting the parameter of `ShowCursor` to `TRUE` will show the mouse again. Actually, `ShowCursor` is implemented with a counter, which means that you have to call `ShowCursor` with parameter `TRUE` as many times as you called it with `FALSE` in order to get the mouse cursor to reappear—remember this later when your mouse cursor doesn't reappear when you think it should.

Having cleared everything with the operating system, we are now ready to get down to business. A call to my function `InitDirectDraw`, which is found in `Ddsetup.cpp`, attempts to initialize DirectDraw and returns `TRUE` if it succeeds. We store the return value in a Boolean variable called `OK`.

```
BOOL OK=InitDirectDraw(hwnd);//initialize DirectDraw
```

If the call to `InitDirectDraw` succeeded, we attempt to load the image from disk with a call to my function `LoadImages`, which we will also describe in more detail later. In addition to loading the image from disk, `LoadImages` also displays the background image to the screen. It returns `TRUE` if it succeeds, so again we store the return result in `OK`.

```
if(OK)OK=LoadImages(); //load images from disk
```

If either `InitDirectDraw` or `LoadImages` fails, `OK` will be `FALSE`. If this happens, we call the API function `DestroyWindow` to clean up the window we created, and bail out.

```
if(!OK){ //bail out if initialization failed
  DestroyWindow(hwnd); return FALSE;
}
```

The last thing we have to do in `WinMain` is start a message pump:

```
while(TRUE)
  if(PeekMessage(&msg,NULL,0,0,PM_NOREMOVE)){
    if(!GetMessage(&msg,NULL,0,0))return msg.wParam;
    TranslateMessage(&msg); DispatchMessage(&msg);
  }
  else if(!ActiveApp)WaitMessage();
```

The message pump handles the Windows message passing process. If our application is not the active app (the one that Windows is currently focusing on), then `ActiveApp` will have been set to `FALSE` elsewhere in the program, and our app will simply wait for messages (most importantly, for the message that makes our app active again). Otherwise it does the Windows default message processing action, which is beyond the scope of this book.

Creating a Full-screen Window

You will recall that `WinMain` uses the function `CreateDefaultWindow`, found in `Ddsetup.cpp`, to set up a default display window. `CreateDefaultWindow` has two parameters, `name`, a string name for our app, and `hInstance`, the instance handle for our program. It begins with the declaration of a local variable `wc`, a structure of type `WNDCLASS`, which we will load with information about the kind of window we want to open. We will pass this structure to the operating system when we open the window.

```
WNDCLASS wc; //window registration info
```

The first thing we do in `WinMain` is fill in various fields in local variable `wc` to describe what kind of window we want to open. The style field is an example of something we will see a lot of: a Windows flag. This is essentially an unsigned integer with a single bit reserved for each property. Here we want to set two of these bits, corresponding to "redraw the screen on horizontal movement or width change," and "redraw the screen on vertical movement or width change." Luckily for us, we don't have to remember which bits to set. The Windows API gives us predefined constants, `CS_HREDRAW` and `CS_VREDRAW`, which are powers of two corresponding to these bit positions. To set both of these bits, simply OR together both of these values using the bitwise-OR operator "`|`" (not the Boolean OR operator "`||`").

```
wc.style=CS_HREDRAW|CS_VREDRAW; //style
```

The `lpfnWndProc` field is a pointer to the window procedure, which is `WindowProc` in this example:

```
wc.lpfnWndProc=WindowProc; //window message handler
```

The next two fields are not used in our program and can safely be set to zero:

```
wc.cbClsExtra=wc.cbWndExtra=0;
```

The `hInstance` field must be set to the instance handle for our program, which is given to us as a parameter to `CreateDefaultWindow`:

```
wc.hInstance=hInstance;
```

We can create a custom icon for our program. This is the icon that will show up on the desktop, among other places. But here we will satisfy ourselves with the default application icon.

```
wc.hIcon=LoadIcon(hInstance,IDI_APPLICATION);
```

Similarly, we will use the default arrow mouse cursor:

```
wc.hCursor=LoadCursor(NULL,IDC_ARROW);
```

We can direct the operating system to color the background of the window, but here we will tell it not to bother. We will take care of all drawing ourselves.

```
wc.hbrBackground=NULL;
```

We are not going to be using a menu in this program, so set the menu name field to `NULL`:

```
wc.lpszMenuName=NULL;
```

Set the class name to the name parameter:

```
wc.lpszClassName=name;
```

Now we register our window with the operating system:

```
RegisterClass(&wc);
```

Having described our window, we can now request that the operating system go ahead and create it using the `CreateWindowEx` API function:

```
hwnd=CreateWindowEx(WS_EX_TOPMOST,name,name,
    WS_POPUP,0,0,GetSystemMetrics(SM_CXSCREEN),
    GetSystemMetrics(SM_CYSCREEN),NULL,NULL,hInstance,NULL);
```

`CreateWindowEx` has 12 parameters. The first parameter to this function is the extended window style, and we use it to specify that the window is a topmost window, that is, it should stay above all nontopmost windows. The second parameter is the class name, which should be the same as that provided in the earlier call to `RegisterClass`. The third parameter is a window name; it really does not matter what we use here. The fourth parameter is the window style, for which we choose a popup window style `WS_POPUP`; again it really does not matter what we use here, since we are going to be running full screen. The fifth and sixth parameters, which are set to zero, are the screen coordinates of the top left corner of the window. The seventh and eighth parameters are the width and height of the window, which we set to the screen height and width, ascertained by calls to the API function `GetSystemMetrics`. The ninth parameter is a handle to the parent window, which can be `NULL` since we specified the `WS_POPUP` style. The 10th parameter is a handle to the menu, which is `NULL` again since we are not using a menu. The 11th parameter is the instance handle, and we are not using the 12th and last parameter, so we can set it to `NULL`.

Setting Up DirectDraw

Setting up DirectDraw takes several steps. We will declare a set of global variables to give easy access to the various parts of DirectDraw that we will be using. Then, we need to set up a DirectDraw object, a primary surface, and a palette.

Declarations

Now we can get back to those global variables that we promised we would return to later. First, we need a *DirectDraw object*, which is an object that will manage the video hardware for us. We reserve space for a pointer to the DirectDraw object, and will create it later.

```
LPDIRECTDRAW lpDirectDrawObject; //direct draw object
```

Second, we will need a *primary surface*. A *surface* is the DirectDraw term for an object used to store an image. Modern video cards carry large amounts of memory that allow us to store several images in video memory, but only one of these—the primary surface—will be displayed at any given time. The primary surface, then, is a surface that is stored in video memory on the video card and contains the image that is currently displayed on the monitor. Again, we reserve space for a pointer to the primary surface, which is to be created later.

```
LPDIRECTDRAWSURFACE lpPrimary; //primary surface
```

Third, since we are going to be in 8-bit color, we are going to need a palette for the primary surface:

```
LPDIRECTDRAWPALETTE lpPrimaryPalette; //its palette
```

The DirectDraw Object

I have encapsulated the DirectDraw initialization into a function called InitDirectDraw, found in Ddsetup.cpp. This function takes a window handle as a parameter, and returns TRUE if it succeeds.

```
BOOL InitDirectDraw(HWND hwnd){ //direct draw initialization
```

The first thing it does is create a DirectDraw object and place a pointer to it in the global variable lpDirectDrawObject. We need to save a pointer to it because the DirectDraw object is a video hardware manager—once created it takes control of the video hardware from the operating system, and we will then be able to ask it to perform various video hardware oriented tasks for us; we ask it by calling the relevant member function of the DirectDraw object. The DirectDraw object is created by calling the DirectDraw function DirectDrawCreate. This function takes three parameters, the first of which should be NULL, and the last of which *must* be NULL. The second parameter is the address where you would like

DirectDraw to put a pointer to the DirectDraw object after it is created. `DirectDrawCreate` will return `DD_OK` if it succeeds; if it fails we will bail out and return `FALSE`. Rather than checking the return value of `DirectDraw-Create` against `DD_OK`, it is slightly more readable to make use of the Windows API macros `SUCCEEDED` and `FAILED`.

```
if(FAILED(DirectDrawCreate(NULL,&lpDirectDrawObject,NULL)))
  return FALSE;
```

The DirectDraw object is a powerful tool, so powerful that we can take control of the video hardware away from the operating system. The next thing we have to do is specify how much of this power we will use, that is, to what extent we will share the video hardware with the operating system, and through it, with other applications. This is done with the DirectDraw object's `SetCooperativeLevel` member function. The first parameter to this function is a window handle, and the second parameter is a flag word that contains one bit for each of several properties. Simply set the corresponding bits by performing a logical OR of the predefined constants for each property. We will be asking for exclusive mode, meaning that we will not share the video hardware, and fullscreen mode, meaning we will take over the whole desktop. We get this set of properties by ORing together the two values `DDSCL_EXCLUSIVE` and `DDSCL_FULLSCREEN`. `SetCooperativeLevel` returns `DD_OK` if it succeeds, and we bail if it fails. (For that matter, all of the DirectDraw functions used in the rest of this section return `DD_OK` if they succeed, and we bail out if any one of them fails—so I won't mention it again.)

```
if(FAILED(lpDirectDrawObject->SetCooperativeLevel(hwnd,
DDSCL_EXCLUSIVE|DDSCL_FULLSCREEN)))
  return FALSE;
```

Now we have complete control of the screen. The first thing we do with this control is change screen resolution using the `SetDisplayMode` member function of the DirectDraw object. This function takes three parameters, from left to right, the screen width, screen height, and color depth. We will use constants `SCREEN_WIDTH`, `SCREEN_HEIGHT`, and `COLOR_DEPTH` defined in `Defines.h`. Note that the parameters have to correspond to some sensible values corresponding to some hardware supported video mode, such as 640x480, 800x600, 1024x768, etc., with 8-, 16-, 24-, or 32-bit color.

```
if(FAILED(lpDirectDrawObject->
SetDisplayMode(SCREEN_WIDTH,SCREEN_HEIGHT,COLOR_DEPTH)))
  return FALSE;
```

The Primary Surface

Now we create the primary surface. We should do this only after the display mode has been set, since the primary surface will automatically be created to be the same size and color depth as the display mode. DirectDraw will let you create surfaces of many different sizes and flavors. This is done using the DirectDraw object's `CreateSurface` member function, the first parameter of which is a *DirectDraw surface descriptor*, which is a structure that describes the type of surface to be created. First, we declare a local DirectDraw surface descriptor.

```
DDSURFACEDESC ddsd; //direct draw surface descriptor
```

Then we fill in the relevant fields. Like many Windows structures, it has a size field that *must* be set to the size of the structure:

```
ddsd.dwSize=sizeof(ddsd);
```

A second feature common to this type of structure is the flags field. Since the structure has many fields that may or may not be used, for speed we can specify exactly which of the fields contain sensible values; the rest can be skipped over and ignored by `CreateSurface`. As always, this is performed by doing a logical OR of the relevant predefined constants, which can be found in the DirectX help files. In this instance it is easy, as we will be using only one field, the capabilities field. We set the `dwFlags` field of `ddsd` accordingly.

```
ddsd.dwFlags=DDSD_CAPS;
```

Now, we set the capabilities field to indicate that this will be the primary surface:

```
ddsd.ddsCaps.dwCaps=DDSCAPS_PRIMARYSURFACE;
```

Now we can pass the DirectDraw surface descriptor containing the specifications for the primary surface as the first parameter to the `CreateSurface` member function of the DirectDraw object. The second parameter is the address of a pointer that we will use later to access the primary surface; after all, we will need to draw an image there so it can be displayed on the video screen. The third parameter must be set to NULL.

```
if(FAILED(lpDirectDrawObject->
CreateSurface(&ddsd,&lpPrimary,NULL)))
  return FALSE;
```

The Palette

Having created the primary surface, we attach a palette to it using my `Create-Palette` function (to be described in more detail in a moment), and save a pointer to it so that we can load color values later:

```
lpPrimaryPalette=CreatePalette(lpPrimary);
```

If we get to this point in the code we can assume that DirectDraw initialization has succeeded, and so we

```
return TRUE;
```

My `CreatePalette` function, also found in `Ddsetup.cpp`, will create a DirectDraw palette, set every color entry in the palette to black, attach that palette to the surface given to it as a parameter, and return a pointer to the palette:

```
LPDIRECTDRAWPALETTE CreatePalette(LPDIRECTDRAWSURFACE surface){
```

The function has two local variables: a `PALETTEENTRY` array `pe` that we will use to set the initial colors in the DirectDraw palette, and a pointer that we will use to point to the DirectDraw palette that we create. The `PALETTEENTRY` array has 256 entries, which is specified using the constant `COLORS` defined in `Defines.h`.

```
PALETTEENTRY pe[COLORS]; //new palette
LPDIRECTDRAWPALETTE lpDDPalette; //direct draw palette
```

We start by setting each color in `pe` to black:

```
for(int i=0; i<COLORS; i++)
  pe[i].peRed=pe[i].peGreen=pe[i].peBlue=0;
```

Then we use the `CreatePalette` member function of the DirectDraw object to create the palette. The first parameter specifies that we want 8-bit color, and the second is the address of a pointer to the new palette. The third parameter must be `NULL`.

```
if(FAILED(lpDirectDrawObject->
CreatePalette(DDPCAPS_8BIT,pe,&lpDDPalette,NULL)))
  return NULL;
```

Having created the DirectDraw palette and gotten a pointer to it in the local variable `lpDDPalette`, we now attach the palette to the surface that was specified as the parameter to my `CreatePalette` function, using the surface's `SetPalette` member function:

```
surface->SetPalette(lpDDPalette);
```

Finally, we return a pointer to the newly created DirectDraw palette:

```
return lpDDPalette;
```

Loading Graphics

The graphics images are loaded by my `LoadImages` function. All of the real work is going to be done by a global `CBmpFileReader` class object, which we will describe in more detail later. For now, let's just look at how the object is used. There is only one image to be loaded, a file named `Bckgnd.bmp`. We load it from disk into the global `CBmpFileReader` class object `background`, and bail out if the load fails.

```
if(!background.load("bckgnd.bmp")) //read from file
   return FALSE; //read failed
```

The load operation got us the image data and the palette. We first load the palette to the primary surface palette. Recall that we kept a pointer to that palette in the global variable `lpPrimaryPalette`.

```
if(!background.setpalette(lpPrimaryPalette)) //set palette
   return FALSE; //set palette failed
```

Having done that, we load the image to the primary surface. Note that we load the palette, then load the image to the primary surface in that order. Note that if we already had an image that uses a different palette drawn to the primary surface (we didn't—all we had was black, but just suppose for a moment that we did), then there would have been a small amount of time during which we had the old image drawn with the new palette, which would make it look pretty awful, depending on how different the palettes were. Doing it the other way would display the new image in the old palette, which would look just as bad. However, loading a palette means moving 256 color entries of 3 bytes each, for a total of 768 bytes. Loading a 640x480 image means moving 307,968 bytes—more than 400 times as much data. Which would be faster? Doesn't it make more sense to have things looking bad while we are loading a small palette than have things looking bad for longer while we draw a large image? That is why we load the palette first, then draw the image.

```
if(!background.draw(lpPrimary)) //draw to surface
   return FALSE; //draw failed
```

If all is well, we should now see the image displayed on the screen using the correct palette, so we can

```
return TRUE; //all steps succeeded
```

The Window Procedure

The window procedure `WindowProc` is the function that is called by the operating system whenever a message is to be passed to your program. You'll find it in `Main.cpp`. It has four parameters, which are set by the operating system. The first is the handle of the window to which the message is being sent, which is important if your application has more than one window; ours does not, so we will pretty much ignore it. The second is an unsigned integer encoding of the message. Fortunately for us, the Windows API has predefined constants for these messages, including, for example, `WM_KEYDOWN` for the message sent when the player hits a key on the keyboard. The last two function parameters carry the parameters of the message, which differ from message to message. For example, for the `WM_KEYDOWN` message, the third parameter to `WindowProc` is set to a value that encodes the actual key that was hit.

```
long CALLBACK WindowProc(HWND hwnd,UINT message,
                    WPARAM wParam,LPARAM lParam){
```

The body of `WindowProc` is a simple switch statement that specifies the action to be taken for each message. We begin with five simple cases. The first is `WM_ACTIVATEAPP`, which is sent whenever our application becomes the active application or becomes inactive; `wParam` will be `TRUE` in the first case, and `FALSE` in the latter. We will record this in the global variable `ActiveApp`.

```
case WM_ACTIVATEAPP: ActiveApp=wParam; break;
```

The second case is `WM_CREATE`, which is sent when the `CreateWindowEx` function called from our function `CreateDefaultWindow` (found in `Ddsetup.cpp`) creates the window for our application. This is where we can do initialization that should take place immediately after the window has actually been created. We will do nothing, but it is good practice to include this for later.

```
case WM_CREATE: break;
```

The third case is `WM_KEYDOWN`, which is sent when a keyboard key goes down. We notify a keyboard handler function to take care of it (we'll come back to this at the end of this section).

```
case WM_KEYDOWN: //keyboard hit
  if(keyboard_handler(wParam))DestroyWindow(hwnd);
  break;
```

The fourth case is `WM_DESTROY`, which is our signal to shut down the game. The DirectDraw object and the DirectDraw surfaces are Windows COM objects, which for the purposes of this book means that they are just like C++ classes except for the fact that they don't have constructors and destructors. Instead of a destructor, they have a function `Release` which we must call explicitly on shutdown. Every surface we create must be released, and it must be released *before* we release the DirectDraw object. So, when exiting the game, we release the primary surface, then release the DirectDraw object. After the DirectDraw object has been released, we show the mouse cursor. The last thing that we must do when shutting down is call the Windows API function `PostQuitMessage` to indicate to the operating system that our program is ready to quit.

```
case WM_DESTROY: //end of game
  if(lpDirectDrawObject!=NULL){ //if DD object exists
    if(lpPrimary!=NULL) //if primary surface exists
      lpPrimary->Release(); //release primary surface
    lpDirectDrawObject->Release(); //release DD object
  }
  ShowCursor(TRUE); //show the mouse cursor
  PostQuitMessage(0); //and exit
  break;
```

Finally, we have a handler for all of the other messages; we just pass them back to the operating system using the Windows API function `DefWindowProc`:

```
default: //default window procedure
  return DefWindowProc(hwnd,message,wParam,lParam);
} //switch(message)
```

Finally, we return zero and exit from the window procedure.

For convenience, we moved the keyboard handler into a separate function in `Main.cpp` rather than just put the code in the switch statement in the window procedure. As you might image, this function will become *much* more complicated as our game develops. We pass the keyboard handler the `wParam` parameter that was given to the window procedure as an argument to the `WM_KEYDOWN` message. If an alphabetic or numeric key went down, `wParam` contains the ASCII code of that key. For example, if it was the "A" key, then `wParam` contains `'A'`. There is a set of predefined constants called *virtual key codes* for the rest of the keys. We will check to see whether `wParam` is the Esc key by comparing `wParam` to `VK_ESCAPE`. We'll have the keyboard handler return `TRUE` if this happens.

```
BOOL keyboard_handler(WPARAM keystroke){ //keyboard handler
  BOOL result=FALSE; //return TRUE if game is to end
  switch(keystroke){
    case VK_ESCAPE: result=TRUE; break; //exit game
  }
  return result;
} //keyboard_handler
```

The Bmp File Reader

The bmp file reader class `CBmpFileReader` will input bmp files and store them in an internal format ready to be drawn to a DirectDraw surface. We will keep this internal format image around even after it has been drawn to a surface because all surfaces are prone to *surface loss*, which is as catastrophic as it sounds. It means that the memory that has been allocated to your surface, along with the image in that memory, has been taken away from you by the operating system or the video hardware. After surface loss, we will need to restore all of the surfaces and redraw what was on them. Why not reload the images from disk when surfaces need to be restored? Well we could, but that would take longer than keeping them in memory. But won't that waste memory? Well, the Windows memory manager will swap them out of real memory onto virtual memory on disk if real memory is low, because it automatically pages out memory that is not being accessed often. But isn't reloading paged-out memory on disk just as slow as reloading the image? At worst it is no slower, and at best the image won't be on disk at all, and we will have a real speed win. So, it is to our advantage to just leave a copy of each image in a `CBmpFileReader` class instance and just let Windows manage resources for us.

Palettized Art

As you may recall, we're going to be using fixed-palette, 256-color artwork. That means that we can use up to 256 different colors, with each color described using 24 bits. The palette is specified as a color table with 256 entries, each entry being 3 bytes long, for a total of 768 bytes. The 3 bytes for each color is used as follows: one byte for the intensity of red, one byte for green, and one byte for blue, in that order. Black has zero intensity in all three colors, which we will express as having an *RGB value* of (0,0,0). White has full intensity in all three colors, that is, an RGB value of (255,255,255).

The best way of thinking of palettized art is to think of it as a paint-by-numbers set. Once the 256 colors in the palette have been specified, we can list the pixels in the image in row-major order using one byte for each pixel to specify which of the 256 palette positions is used to paint that pixel. The image in file `Bckgnd.bmp` is shown in Figure 2.2 next to its palette of 256 colors arranged in 16 rows of 16 colors. Palette position 0, which is filled with a shade of dark red, is at the top left corner of the palette as it is drawn in that figure. Palette position 255, which is filled with an obnoxious shade of pink (technically called magenta) with an RGB value of (255,0,255), is at the lower right corner. The palette entries in between are drawn in row-major order in Figure 2.2.

Figure 2.2
Bckgnd.bmp
(left) and its
palette
(right)

While each palette entry can potentially hold a different color, it doesn't have to; we could have several palette entries containing the same 24-bit color. If we change the color in one of the palette entries, then all of the pixels that are drawn using that palette index are changed too. For example, Figure 2.3 shows `Bckgnd.bmp` with color number 73 changed from off-white with an RGB value of (244,243,254) in Figure 2.2 to black. We can see that palette position 73 (indicated by the large arrow in Figure 2.3) was used to draw many of the pixels in the clouds, the ones that have turned black.

Figure 2.3
Bckgnd.bmp
from Figure
2.2 with one
palette
entry
changed to
black

The Bmp File Format

The bmp file format that we will be using is as follows (see Figure 2.4). First, there is a file header, then an info header. The info header contains useful information such as the width, height, and color depth of the image. Then there are 768 bytes of palette, listed as 256 24-bit RGB values. Lastly, the image data is listed, one byte for each pixel, using 640x480=307,200 bytes of image data in `Bckgnd.bmp`. Although this is not important in Demo 0, there's a subtlety that you should remember if you want to read bmp files of nonstandard sizes—the rows of the image are rounded up in size to the next multiple of 4, so that, for example, an image that is 21 pixels wide and 10 pixels high will use 24x10=240 bytes of image data, not 21x10=210 bytes as you might expect.

There is one other subtlety about bmp files—they are stored upside-down. That is, the order of the rows is reversed. The first row of the image is actually where you would expect the *last* row to be stored (see Figure 2.5).

Figure 2.4
The bmp file format

| File Header |
| File Info |
| Palette (256 entries each 3 bytes long) |
| Image (Indices into palette, one byte per pixel) |

Figure 2.5
How the image is stored in a bmp file

Last row	Filler
...	Filler
Second row	Filler
First row	Filler

Bmp File Reader Overview

The header file for `CBmpFileReader` is `Bmp.h`. It starts with a small set of includes for the Windows API and DirectDraw, and our defines file `Defines.h`.

```
#include <windows.h>
#include <windowsx.h>
#include <ddraw.h>

#include "defines.h"
```

Notice that the entire file is bracketed by an `ifndef`. This is just to keep the compiler happy. We will be including our header files in many different code files, which will cause the compiler to complain the second time it sees the definition of `CBmpFileReader`. To prevent this, we define a unique symbol `__bmp_h__` the first time the compiler sees `Bmp.h`, and prevent the compiler from seeing it again by placing an #ifndef of the same symbol in front of everything. I usually use the name of the file with the period replaced by an underscore, with two underscores in front of and two underscores behind the name, just to make sure it is unique. If you let Visual C++ create the file for you, it will do the same thing using a very long, very obscure string that it creates automatically.

```
#ifndef __bmp_h__
#define __bmp_h__
  . . .
#endif
```

CBmpFileReader has four protected member variables—they could be private, but I have chosen to make them protected because we will be deriving a new class from CBmpFileReader in Chapter 5. They are, respectively, the file header, the file info, the palette, and the image data. Note that we know ahead of time that the palette will be 768 bytes long, whereas the size of image data will depend on the file width and height. The bmp file reader class is designed to read in files of any size, not just 640x480, so we will declare the image data to simply be a pointer to BYTE data, and we will allocate enough memory later when we know the image resolution.

```
BITMAPFILEHEADER m_BMPFileHead; //bmp header
BITMAPINFOHEADER m_BMPFileInfo; //bmp file information
RGBQUAD m_rgbPalette[COLORS]; //the palette
BYTE *m_cImage; //the image
```

CBmpFileReader has five public member functions, starting with a constructor and a destructor:

```
CBmpFileReader(); //constructor
~CBmpFileReader(); //destructor
```

Function load is given a filename, and loads the bmp file with that name into the protected member variables, returning TRUE if it succeeds:

```
BOOL load(char *filename); //load from file
```

Function draw will draw the image pointed to by private member variable m_cImage to a DirectDraw surface:

```
BOOL draw(LPDIRECTDRAWSURFACE surface); //draw image
```

Function setpalette will load a palette from private member variable m_rgbPalette to a DirectDraw palette:

```
BOOL setpalette(LPDIRECTDRAWPALETTE palette); //set palette
```

The code file for CBmpFileReader is Bmp.cpp. The constructor sets the image pointer m_cImage to zero. The destructor deletes the memory pointed to by m_cImage. Note that if no memory has been allocated for the image, the destructor still does not crash, since the C++ `delete` operation will do nothing to a zero pointer. If, however, we had failed to initialize `m_cImage` in the constructor, and accidentally deleted it before assigning any memory to it, we might find ourselves garbage-collecting part of our program (or even the operating system) code, leading to a messy crash. We assume, however, that in the normal course of events memory has been allocated to `m_cImage`, which then is garbage-collected by the destructor. Note also the use of `delete[]`, which deletes a whole array of `BYTE`s, instead of plain `delete`, which would delete only the first `BYTE` pointed to by `m_cImage`.

```
CBmpFileReader::CBmpFileReader(){ //constructor
m_cImage=0; //memory not yet allocated
}

CBmpFileReader::~CBmpFileReader(){ //destructor
  delete[]m_cImage; //reclaim memory from image data
}
```

Loading Bmp Files

The `CBmpFileReader` `load` function begins with four local variables: a handle `hfile` to the input file, two counters `actualRead` (the number of bytes actually read) and `image_size` (the size of the image part of the bmp file, that is, the image width times the image height), and a helper Boolean called `OK` that we will use for the return value of the function, keeping set to `TRUE` as long as no error has yet occurred:

```
HANDLE hfile; //input file handle
DWORD actualRead; //number of bytes actually read
int image_size; //size of image (width*height)
BOOL OK=TRUE; //no error has occurred yet
```

We open the file for reading using the Windows API function `CreateFile`, bailing out if the open failed:

```
hfile=CreateFile(filename,GENERIC_READ,FILE_SHARE_READ,
  (LPSECURITY_ATTRIBUTES)NULL,OPEN_EXISTING,
  FILE_ATTRIBUTE_NORMAL,(HANDLE)NULL);
if(hfile==INVALID_HANDLE_VALUE)return FALSE;
```

We then read the file header and the file info. You will notice that I carefully have not said how large the file info and the file header are. That's because we don't really need to know. The Windows structures `BITMAPFILEHEADER` and `BITMAPINFOHEADER` are exactly the right size, so we'll just read in `sizeof(m_BMFileHead)` and `sizeof(m_BMPFileInfo)` bytes, respectively, using the Windows API function `ReadFile`.

```
OK=ReadFile(hfile,&m_BMPFileHead,sizeof(m_BMPFileHead),
  &actualRead,NULL);
if(OK)OK=ReadFile(hfile,&m_BMPFileInfo,
  sizeof(m_BMPFileInfo),&actualRead,NULL);
```

We immediately put the file info to good use by verifying that the file is a 256-color (8-bit color) file:

```
if(OK)OK=m_BMPFileInfo.biBitCount==COLOR_DEPTH;
```

We read the palette:

```
if(OK)OK=ReadFile(hfile,m_rgbPalette,sizeof(m_rgbPalette),
  &actualRead,NULL);
```

At this point, we bail out if something went wrong, before we allocate any memory for the image:

```
if(!OK){CloseHandle(hfile); return FALSE;}
```

We calculate the image size from information in the file info structure:

```
image_size=m_BMPFileInfo.biWidth*m_BMPFileInfo.biHeight;
```

We allocate memory for the image, carefully deleting any that has already been allocated, thinking ahead that someday someone may want to reuse a CBmpFileReader class instance to read in several bmp files. We bail out if the memory allocation fails.

```
if(m_cImage)delete[]m_cImage; //dispose of any old space
m_cImage=new BYTE[image_size]; //allocate new space
if(!m_cImage){ //bail if alloc failed
  CloseHandle(hfile); return FALSE;
}
```

Recall that I mentioned that rows of a bmp image are rounded up in size to the next multiple of 4. The width that we read from the file into m_BMPFileInfo. biWidth is the expected width of the image (which may not be a multiple of 4), not the padded width found in the image data in the file (which *is* a multiple of 4). We can round it up to the next multiple of 4 using the following slightly obscure line of C++ code.

```
int width=(m_BMPFileInfo.biWidth+3)&~3;
```

Here's how it works: ~3 is the bitwise complement of 3, that is, a word with all ones except for the least significant 2 bits, which are zero. (OK, so I'm forgetting the sign bit... so don't use this code to read in huge bmp files.) So, performing a bitwise & of any number with ~3 will set its least significant 2 bits to zeros, which is the same as rounding it down to the next lower multiple of 4. Therefore, taking m_BMPFileInfo.biWidth, adding 3, then performing a bitwise & of it with ~3 will round it up to the next multiple of 4. To convince yourself of this last step of my reasoning, consider the four possible remainders when m_BMPFile-Info.biWidth is divided by 4, and recall that &~3 rounds down to the next lowest multiple of 4, which implies that:

```
4i&~3=(4i+1)&~3=(4i+2)&~3=(4i+3)&~3=4i.
```

Case 1: m_BMPFileInfo.biWidth=4i. Then, width=(4i+3)&~3=4i.

Case 2: m_BMPFileInfo.biWidth=4i+1. Then, width=(4i+4)&~3=(4(i+1))&~3=4(i+1).

Case 3: m_BMPFileInfo.biWidth=4i+2. Then, width=(4i+5)&~3=(4(i+1)+1)&~3=4(i+1).

Case 4: m_BMPFileInfo.biWidth=4i+3. Then width=(4i+6)&~3=(4(i+1)+2)&~3=4(i+1).

In all four cases, width gets set to the smallest multiple of 4 that is greater than or equal to m_BMPFileInfo.biWidth, as required.

We declare a line counter, and 4 bytes in which to hold the (at most) 4 bytes of filler at the end of each row of pixels in the image data:

```
int i=0; //counter
BYTE trash[4]; //to hold the trash at the end of each line
```

Then, we compute the number of filler bytes at the end of each row, which will be a number between 0 and 3, inclusive:

```
int remainder=width-m_BMPFileInfo.biWidth; //width of trash
```

We use i to count the number of rows, reading one row per iteration of a while loop, bailing out of the loop if any of the reads fail. We use two calls to the API function ReadFile, first reading the real data, then the filler (if any) at the end of the row.

```
while(OK&&i<m_BMPFileInfo.biHeight){
  //read data
  OK=OK&&ReadFile(hfile,
    (BYTE*)(m_cImage+i*m_BMPFileInfo.biWidth),
    m_BMPFileInfo.biWidth,&actualRead,NULL);
  //read trash at end of line
  OK=OK&&ReadFile(hfile,trash,remainder,&actualRead,NULL);
  i++; //next line
}
```

If the read failed, we clean up, close the file handle, and exit:

```
if(!OK)delete[]m_cImage; //clean up if failed
//close up and exit
CloseHandle(hfile);
return OK;
```

Drawing to a Surface

The `CBmpFileReader draw` function draws the image from the member variable `m_cImage` to a DirectDraw surface. It has a single parameter, a pointer to a DirectDraw surface called `surface`. It begins with four local variables, first a DirectDraw surface descriptor that we will use to get information about the surface pointed to by `surface`.

```
DDSURFACEDESC ddsd; //direct draw surface descriptor
```

Next, we declare a pair of source and destination pointers that we will use to move byte data from `m_cImage` to `surface`:

```
BYTE *dest,*src; //destination and source pointers
```

Finally, we declare a variable to hold the width of the image in `m_cImage`:

```
int src_width; //width of source
```

We prepare the surface descriptor by filling it with zeros, and setting its size field to its size:

```
memset(&ddsd,0,sizeof(DDSURFACEDESC));
ddsd.dwSize=sizeof(ddsd);
```

We need to get access to the portion of the DirectDraw surface that contains the byte data for the image. While we load our image to that location, we have to ensure that nothing else accesses that memory. This is done by *locking down* the surface. Locking down a surface is potentially time-consuming, so we lock it only when we need to and unlock it as soon as we are able. Surfaces are locked and unlocked using their `Lock` and `Unlock` member functions. The call to `Lock` has four parameters. The first parameter can be set to a pointer to a rectangle within the surface that we wish to lock down; setting it to `NULL` will lock down the entire surface. The second parameter is a pointer to our DirectDraw surface descriptor, which will receive useful information about `surface`. The third parameter is a flag word, which we will set to `DDLOCK_WAIT`, which instructs DirectDraw to only return when either a lock has been achieved or an error has occurred. Conceivably, we could instead allow the `Lock` to fail and go off to do some other work instead, but there's no need to get that complicated here. The fourth parameter must be set to `NULL`. If the `Lock` fails, we will bail out of the `draw` function.

```
if(FAILED(surface->Lock(NULL,&ddsd,DDLOCK_WAIT,NULL)))
    return FALSE;
```

Now we start using the information stored in the DirectDraw surface descriptor `ddsd` by the `Lock` function. We set `dest` to point to the place in the surface where we want to store the byte data for the image.

```
dest=(BYTE*)ddsd.lpSurface; //destination
```

Similarly, we set `src` to point to the place within `m_cImage` that we want to start moving bytes from. Recall that bmp files are stored upside-down and so the first row of the image is actually where you would expect the last row to be stored (see Figure 2.5).

```
src=m_cImage+
  ((m_BMPFileInfo.biHeight-1)*m_BMPFileInfo.biWidth);
```

The width in bytes of the surface is stored in `ddsd.lPitch`; if the image is too wide for the surface, we clip it, which may look strange but is better than crashing.

```
if(m_BMPFileInfo.biWidth>ddsd.lPitch)src_width=ddsd.lPitch;
else src_width=m_BMPFileInfo.biWidth;
```

Now we move data to the surface. Note the careful way that we do it. We move one row at a time, subtracting `src_width` from `src` each time (to get to the start of the previous row of the source) and adding `ddsd.lPitch` to `dest` (to get to the start of the next row of the destination). Don't make the mistake of assuming that each row of the image in the surface is adjacent to the previous one. In reality, there is space left at the end of each row, which is used by DirectDraw for various purposes (see Figure 2.6). By using `dest+=ddsd.lPitch`, we make sure that we skip over it.

```
for(int i=0; i<m_BMPFileInfo.biHeight; i++){
  memcpy(dest,src,src_width);
  dest+=ddsd.lPitch; src-=src_width;
}
```

Now we are done, so we can unlock the surface and exit:

```
surface->Unlock(NULL);
return TRUE;
```

Figure 2.6
How the image is stored in a DirectDraw surface

First row	Used by DirectDraw
Second row	Used by DirectDraw
. . .	Used by DirectDraw
Last row	Used by DirectDraw

Setting the Palette

The CBmpFileReader setpalette function loads the palette from the member variable m_rgbPalette to a DirectDraw palette. It has a single parameter, a pointer to a DirectDraw palette called palette. It begins with a local variable, an array of PALETTEENTRYs called pe.

```
PALETTEENTRY pe[COLORS]; //intermediate palette
```

We load pe from m_rgbPalette:

```
for(int i=0; i<COLORS; i++){ //for each palette entry
  pe[i].peRed=m_rgbPalette[i].rgbRed; //set red
  pe[i].peGreen=m_rgbPalette[i].rgbGreen; //set green
  pe[i].peBlue=m_rgbPalette[i].rgbBlue; //set blue
}
```

Then, we load the palette from pe to palette using the DirectDraw palette's member function SetEntries. SetEntries has four parameters. The first must be NULL. The second and third allow us to load only part of the palette by specifying the lower and upper indices of the entries to be loaded; we will load the entire palette, from index 0 to index COLORS (which, you will recall, is set to 256 in Defines.h). The last parameter is a pointer to the PALETTEENTRY array pe.

```
palette->SetEntries(NULL,0,COLORS,pe);
```

Demo 0 Files

Code Files

The following files are used in Demo 0:

- ◎ `Bmp.h`
- ◎ `Bmp.cpp`
- ◎ `Ddsetup.cpp`
- ◎ `Defines.h`
- ◎ `Main.cpp`

Media Files

The following image files are used in Demo 0:

- ◎ `Bckgnd.bmp`

Required Libraries

- ◎ `Ddraw.lib`

Chapter 3

Here's what you'll learn:

- How the video serializer works

- What tearing is and how to avoid it

- How to implement page flipping in DirectDraw

- How to create a secondary surface in DirectDraw

- What surface loss is, and how to deal with it by restoring and reloading

Page Flipping

In Demo 1, we learn how to do page flipping in video memory to avoid the animation flaw known as tearing. Along the way, we'll learn a little about how the video hardware inside your computer works. Demo 1 reads in a bmp file called Up.bmp from disk and displays it on the screen. The image in Up.bmp looks very similar to the one in Bckgnd.bmp from Demo 0 (see Chapter 2), with the addition of a crow with its wings up in the center of the screen (see Figure 3.1). When you hit the Spacebar, this image is replaced by the one in Down.bmp, which has the crow with its wings down (see Figure 3.2). Each time you hit the Spacebar, the image on the screen flips between the two images in a process called *page flipping*. The transition between the two images is clean, clear, and crisp.

Figure 3.1
Single frame
of crow with
wings up

Figure 3.2
Single frame
of crow with
wings down

Experiment with Demo 1

Take a moment now to run Demo 1.

- You should see the picture shown in Figure 3.1.
- Hit the Spacebar; you should see Figure 3.2.
- Each time you hit the Spacebar, it should flip between the two images.
- After reading this chapter, hold down the Spacebar and let autorepeat make the crow look like it is flapping its wings. Look for tearing.
- Hit the Esc key to exit the program.
- Double-click on Up.bmp and Down.bmp to fire up the default paint program on your computer (usually Microsoft Paint) to verify to yourself that when you ran Demo 1 you were seeing the images that are stored in those files.

Why Flip Pages?

Before we get to the programming part of this chapter, let's take a quick look at how the graphics hardware on your PC works.

The Video Serializer

Think about your game as an interactive movie. You will be composing frames of this movie on-the-fly in response to the player's actions, and displaying them on the monitor. Obviously, each frame is composed by the CPU using system memory. So how does it get from system memory to the monitor? Your video card has two important pieces of hardware on it: *video memory* and the *video serializer.* The video memory contains the image to be displayed on the monitor, and it is the video serializer's job to display it. The video serializer takes the image from the video memory and sends it to the monitor at a constant rate, usually somewhere between 60 and 80 times per second. It does this even if the image doesn't change, because your monitor can only display an image for a fraction of a second before it begins to fade from the screen. While it is doing this, the CPU is attempting to send the next frame of animation to video memory. The process is shown in Figure 3.3. We can see from this description that both the CPU and the video serializer need access to video memory.

Figure 3.3
How the image gets to your monitor

Here's how the typical CRT computer monitor works, described in broad terms (the details are actually more complicated, but not important here). The surface of the screen is divided into rows and columns of pixels. Each pixel is coated with a special phosphor, which glows when it is hit with electrons, and will continue to glow for a fraction of a second afterwards. An electron beam scans the pixels from left to right, top to bottom, firing the right amount of electrons at each pixel in response to information provided by the video serializer. The video serializer has preferential access to video memory so that it can keep to a regular clock-like refresh schedule, thus ensuring that the image on your monitor stays clear and bright at all times. In order to do this, the video serializer takes the majority of available access cycles to the video memory, while the CPU often has to wait. As a result, the video serializer can read from video memory faster than the CPU can write to it. This leads to a problem known as tearing, which results from having a new frame only partially replace the frame before it.

Tearing

Consider the two frames of animation shown in Figures 3.4 and 3.5. Frame 1 (Figure 3.4) shows an outhouse, a silo, and a barn. In Frame 2 (Figure 3.5), the camera has panned 6 pixels to the left, and so everything in the image has shifted 6 pixels to the right. Ideally, we would like to show Frame 1, then Frame 2, and then move on to Frame 3, etc.

Figure 3.4
Frame 1 of
animation

Figure 3.5
Frame 2 of
animation:
the camera
pans left
from Frame
1 (Figure
3.4)

Suppose that Frame 1 has already been loaded to video memory, and that the video serializer has already drawn it to the monitor, perhaps several times. When the video serializer is drawing from the bottom of Frame 1 in video memory, we quickly start to draw Frame 2 over it, starting at the top. However, since the video serializer has preferential access to video memory, it will read faster than the CPU can write. After a while we get the situation shown in Figure 3.6, where the CPU is still drawing Frame 2 on top of Frame 1, but the video serializer is catching up. Eventually it will pass the point at which the CPU is writing Frame 2 into video memory and start reading from Frame 1 again. We will see displayed on the monitor a frame that consists of the top of Frame 2 pasted on the bottom of Frame 1, as shown in Figure 3.7. It looks like the bottom of the frame has been torn off and shifted slightly to the left, hence the term *tearing*.

Figure 3.6
Animation
with one
page of
video
memory

Figure 3.7
What is actually drawn in one-page animation (see Figure 3.6): the top of Frame 2 (Figure 3.5) and the bottom of Frame 1 (Figure 3.4), leaving a tear

This is a very simplified account of what is going on; in reality you will probably see many tears, not just one. The tears occur very quickly, in the blink of an eye. They can be in different places on each frame, and there can be a different number of tears on each frame. It takes a fast eye to see them, and unless you are aware of what is going on and are really watching for them, you probably won't notice them consciously. Subconsciously, however, you will be aware that the animation looks *bad* without being able to put your finger on exactly what the problem is. You will see this behavior exhibited by many old DOS games, Mac games, and games that you play in a web browser. Now that you know what to look for, go look carefully at one of these types of games and look for tearing.

How to Avoid Tearing

The only way to avoid tearing is to grab control of the video hardware, and take advantage of the large amounts of video memory that are now available on even quite low-end video cards. Unfortunately, Windows, like any sensible operating system, will not let you take control of the video hardware when other applications are likely to be using it. Fortunately, DirectX gives you the power to do so when your game is running in full-screen mode. That's why we are running full screen in this book.

When the CPU is writing to video memory, it simply takes a pointer to video memory and moves that pointer down the memory while writing bytes of data. Likewise, the video serializer reads data from a pointer. Our solution to the tearing problem is to use two frames' worth of video memory, and allow the video serializer to draw from a completed frame while the CPU is drawing the next frame someplace else in video memory (see Figure 3.8). These frames in video memory are called *pages*. When the CPU has finished writing its frame, we do what is called *page flipping*, which puts the video serializer's pointer at the top of the new frame, and puts the CPU's pointer at the top of the old frame that the serializer just finished with (see Figure 3.9). In this way, the video serializer always has a complete frame to draw from except for a brief period while the pointers are being moved, which is so small that it can usually be done in the *vertical retrace interval*, which is the time period during which your monitor's electron beam moves from the lower-right pixel on the screen to the top-left pixel.

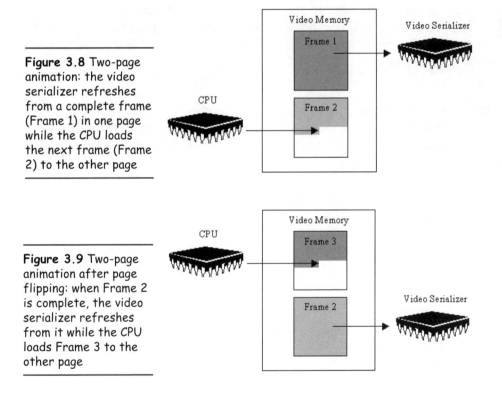

Figure 3.8 Two-page animation: the video serializer refreshes from a complete frame (Frame 1) in one page while the CPU loads the next frame (Frame 2) to the other page

Figure 3.9 Two-page animation after page flipping: when Frame 2 is complete, the video serializer refreshes from it while the CPU loads Frame 3 to the other page

The page that the CPU is writing to is called the *front buffer*, while the page that the video serializer is reading from is called the *back buffer*. Page flipping is the process of swapping the front buffer and the back buffer, but keep in mind that this does not involve moving the image data in the pages, just moving two pointers.

The Secondary Surface

The back buffer is a secondary surface that we request from the DirectDraw object. We declare in Main.cpp a pointer for the back buffer, which we will call lpSecondary, and one for its palette, lpSecondaryPalette.

```
LPDIRECTDRAWSURFACE lpSecondary=NULL; //back buffer
LPDIRECTDRAWPALETTE lpSecondaryPalette; //its palette
```

These are externed at the top of Ddsetup.cpp. In InitDirectDraw, we change the flags slightly in ddsd to show that we will be requesting a number of back buffers, in our case only one, but DirectDraw will let us attempt to use more than one back buffer if we wish. This is done by ORing in DDSD_BACKBUFFER-COUNT to ddsd.dwFlags.

```
ddsd.dwFlags=DDSD_CAPS|DDSD_BACKBUFFERCOUNT;
```

In order to get DirectDraw to let us page flip, we modify the dwCaps field to allow a flippable, complex surface by ORing in the appropriate two flags. A complex surface means one that has other surfaces attached to it; the secondary surface will be attached to the primary surface.

```
ddsd.ddsCaps.dwCaps=DDSCAPS_PRIMARYSURFACE|DDSCAPS_FLIP
    |DDSCAPS_COMPLEX;
```

We specify that there will be one back buffer:

```
ddsd.dwBackBufferCount=1;
```

We add code at the end of InitDirectDraw to attach a secondary surface to the primary surface (while we asked the DirectDraw object to create the primary surface, we must ask the primary surface to attach a secondary surface). This is done using a call to the primary surface's GetAttachedSurface member function and specifying that we need a back buffer using a DDSCAPS structure.

```
DDSCAPS ddscaps;
ddscaps.dwCaps=DDSCAPS_BACKBUFFER;
```

We attach the secondary surface to the primary surface, and create a palette for it:

```
if(FAILED(lpPrimary->
GetAttachedSurface(&ddscaps,&lpSecondary)))
  return FALSE;
lpSecondaryPalette=CreatePalette(lpSecondary);
```

Returning to Main.cpp, we declare two CBmpFileReader class instances, frame0 and frame1, to hold the two frames of animation.

```
CBmpFileReader frame0; //first frame
CBmpFileReader frame1; //second frame
```

Function `LoadImages` loads `Up.bmp`, draws it to the primary surface, and sets the palette using the `CBmpFileReader` class instance `frame0`:

```
if(!frame0.load("up.bmp"))return FALSE; //read from file
if(!frame0.setpalette(lpPrimaryPalette)) //set palette
  return FALSE;
if(!frame0.draw(lpPrimary))return FALSE; //draw
```

Then it loads `Down.bmp`, draws it to the secondary surface, and sets the palette using the `CBmpFileReader` class instance `frame1`:

```
if(!frame1.load("down.bmp"))return FALSE; //read from file
if(!frame1.setpalette(lpSecondaryPalette)) //set palette
  return FALSE;
if(!frame1.draw(lpSecondary))return FALSE; //draw
```

Page flipping is done using the primary surface's `Flip` member function. Unfortunately, DirectDraw surfaces are not just set-and-forget structures. They can be lost at awkward times that are out of the programmer's control (for example, if the user hits Alt+Tab to select another running application as the active app, it has the unpleasant side effect of causing all surfaces in our game to become lost). In particular, we may find out that surfaces have been lost when we attempt to page flip. If so, the surfaces must be restored. We will write a function `RestoreSurfaces` to take care of this detail. The page flipping operation, then, consists of calling the primary surface's `Flip` member function and restoring the surfaces if it reports surface loss by returning `DDERR_SURFACELOST`.

```
BOOL PageFlip(){ //return TRUE if page flip succeeds
  if(lpPrimary->Flip(NULL,DDFLIP_WAIT)==DDERR_SURFACELOST)
    return RestoreSurfaces();
  return TRUE;
} //PageFlip
```

The primary and secondary surfaces are restored by calling their `Restore` member functions. This reallocates the memory but does not redraw the image; we have to do that ourselves using the appropriate `CBmpFileReader` class instances.

```
BOOL RestoreSurfaces(){ //restore all surfaces
  BOOL result=TRUE;
  if(SUCCEEDED(lpPrimary->Restore()))
    result=result&&frame0.draw(lpPrimary)&& //redraw image
      frame0.setpalette(lpPrimaryPalette); //set palette
  else return FALSE;
  if(SUCCEEDED(lpSecondary->Restore()))
    result=result&&frame1.draw(lpSecondary)&& //redraw image
      frame1.setpalette(lpSecondaryPalette); //set palette
  else return FALSE;
```

```
    return result;
} //RestoreSurfaces
```

To make the page flip happen in response to the Spacebar, we need to add the following case to the switch statement in function `keyboard_handler`:

```
case VK_SPACE: result=!PageFlip(); break;
```

Lastly, in response to the `WM_DESTROY` message case in `WindowProc`, we need to release the secondary surface. Since it is attached to the primary surface, we make sure that we release the secondary surface first, then the primary surface.

```
if(lpSecondary!=NULL) //if secondary surface exists
    lpSecondary->Release(); //release secondary surface
```

We will be adding a lot more surfaces to our game as we move from demo to demo. The process will be same for each new surface; they will each need to be:

- Created by the DirectDraw object.
- Drawn to (when initializing and when restoring) from a `CBmpFileReader` object.
- Restored (and redrawn to) in function `RestoreSurfaces` when surfaces are lost.
- Released in `WindowProc` in response to the `WM_DESTROY` message. Take care though; the `Release` function of each surface must be called only once. Calling it more often is a common cause of crashes.

Demo 1 Files

Code Files

The following files in Demo 1 are used without change from Demo 0:

- Bmp.h
- Bmp.cpp
- Defines.h

The following files in Demo 1 have been modified from Demo 0:

- Ddsetup.cpp
- Main.cpp

Media Files

The following image files are new in Demo 1:

- Down.bmp (to be used only in Demos 1 and 2)
- Up.bmp (to be used only in Demos 1 and 2)

Required Libraries

- Ddraw.lib

Chapter 4

Here's what you'll learn:

- How to implement a game timer using the Windows API function timeGetTime

- How to use the timer to regulate animation speed

- How to modify the message loop to allow full-screen animation

Full-screen Animation

In Demo 2, we learn how to perform full-screen animation using three frames of animation to make the crow from Demo 1 look like it is flying (well, flying against a headwind—it flaps like crazy but never gets anywhere). The trick is to make the crow's wings beat at about the same speed whether you have an antique 90 MHz Pentium I or one of the new gigahertz plus Pentium IVs that are the hottest thing on the market at the time of this writing (but won't be by the time this book reaches the stores). We will achieve this by using a *timer* to control the rate at which the frames are displayed. The timer is a simple class that we will use a lot. In a game, everything must be time-based to ensure that it is playable on a range of available hardware. The advantage to making it a class is that we can reuse it in multiple projects, and if we wish, we can change the implementation of the timer midway through the project with a minimum of recoding and recompilation.

Experiment with Demo 2

Take a moment now to run Demo 2.

- You should see the crow from Demo 1 flapping its wings.
- Hit Alt+Tab to make the game inactive. All the surfaces have just been lost. Reactivate it from the Windows taskbar; the surfaces will be restored and reloaded.
- If you can, try it on several computers of different speeds. Note that the crow flaps its wings at about the same speed on all of them.
- Hit the Esc key to exit the program.

The Timer

The header file for the timer class CTimer is Timer.h. The timer acts like a stopwatch, counting the time that has elapsed in milliseconds since it was started. CTimer has a single protected member variable that records the time at which the timer was started.

```
int m_nStartTime; //time that timer was started
```

The public member functions include a constructor and a start function.

```
CTimer(); //constructor
virtual void start(); //start the timer
```

The time function, also virtual, will return the number of milliseconds since the start function was called:

```
virtual int time(); //return the time in ms
```

Finally, the elapsed function takes two parameters, start and interval. If interval milliseconds have elapsed since start, the function returns TRUE and sets start to the current time. Otherwise, it returns FALSE. Notice that start is declared as a call-by-reference parameter, int &start. This function will be used extensively for events that must repeat after a certain amount of time. We will keep a variable for each repeating event and use it to record the last time that the event occurred. This variable will be passed to the timer's elapsed function as the first parameter.

```
BOOL elapsed(int &start,int interval);
```

The CTimer functions are all very simple. Their implementation can be found in Timer.cpp. The constructor sets the member variable to a sensible value.

```
CTimer::CTimer(){ //constructor
  m_nStartTime=0;
}
```

The start function sets the start time using the Windows API function timeGetTime, which returns the number of milliseconds since Windows was rebooted. The value returned by timeGetTime wraps around to zero every 2^{32} milliseconds, which is about 49.71 days. If you think that your game will be running when Windows has been up for that long, then you will need to take further action. Personally, I can't keep Windows from crashing for more than a few hours, so I'm going to be lazy and assume that the same is true of my customers. The timeGetTime function is not a very good timer on some hardware. In general, it is accurate only down to about 5 milliseconds—but this is accurate enough for *Ned's Turkey Farm*.

```
void CTimer::start(){ //start the timer
  m_nStartTime=timeGetTime();
}
```

The CTimer time function simply subtracts the start time from the current time returned by the API function timeGetTime:

```
int CTimer::time(){ //return the time
  return timeGetTime()-m_nStartTime;
}
```

Finally, the elapsed function checks to see whether the current time is later than (or equal to) start+interval, sets start to the current time, and returns TRUE if so and FALSE if not:

```
int CTimer::elapsed(int &start,int interval){
  //has interval elapsed from start?
  int current_time=time();
  if(current_time>=start+interval){
    start=current_time; return TRUE;
  }
  else return FALSE;
}
```

Using the Timer

In `Main.cpp` we must, of course, include the header for the timer class:

```
#include "timer.h" //game timer
```

Then, we have some new declarations. We add a `CBmpFileReader` object for frame 2 of the animation.

```
CBmpFileReader frame0,frame1,frame2;
```

A frame counter is used to keep track of which frame is currently being displayed:

```
int current_frame=0; //current frame of animation
```

A `CTimer` object is declared for the game timer:

```
CTimer Timer; //game timer
```

The body of `LoadImages` is changed to load the three frames of animation from `Down.bmp`, `Middle.bmp`, and `Up.bmp`. All three of the images will use the same palette, which we will load from `frame0`. The artist must, of course, be aware that all artwork used in the body of the game will use the same palette. We won't bother to check that the artist has done this; if the palettes don't match, you will notice it pretty quickly during play testing.

```
BOOL LoadImages(){ //load graphics from files to surfaces
  //load the first frame
  if(!frame0.load("down.bmp"))return FALSE; //read from file
  frame0.draw(lpPrimary); //draw to primary surface
  //set palettes in all surfaces
  if(!frame0.setpalette(lpPrimaryPalette))return FALSE;
  if(!frame0.setpalette(lpSecondaryPalette))return FALSE;
  //load the other frames
  if(!frame1.load("middle.bmp"))return FALSE; //read from file
  if(!frame2.load("up.bmp"))return FALSE; //read from file
  return TRUE;
} //LoadImages
```

Recall the movie analogy that we used for game animation in Chapter 3. Our aim is to compose and display movie frames as fast as we possibly can. In Windows API programming, this can be done in the message loop—when your application isn't processing messages, it should be processing frames. The message loop from Demos 0 and 1 looked like this:

```
while(TRUE)
  if(PeekMessage(&msg,NULL,0,0,PM_NOREMOVE)){
    if(!GetMessage(&msg,NULL,0,0))return msg.wParam;
    TranslateMessage(&msg); DispatchMessage(&msg);
  }
  else if(!ActiveApp)WaitMessage();
```

We modify the last line of this code to say that if the app is active, then we process a frame, otherwise we do the `WaitMessage()`:

```
while(TRUE)
  if(PeekMessage(&msg,NULL,0,0,PM_NOREMOVE)){
    if(!GetMessage(&msg,NULL,0,0))return msg.wParam;
    TranslateMessage(&msg); DispatchMessage(&msg);
  }
  else if(ActiveApp)ProcessFrame(); else WaitMessage();
```

Function `ProcessFrame` processes a frame—that is, it composes it in the secondary surface, then flips it to the primary surface:

```
BOOL ProcessFrame(){ //process a frame of animation
  ComposeFrame(); //compose a frame in secondary surface
  return PageFlip(); //flip video memory surfaces
} //ProcessFrame
```

Function `ComposeFrame` composes a frame of animation to the secondary surface. We will change frames 10 times per second. (It is not a good idea in general to constrain your frame rate this way—we are just doing this as an example. Later, we will let the frame rate get as high as it can, and use similar techniques to govern the animation of objects within the game instead.) We start with a static local variable (that is, one that persists after the function has been called) `last_time` to record the last time the frame was changed.

```
static int last_time=Timer.time();
```

Recall that we are using a global variable `current_frame` to keep track of which frame is to be displayed. Sensibly, we first make sure that this value is in range. We allow it to take one of four possible values, from 0 to 3 inclusive so we can draw the frames in this order—frame 0 (wings down), frame 1 (wings middle), frame 2 (wings up), frame 1 (wings middle), then repeat.

```
if(current_frame<0)current_frame=0;
if(current_frame>3)current_frame=3;
```

The `CBmpFileReader draw` function is used to draw the current frame to the secondary surface:

```
switch(current_frame){
  case 0: frame0.draw(lpSecondary); break;
  case 1: frame1.draw(lpSecondary); break;
  case 2: frame2.draw(lpSecondary); break;
  case 3: frame1.draw(lpSecondary); break;
}
```

Finally, we increment `current_frame`, wrapping around to zero again when it exceeds three. Note the use of the `CTimer elapsed` function: If 100 milliseconds (one-tenth of a second) has elapsed, then we increment `current_frame`. Remember that the `CTimer elapsed` function has a side effect of setting `last_time` to "now" when it returns `TRUE`, so that the frame is changed on a regular schedule, 10 times per second.

```
if(Timer.elapsed(last_time,100))
  if(++current_frame>=4)current_frame=0;
```

But wait a second. We compose a frame to the secondary surface and then page flip. Doesn't that mean that the next frame—and every second frame thereafter—should be composed to the primary surface? The answer is no. DirectDraw takes care of swapping `lpPrimary` and `lpSecondary` for us every time we page flip. So the rule is, the primary surface is the one that the video serializer displays on the monitor, and the secondary surface is the one that we compose frames on.

The last thing we must remember to do is to start the timer during the initialization period, before we enter the message loop:

```
Timer.start();
```

Demo 2 Files

Code Files

The following files in Demo 2 are used without change from Demo 1:

- ◎ Bmp.h
- ◎ Bmp.cpp
- ◎ Ddsetup.cpp
- ◎ Defines.h

The following files in Demo 2 have been modified from Demo 1:

- ◎ Main.cpp

The following files are new in Demo 2:

- ◎ Timer.h
- ◎ Timer.cpp

Media Files

The following image files are new in Demo 2:

- ◎ Middle.bmp (to be used only in Demo 2)

Required Libraries

- ◎ Ddraw.lib
- ◎ Winmm.lib

Chapter 5

Here's what you'll learn:

- What a sprite is and how to set up a sprite file

- What blitting is

- How to do transparent blitting in DirectDraw

- Why you should separate an object's image from its other physical properties

- How to load and draw multi-framed sprites to the screen

- What happens if you try to draw outside the screen

Sprite Animation

In Demo 3, we learn how to do sprite animation. A *sprite* is a small piece of artwork that moves across the screen. *Sprite animation*, then, is the process of animating a sprite. Sprites may have several frames of animation, but in this example, we simply move a single-frame sprite depicting a plane across the background (see Figure 5.1). The process of drawing a sprite on top of the background is called *blitting*. DirectDraw allows us to blit from one surface to another with *transparency*, which means that we can designate one or more palette positions as transparent, that is, undrawn. This allows us to draw sprites with holes in them through which we can see the background.

Figure 5.1
A plane
sprite flying
across the
background

Experiment with Demo 3

Take a moment now to run Demo 3.

◉ You should see a plane flying from right to left across the background.

◉ Notice that the plane disappears as soon as its leftmost pixel leaves the screen. DirectDraw refuses to draw anything that goes outside the target surface. This is for a simple reason—if it didn't, you could accidentally end up drawing the plane anywhere in memory, for example, in the middle of the executable code for your game, or in the middle of the operating system. This would be a Bad Thing. So, remember this: If you try to draw a sprite but see nothing, it may mean that you have missed the surface completely.

◉ If you wait long enough, the plane will reappear on the right—as soon as its rightmost pixel is on the screen, that is.

◉ Hit the Esc key to exit the program.

The Sprite File

The sprites for our game were drawn by the artist in the file `Sprites.bmp` (see Figure 5.2). Notice that there are many sprites included in that file. Many artists prefer to put multiple sprites into a single file so that they can easily compare frames of animation to make sure they are consistent with each other. `Sprites.bmp` uses the same palette as `Bckgnd.bmp`. You must make sure that the artist realizes that all of the artwork to be used in the game must be drawn with the same palette.

Figure 5.2
The sprite file
Sprites.bmp

The background color used in `Sprites.bmp` is magenta, with an RGB value of (255,0,255). The important thing is not the color that is used, but its palette position. You and the artist must agree on a palette position that will be used for the background so that you can use that palette position to indicate transparent pixels—if the artwork is inconsistent with your program, the plane will be drawn with a rectangular block around it (see Figure 5.3). Although in principle any palette position can be used, it is normal to use either the first or last palette position (that is, either palette position 0 or palette position 255). This helps the artist to locate it in the palette. However, many art tools do not give any indication to the artist which end of the palette is which, so don't blow a fuse if the artist gets it wrong initially. In addition, you should know that the same art tool on two different platforms (such as PC and Mac) has been known to reverse the palettes on their images.

Figure 5.3
What you will see if you mess up the transparent color

It doesn't matter to the game what color you put in the transparent palette position, since pixels in that palette position aren't ever drawn. However, it is best that you put some color that isn't used elsewhere in the game so that the artist (or more accurately, the automated art tools that the artist may use) isn't tempted to use that palette position expecting it to actually be drawn. You can use the same color in another palette position if you have to, but the artist must be sure that the transparent palette position is used only for transparent pixels; otherwise your sprites will get holes in them where you don't necessarily want them.

You must also tell your artist not to antialias the sprites to the background. *Antialiasing* is the process of blurring the outer pixels of the sprites into the background. It is used to reduce the jaggedness of edges where the pixelation makes it look rough. Antialiasing our sprites onto the background will just give a pink haze around them when they are drawn onto the blue sky, which is an effect that we can live without. Tell the artist that the sprite will be drawn onto a variety of colored backgrounds, so there is nothing that we can antialias to. Be forewarned that it is normal for an artist, particularly a novice, to forget to turn off antialiasing occasionally. This is why I like to put magenta into the transparent palette position—when the artist forgets, it is immediately obvious to the naked eye, whereas antialiasing to black or white (which is a popular choice among artists) may go undetected for a long time.

You will notice if you take another look at Figure 5.2 that most of the sprites have a black rectangle around them. This is called the *bounding rectangle*. The bounding rectangle should be the smallest rectangle that will fit around the object. I have chosen in this game to have all of the frames in a multi-frame sprite have the same height and width, even though some frames may be smaller than others. Wasting transparent pixels around an image will slow your game slightly, so it should be avoided, but it is not a major issue.

Somebody—either you or the artist—must measure each of the sprite frames, recording the height and width of the sprite, and the position of the top left pixel of each frame (the top left pixel of the image is pixel (0,0), and the bottom right pixel is pixel (639,479) in our 640x480 resolution images). Explicitly drawing a bounding rectangle around each sprite frame will help you to identify the top left pixel easily even when the top left portion of the image is transparent, and it will have another positive effect: You will undoubtedly mess up your measurements at least once—I almost never manage to get them all right the first time. If you make the frame too small, the sprite image will be clipped along at least one edge. If you make it too big, it may infringe on the neighboring sprite by as little as one pixel, which will give you a floating pixel off to one side of your sprite. A single floating pixel is easy to miss. Using a bounding rectangle will ensure that if you make your sprite too large, one edge of the bounding box will appear on the screen. This is easy to spot (see Figure 5.4, for example) and the problem can then be quickly corrected.

Figure 5.4
Drawing part of the bounding box by accident

The Bmp Sprite File Reader

Since sprite files may contain multiple frames of sprite images within a single file, we need a way to read rectangles from a bmp file. The bmp sprite file reader class CBmpSpriteFileReader is derived from CBmpFileReader and adds to it a new public member draw function that draws to a surface, from the image stored in the CBmpFileReader member variable m_cImage, a rectangle of a given width and height with the top left pixel at a given pair of coordinates. The header file for CBmpSpriteFileReader is Sbmp.h, in which we find the following declaration:

```
class CBmpSpriteFileReader:
public CBmpFileReader{ //bmp sprite file input class
  public:
    BOOL draw(LPDIRECTDRAWSURFACE surface,
      int width,int ht,int x,int y); //draw sprite
};
```

Naturally, the code for CBmpSpriteFileReader::draw, found in Sbmp.cpp, is very similar to the code for CBmpFileReader::draw. The first difference is that the source pointer src is now initially set to point y rows up from the bottom of the image (recall from Chapter 2 that bmp files are stored upside-down) and x pixels across, where x and y are parameters to the draw function:

```
src=m_cImage+ //source pointer
  ((m_BMPFileInfo.biHeight-1-y)*m_BMPFileInfo.biWidth+x);
```

The second difference is that the for loop that moves data from the image to the surface now only move ht rows of data, and each row has width width, where ht and width are also parameters to the draw function:

```
for(int i=0; i<ht; i++){ //for each row
  memcpy(dest,src,width); //copy
  dest+=ddsd.lPitch; src-=m_BMPFileInfo.biWidth; //next row
}
```

The Base Sprite

A sprite is our abstraction of the image of an object. I find that it helps to abstract out the concept of the image of an object from its other features. That way, if we have multiple objects in the game that have the same image (for example, we will have multiple crows), we can share the image data and not waste memory on multiple copies of the same image. Our base sprite class is called CBaseSprite.

Base Sprite Overview

The header file for CBaseSprite is Bsprite.h. CBaseSprite has four private member variables and a private member function. The first private member variable is an array of pointers to DirectDraw surfaces. We will use one surface for each frame of the sprite. Because we have no way of knowing at compile time how many surfaces there will be, we declare it as a pointer to pointers to a DirectDraw surface and will new ourselves enough space in the CBaseSprite constructor.

```
LPDIRECTDRAWSURFACE *m_lpDDImage; //sprite image
```

The next three private member variables record how many frames of animation the sprite has, and the width and height of those frames. Recall that in this simple game, we will insist that all frames of animation in a given sprite have the same width and height (although they may be different for different sprites). This means that they must be as large as the largest frame, which is usually not too wasteful of space unless the sprite is *much* larger in some frames than others. I wouldn't use this technique, for example, in a maritime game in which the sprite frames record how a ship looks from different angles, since the face-on view of a ship can be very narrow compared to the side-on view.

```
int m_nFrameCount; //how many frames used in sprite
int m_nWidth,m_nHeight; //dimensions of sprite images
```

The private member function CreateSurfaces creates the surfaces for the sprite frames, assuming that the three private member variables m_nFrameCount, m_nWidth, and m_nHeight have been set:

```
void CreateSurfaces(); //create surfaces
```

CBaseSprite has, in addition to a constructor and a destructor, seven public member functions. The constructor has three parameters, the number of frames, and the frame width and height.

```
CBaseSprite(int frames,int w,int h); //constructor
~CBaseSprite(); //destructor
```

The CBaseSprite load function loads a frame from a CBmpSpriteFileReader image. It has four parameters, a pointer to the CBmpSpriteFileReader class instance containing the sprite frame, the number of the frame to be loaded, and the x and y coordinates from which the frame is to be loaded.

```
BOOL load(CBmpSpriteFileReader *image,int frame,
    int x,int y); //load sprite image
```

The CBaseSprite draw function is a virtual function because we will derive a more general sprite class from CBaseSprite in the next chapter. It takes four parameters, the number of the frame to be drawn, the x and y coordinates that the lower center pixel of the sprite is to be drawn to, and a pointer to the surface on which to draw it at those coordinates.

```
virtual void draw(int frame,int x,int y,
    LPDIRECTDRAWSURFACE destination); //draw sprite
```

Recall from Chapter 4 that every surface must be restored when surfaces are lost, and released when the game is over. Therefore, every class that contains member surfaces should have a restore and a release function.

```
void Release(); //release direct draw surfaces
BOOL Restore(); //restore surfaces
```

Finally, CBaseSprite has three public *reader functions*, which are used to provide read-only access to private member variables:

```
int frame_count(); //return number of frames
int height(); //return height
int width(); //return width
```

Creation and Destruction

The code for CBaseSprite can be found in Bsprite.cpp. The CBaseSprite constructor first records the number of frames, width, and height of the sprite.

```
CBaseSprite::CBaseSprite(int frames,int width,int height){
  //settings
  m_nWidth=width; m_nHeight=height; //width and height
  m_nFrameCount=frames; //assign number of frames
```

Then, it allocates space for the array of frame pointers, m_lpDDImage, and sets all of the pointers in the array to NULL:

```
m_lpDDImage=new LPDIRECTDRAWSURFACE[frames];
for(int i=0; i<frames; i++)m_lpDDImage[i]=NULL;
```

Finally, it calls private member function CreateSurfaces to create the surfaces in the frame array lpDDImage, and returns:

```
CreateSurfaces();
}
```

The CBaseSprite destructor merely deletes the memory allocated in the constructor:

```
CBaseSprite::~CBaseSprite(){ //destructor
  //deallocate memory allocated in constructor
  delete[]m_lpDDImage;
}
```

The CBaseSprite private member function CreateSurfaces has the task of creating and initializing one surface for each frame of the sprite:

```
void CBaseSprite::CreateSurfaces(){ //create surfaces
```

It has a single local variable, a DirectDraw surface descriptor:

```
DDSURFACEDESC ddsd; //direct draw surface descriptor
```

As we did the last time we used a DirectDraw surface descriptor, we set the size field of ddsd to the structure's size:

```
ddsd.dwSize=sizeof(ddsd); //required field
```

We indicate in the flags field that we're going to set the surface capabilities, height, and width:

```
ddsd.dwFlags=DDSD_CAPS|DDSD_HEIGHT|DDSD_WIDTH; //attributes
```

In the capabilities field, we ask for a plain offscreen surface, that is, one that will reside in system memory as opposed to video memory. Then, we set the width and height of the surface to be the sprite frame height and width.

```
ddsd.ddsCaps.dwCaps=DDSCAPS_OFFSCREENPLAIN; //offscreen
ddsd.dwHeight=m_nHeight; //sprite height
ddsd.dwWidth=m_nWidth; //sprite width
```

In order to set the transparent palette position, we declare a local variable ddck of type DDCOLORKEY. Actually, we can set a range of palette positions to use for the transparent color, so we set both the lower value for the range and the upper value equal to TRANSPARENT_COLOR, which is defined to be 255 in Defines.h.

```
DDCOLORKEY ddck; //direct draw color descriptor
ddck.dwColorSpaceLowValue=
  ddck.dwColorSpaceHighValue=
    TRANSPARENT_COLOR; //one color
```

Finally, we create the surfaces in a "for each frame" style for loop. Each surface is created with a call to the DirectDraw object's CreateSurface member function, and then we set the transparent color in the new surface using its Set-ColorKey member function. SetColorKey has two parameters. We set the first to DDCKEY_SRCBLT to indicate that when a sprite surface is blitted the color key is in the source surface. The second parameter is a pointer to the DDCOLORKEY local variable that we loaded with the transparent color for our game.

```
for(int i=0; i<m_nFrameCount; i++){ //for each frame
  //create surface
  if(FAILED(lpDirectDrawObject->
  CreateSurface(&ddsd,&(m_lpDDImage[i]),NULL)))
    m_lpDDImage[i]=NULL;
  //set the transparent color
  m_lpDDImage[i]->SetColorKey(DDCKEY_SRCBLT,&ddck);
}
}
```

The CBaseSprite Release function calls the Release member function of each surface in the m_lpDDImage array:

```
void CBaseSprite::Release(){ //release all sprite surfaces
  for(int i=0; i<m_nFrameCount; i++) //for each frame
    if(m_lpDDImage[i]!=NULL) //if it is really there
      m_lpDDImage[i]->Release(); //release it
}
```

Loading and Drawing

The CBaseSprite load function loads a sprite frame from a CBmpSprite-FileReader class instance. It simply calls the CBmpSpriteFileReader draw function to draw from the appropriate rectangle in its stored image into the correct frame in its m_lpDDImage array.

```
BOOL CBaseSprite::load(CBmpSpriteFileReader *buffer,
                       int frame,int x,int y){
//grab sprite image from (x,y) in *buffer
//and store in m_lpDDImage[frame]
  return buffer->draw(m_lpDDImage[frame],
    m_nWidth,m_nHeight,x,y);
}
```

The CBaseSprite draw function uses the destination surface's BltFast member function to blit the image from the correct frame in its lpDDImage array. The flags field is set to DDBLTFAST_SRCCOLORKEY|DDBLTFAST_WAIT, indicating respectively that the source surface has a transparency palette range set, and that if the blitter is busy the blit function is to wait and return only after the blitter has responded. The DirectDraw BltFast function takes as its first two parameters the x and y coordinates at which the *top left* pixel of the sprite is to appear. We will find it more convenient for the CBaseSprite draw function to take instead the x and y coordinates at which the *lower center* pixel of the sprite is to appear. Hence, the CBaseSprite draw function must subtract half of the sprite width from the x coordinate, and the sprite height from the y coordinate to get the target coordinates of the top left pixel. The third parameter to BltFast is a pointer to the source surface, and the fourth parameter is a pointer to a rectangle from which to blit from within the source surface. Leaving the rectangle pointer NULL will draw the whole surface.

```
void CBaseSprite::draw(int frame,int x,int y,
                       LPDIRECTDRAWSURFACE dest){
  dest->BltFast(x-m_nWidth/2,y-m_nHeight,m_lpDDImage[frame],
    NULL,DDBLTFAST_SRCCOLORKEY|DDBLTFAST_WAIT);
}
```

Other Member Functions

The CBaseSprite Restore function calls the Restore member function of each surface in the m_lpDDImage array:

```
BOOL CBaseSprite::Restore(){ //restore surfaces
  BOOL result=TRUE; //return TRUE if all surfaces restored OK
  for(int i=0; i<m_nFrameCount; i++) //for each frame
    if(m_lpDDImage[i]) //if it exists
      result=result&&
        SUCCEEDED(m_lpDDImage[i]->Restore()); //restore it
  return result;
}
```

The remaining three CBaseSprite reader functions frame_count, height, and width return the values in the respective private member variables. Rather than list these simple functions here, we will leave it for you to read them in the listing of Bsprite.cpp in the pdf supplement.

The Object Class

Each of the objects in our game will be described using a class called CObject. CObject will encapsulate everything about an object, including its physical characteristics and its image.

Object Overview

The header file for CObject is Objects.h. CObject has six private member variables that together comprise the internal state of an object—its location in the virtual universe (which in this game is two-dimensional), its speed, the last time it moved, and a pointer to a sprite that represents its image. For memory efficiency we use a *pointer to a sprite* instead of a sprite, so that multiple objects can share the same sprite.

```
int m_nX,m_nY; //current location
int m_nXspeed,m_nYspeed; //current speed
int m_nLastXMoveTime; //last time the object moved
CBaseSprite *m_pSprite; //pointer to sprite
```

In addition to a constructor, CObject has four public member functions. The CObject draw function takes a pointer to a DirectDraw surface, and draws the object on that surface. Notice that the draw function has no other parameters, which implies that the object is responsible for determining where it should be drawn on the screen from its location in the virtual universe.

```
void draw(LPDIRECTDRAWSURFACE surface); //draw
```

The CObject create function sets the initial state of the object. The parameters to that function list the object's initial position, speed, and a pointer to its shared sprite.

```
void create(int x,int y,int xspeed,int yspeed,
    CBaseSprite *sprite); //create instance
```

The CObject accelerate function changes the x and y components of the object's speed, and takes as parameters the amounts by which those components must change:

```
void accelerate(int xdelta,int ydelta=0); //change speed
```

The CObject move function makes the object move. Notice that this function has no parameters, which implies that the object is responsible for determining how far it should move from its internal state. It does this by modifying its location in the virtual universe depending on its speed and the time since the last move was made. This dependence on time is crucial if our game is to run at the same apparent speed on a variety of hardware. Neglecting the dependence on time—one of the most common mistakes that I have seen novice game programmers make—will make objects that travel at a fixed speed move a fixed distance on every frame. However, a faster computer will have a higher frame rate, which means that objects should move less on each frame if they are to achieve the same apparent motion across the screen as on a slow computer. We must also consider the fact that the frame rate of your game will not remain constant, because Windows is a multitasking operating system, meaning that other applications may be running simultaneously, making demands on the CPU's processing power at random times. We overcome both of these problems by measuring the time since the object last moved (which should have been during the previous frame), and then moving it a distance proportional to that time.

```
void move(); //make a move depending on time and speed
```

Object Code

The code for CObject can be found in Objects.cpp. The CObject constructor puts some reasonable initial values into the private member variables.

```
CObject::CObject(){ //constructor
  m_nX=m_nY=m_nXspeed=m_nYspeed=0;
  m_pSprite=NULL; m_nLastXMoveTime=0;
}
```

Next, we have the CObject draw function, which draws the object to a given surface. It calls the draw function of the object's sprite to draw frame 0 to position (m_nX,m_nY) on surface, where m_nX and m_nY are the CObject private member variables that record the object's location in the virtual universe.

```
void CObject::draw(LPDIRECTDRAWSURFACE surface){ //draw
  m_pSprite->draw(0,m_nX,m_nY,surface);
}
```

The CObject create function initializes the object's private member functions, setting m_nLastXMoveTime to zero, and the rest of them to values provided as parameters:

```
void CObject::create(int x,int y,int xspeed,int yspeed,
                     CBaseSprite *sprite){
  m_nLastXMoveTime=0; //time
  m_nX=x; m_nY=y; //location
  m_nXspeed=xspeed; m_nYspeed=yspeed; //speed
  m_pSprite=sprite; //image
}
```

The CObject accelerate function accelerates the object by adding a delta to its speed in the x and y directions:

```
void CObject::accelerate(int xdelta,int ydelta){
  //change speed
  m_nXspeed+=xdelta; m_nYspeed+=ydelta;
}
```

The Move Function

The CObject move function moves the object a distance that depends on its speed and the time since it last moved. We begin the function with the declaration of two constants. XSCALE is a constant whose value we set by experiment—more about that in a moment. MARGIN is a width of a guard band that extends to the left and the right of the screen by 100 pixels; that is, the virtual universe for this demo consists of the background plus a 100-pixel wide strip to the left of the screen and another to the right of the screen.

```
void CObject::move(){ //move object
  const int XSCALE=8; //to scale back horizontal motion
  const int MARGIN=100; //margin on outside of page
```

We next declare two local variables, xdelta, which will record the distance moved in the x direction (in this demo all motion will be in the x direction), and time, which records the current time as obtained from the global game timer Timer, which is externed at the top of Objects.cpp:

```
int xdelta; //change in position
int time=Timer.time(); //current time
```

We then set a local variable tfactor to the amount of time since the object last moved, which is recorded in private member variable m_nLastXMoveTime:

```
int tfactor=time-m_nLastXMoveTime; //time since last move
```

The distance that the object moves in the x direction is equal to its speed multiplied by the time factor. This value needs to be scaled back slightly. For example, at 30 frames per second (33.33 milliseconds between frames), tfactor will be approximately 33, which means that at a speed of 1 the object will move 33 pixels per frame, which comes out to be approximately 1000 pixels—more than the width of the virtual universe—per second. We scale back the distance moved by dividing it by XSCALE, and experimenting with the value of XSCALE until it looks right. (Remember the First Law of Graphics Programming: If it looks right, it *is* right.) The distance moved in the x direction, xdelta, is added into the object's x location.

```
xdelta=(m_nXspeed*tfactor)/XSCALE; //x distance moved
m_nX+=xdelta; //x motion
```

The object in this demo (the plane) will move left across the screen, and so its x coordinate will eventually become negative. When it reaches the edge of the guard band, we move it to the other guard band at the right-hand side of the screen.

```
if(m_nX<-MARGIN)m_nX=SCREEN_WIDTH+MARGIN; //wrap left
```

Next, we record the time of the current move. It is tempting to just write "m_nLastXMoveTime=time" here, and leave it at that. However, the situation is slightly more subtle than it first appears. The object could move so slowly that it moves only one pixel on every second frame. For example, suppose that the game runs at 60 frames per second, the object has an m_nXspeed of 1, and we set XSCALE to 32. On the first frame, the time-since-last-move will be 16 milliseconds, and xdelta will be 16/32, which will be rounded down to zero. On the next frame we want the time-since-last-move to be 32 milliseconds, so that xdelta will be 32/32=1 pixel. Therefore, we *don't* want to set m_nLastXMoveTime to time unless xdelta is nonzero. Unless, of course, xdelta is zero because m_nXspeed is zero—we don't want our object to take off at light speed after sitting still for a few minutes!

```
if(xdelta||m_nXspeed==0) //record time of move
  m_nLastXMoveTime=time;
```

Although we don't use it in this demo, I have also added code for wrapping an object moving rightwards across the screen:

```
if(m_nX>SCREEN_WIDTH+MARGIN)m_nX=-MARGIN; //wrap right
}
```

Changes to Ddsetup.cpp and Main.cpp

The changes to `Ddsetup.cpp` in Demo 3 are all related to the background surface:

```
extern LPDIRECTDRAWSURFACE lpBackground; //background image
```

At the end of `InitDirectDraw`, we add code to set up the background surface as a plain offscreen surface of the same height and width as the screen. This code is almost identical to that used for setting up the surfaces for the sprite frames in `CBaseSprite` earlier in this chapter.

```
ddsd.dwSize=sizeof(ddsd);
ddsd.dwFlags=DDSD_CAPS|DDSD_HEIGHT|DDSD_WIDTH;
ddsd.ddsCaps.dwCaps=DDSCAPS_OFFSCREENPLAIN;
ddsd.dwHeight=SCREEN_HEIGHT; ddsd.dwWidth=SCREEN_WIDTH;
if(FAILED(lpDirectDrawObject->
CreateSurface(&ddsd,&lpBackground,NULL)))
  return FALSE;
```

The changes to `Main.cpp` involve initializing, using, and cleaning up the objects and their sprites. After the declarations of the pointers for the primary and secondary surfaces that we use from Demo 2, we insert a declaration for a pointer for a surface to hold the background image ready for blitting to the secondary surface during animation.

```
LPDIRECTDRAWSURFACE lpBackground=NULL; //background image
```

Next, we declare a `CBmpFileReader` class instance to load the background file, and a `CBmpSpriteFileReader` class instance to load the sprite file:

```
CBmpFileReader background; //background image
CBmpSpriteFileReader g_cSpriteImages; //sprite images
```

Demo 3 has just one object, Ned's trusty old biplane:

```
CObject plane; //plane object
```

The plane sprite is a different entity from the plane object:

```
CBaseSprite *planesprite=NULL; //plane sprite
```

The LoadPlaneSprite and LoadImages Functions

The first piece of code is the function `LoadPlaneSprite`, which loads the plane sprite by calling the `planesprite load` function. The `load` function has four parameters, the first of which is a pointer to the `CBmpSpriteFileReader` class instance `g_cSpriteImages` that holds the sprite image. The next parameter is 0, indicating that we are loading frame 0 of the sprite (which only has one frame). The next two parameters are 1, 1, which are the coordinates of the top left pixel of the rectangle containing the plane sprite image (the plane sprite is at the top left corner of Sprites.bmp, inside a bounding box of width 1—see Figure 5.2).

```
BOOL LoadPlaneSprite(){ //load plane image
  return planesprite->load(&g_cSpriteImages,0,1,1);
} //LoadPlaneSprite
```

The body of function LoadImages is replaced completely by the following code. First, we load the background image from the file Bckgnd.bmp into the CBmpFileReader class instance background, then draw it to the background surface pointed to by lpBackground.

```
if(!background.load("bckgnd.bmp"))return FALSE; //read file
background.draw(lpBackground); //draw to background surface
```

We then set the palettes of the primary and secondary surfaces:

```
if(!background.setpalette(lpPrimaryPalette))return FALSE;
if(!background.setpalette(lpSecondaryPalette))return FALSE;
```

Next, we load the sprite image file Sprites.bmp into the CBmpSpriteFile-Reader class instance g_cSpriteImages:

```
if(!g_cSpriteImages.load("sprites.bmp"))return FALSE;
```

We then new ourselves a planesprite of type CBaseSprite, a base sprite with one frame, 121 pixels wide and 72 pixels high. How do we figure out the height and width of the plane sprite? We open up the sprite file Sprites.bmp with an art tool, such as Microsoft Paint, and measure the coordinates of the top left pixel and the bottom right pixel of the plane sprite in the top left corner of the file, just inside the bounding box. In general, if the top left pixel is at (x_1, y_1) and the bottom right pixel is at (x_2, y_2), then the sprite is x_2-x_1+1 pixels wide, and y_2-y_1+1 pixels high.

```
planesprite=new CBaseSprite(1,121,72);
if(!LoadPlaneSprite())return FALSE; //load plane images
```

The CreateObjects Function

The function CreateObjects creates the objects in the game. At this stage of development we have just the plane, of course. It calls the CObject plane create function with five parameters. The first two are the initial coordinates of the bottom center pixel of the plane sprite, (320, 271), which puts it approximately at the center of the screen. The next two are the x and y components of its speed, −1, 0, which makes it move left at speed 1. The last parameter is a pointer to its sprite, planesprite.

```
void CreateObjects(){
  plane.create(320,271,-1,0,planesprite); //create plane
} //CreateObjects
```

The RestoreSurfaces Function

In function `RestoreSurfaces`, after some minor changes to how the primary and secondary surfaces are redrawn after they are restored (in Demo 2 they were redrawn from `frame0` and `frame1`, while here in Demo 3 they are redrawn from `background`), we add code to restore and redraw the `lpBackground` surface (using the DirectDraw surface `Restore` function) and the `planesprite` sprite frame surface (using our `CBaseSprite Restore` member function):

```
if(SUCCEEDED(lpBackground->Restore())) //if background restored
  result=result&&background.draw(lpBackground); //redraw image
else return FALSE;
if(planesprite->Restore()) //if plane sprite restored
  result=result&&LoadPlaneSprite(); //redraw image
else return FALSE;
```

The ComposeFrame Function

The body of `ComposeFrame` gets totally rewritten. Now it is beginning to look like a *real* sprite animation engine, except for the fact that Demo 3 has only one object. First, we draw the background to the secondary surface. Setting the `DDBLTFAST_NOCOLORKEY` flag in `BltFast` ensures that no transparencies are used. It is a little inefficient at this point to redraw the whole background on each frame since most of it doesn't change, but later in the development we will add a moving background that will change on almost every frame. If this weren't so, we could just redraw the background behind the plane instead of redrawing the whole thing—such a process is called *dirty rectangle animation*.

```
lpSecondary->BltFast(0,0,lpBackground,NULL,
  DDBLTFAST_NOCOLORKEY|DDBLTFAST_WAIT);
```

Then we move the objects:

```
plane.move();
```

Then, we draw them on top of the secondary surface:

```
plane.draw(lpSecondary);
```

The Window Procedure and WinMain

The final thing we need to do to the new surfaces in `Main.cpp` is to release them when we are finished with them. In the switch statement in `WindowProc`, under the `WM_DESTROY` case, we must add the following code after the primary and secondary surfaces have been released. (And we can delete the `planesprite` while we are cleaning up.) The background surface is released using its DirectDraw surface `Release` function, and `planesprite` is released using our `CBaseSprite Release` member function.

```
if(lpBackground!=NULL) //if background exists
  lpBackground->Release(); //release background
if(planesprite!=NULL) //if plane sprite exists
  planesprite->Release(); //release plane sprite
delete planesprite; //delete plane sprite
```

Finally, a call to CreateObjects in WinMain just before we enter the message loop will create our objects for us:

```
CreateObjects();
```

Demo 3 Files

Code Files

The following files in Demo 3 are used without change from Demo 2:

- Bmp.h
- Bmp.cpp
- Timer.h
- Timer.cpp

The following files in Demo 3 have been modified from Demo 2:

- Ddsetup.cpp
- Defines.h
- Main.cpp

The following files are new in Demo 3:

- Bsprite.h
- Bsprite.cpp
- Objects.h
- Objects.cpp
- Sbmp.h
- Sbmp.cpp

Media Files

The following image files are new in Demo 3:

- Bckgnd.bmp (previously used in Demo 0 but not Demos 1 and 2)
- Sprites.bmp

Required Libraries

- Ddraw.lib
- Winmm.lib

Chapter 6

Here's what you'll learn:

- What sprite clipping is

- How to create and use a DirectDraw clipper

- How to add more objects to the game

Sprite Clipping

In Demo 4, we learn how to clip sprites so that they don't disappear prematurely at the edge of the screen. Fortunately, DirectDraw provides us with a mechanism that can quickly and easily clip sprites for us. So that you can test clipping at the top and bottom of the screen, we have added code to the keyboard handler to allow you to steer the plane using the arrow keys on the keyboard. There are also more objects than there were in Demo 3—we have added two crows who flap their wings as they move across the screen. One moves faster than the other, and flaps its wings faster too. One crow is behind the plane, and the other is in front of it.

Figure 6.1
Screen shot of Demo 4 showing clipped plane sprite

Experiment with Demo 4

Take a moment now to run Demo 4.

◉ You should see a plane and two crows flying from right to left across the background.

◉ Notice that the plane no longer disappears as soon as its leftmost pixel leaves the screen. The plane is clipped, that is, if only part of it is on the screen, only that part is drawn.

◉ If you wait long enough, the plane will reappear on the right.

◉ Use the left and right arrow keys to accelerate and decelerate the plane.

◉ Use the up and down arrow keys to move the plane up and down. Notice how it clips correctly on all four sides of the screen.

◉ Hit the Esc key to exit the program.

Creating a DirectDraw Clipper

Sprite clipping is done with an object called a *DirectDraw clipper*. The code for creating the clipper goes into the `InitDirectDraw` function in `Ddsetup.cpp`. First, we create a local variable `lpClipper` to point to the clipper.

```
LPDIRECTDRAWCLIPPER lpClipper; //pointer to the clipper
```

Next, we ask the DirectDraw object to create the clipper for us, returning a pointer to it in `lpClipper`. If this fails, we bail out of `InitDirectDraw`.

```
if(FAILED(lpDirectDrawObject-> //create the clipper
CreateClipper(NULL,&lpClipper,NULL)))
   return FALSE;
```

The clipper can be set to clip to any rectangle or to the entire window. Since we are running fullscreen, we will use the clipper's `SetHWnd` member function to achieve the latter effect. The `SetHWnd` function gives the clipper a window handle, and says, in effect, "Hey, clip to this window." This is actually a very powerful operation that can be used in windowed mode to clip objects correctly even when other windows partially obscure your game.

```
if(FAILED(lpClipper->SetHWnd(NULL,hwnd)))
   return FALSE;
```

Finally, we attach the clipper to the secondary surface so that every sprite that gets drawn to the secondary surface gets clipped. This is done by calling the secondary surface's `SetClipper` member function with a pointer to the clipper; this is why we need the local variable `lpClipper` in the first place.

```
if(FAILED(lpSecondary->SetClipper(lpClipper)))
   return FALSE;
```

The Clipped Sprite

DirectDraw clippers are set-and-forget objects. We've created it; now it will do its job without any further prompting from us… except for one small detail. In Demo 3 we used the `BltFast` member function to draw sprites to the secondary surface. `BltFast` is actually a scaled-down version of a function called `Blt`, which can do much more than `BltFast` can but, as the name suggests, the smaller stripped-down `BltFast` is much faster than `Blt` at doing the things that it can do. Well, you've probably guessed it by now—`BltFast` is fast but it cannot clip. Because it is sometimes useful to have sprites that aren't clipped (for example, for things like buttons that don't go anywhere near the edge of the screen), we will leave our `CBaseSprite` class the way it is, and derive a new class from it called `CClippedSprite`. `CClippedSprite` essentially looks the same as `CBaseSprite` except for the fact that sprite frames are drawn with `Blt` instead of `BltFast`.

Clipped Sprite Overview

The header file for `CClippedSprite` is `Csprite.h`. `CClippedSprite` is derived from `CBaseSprite`:

```
class CClippedSprite: public CBaseSprite{
```

It has one private variable, a bounding rectangle; `Blt` requires you to specify a rectangle from which to blit in the source surface. We use the Windows API structure `RECT`, which has four fields, `left`, `right`, `top`, and `bottom`. The rectangles specified by `RECT` structures are reminiscent of C arrays, in that the horizontal extent is `left` to `right-1`, and the horizontal extent is `top` to `bottom-1`. Notice that the rectangle has width `right-left` and height `bottom-top`.

```
private:
   RECT m_rectSource; //bounding rectangle
```

It has its own constructor, and of course a virtual override for the `draw` function.

```
public:
   CClippedSprite(int frames,int w,int h); //constructor
   virtual void draw(int frame,int x,int y,
     LPDIRECTDRAWSURFACE destination); //draw sprite
};
```

Clipped Sprite Code

The code file for `CClippedSprite` is `Csprite.cpp`. It begins with the
`CClippedSprite` constructor, which calls the `CBaseSprite` constructor, then
sets the source bounding rectangle to be the same as the sprite frames. Notice that
setting `m_rectSource.left` to 0 and `m_rectSource.right` to w makes the
horizontal extent of the rectangle span from pixel 0 to pixel w−1, that is, a rectangle of width exactly w.

```
CClippedSprite::CClippedSprite(int frames,int w,int h):
CBaseSprite(frames,w,h){ //constructor
  //set bounding rectangle for use with Blt()
  m_rectSource.left=0; m_rectSource.right=w;
  m_rectSource.top=0; m_rectSource.bottom=h;
}
```

Recall from Chapter 5 that the `BltFast` function required the coordinates at
which to draw the top left pixel of the source surface within the destination surface. The `Blt` function requires a destination *rectangle* instead of the x-y
coordinates. The source image will be scaled to fit in the destination rectangle,
which is a cool effect if you need it, but if you *don't* need it, make sure that the
source rectangle is *exactly* the same size as the destination rectangle. If you are off
by one pixel, your rendering speed will take a small hit as the sprite is scaled
unnecessarily, and more importantly, the quality of your artwork will take a perceptible hit because one row or column of pixels of your sprite never gets drawn. The
`CClippedSprite draw` function is an override of the `CBaseSprite draw`
function.

```
void CClippedSprite::draw(int frame,int x,int y,
                         LPDIRECTDRAWSURFACE dest){ //draw
```

It has a local variable holding the destination rectangle. (The source rectangle is
kept in the private member variable `m_rectSource` since its value never
changes, whereas the destination rectangle is potentially different each time the
sprite is drawn.)

```
RECT rectDest; //destination rectangle
```

We compute the horizontal extent of the destination rectangle, remembering that
the coordinates of a sprite in our game are defined to be the coordinates of its bottom center pixel:

```
rectDest.left=x-m_nWidth/2;
rectDest.right=rectDest.left+m_nWidth;
```

It's a good idea to verify with pencil and paper that the destination rectangle is the right width. In this case it is easy to see that `rectDest.right-rectDest.left` is `m_nWidth` as required. Coding it the way we did has made it bulletproof whether `m_nWidth` is odd or even. It may be tempting to you to set `rectDest.right` to `x+m_nWidth/2` to make it symmetrical with `rectDest.left`. However, that would be wrong when `m_nWidth` is odd, because halving an odd integer will round it down. For example, if `m_nWidth` is 21, then `m_nWidth/2=10`, and so `rectDest.left` is set to `x-10` and `rectDest.right` would erroneously be set to `x+10`, resulting in a rectangle of width

```
rectDest.right-rectDest.left=(x+10)-(x+10)=20
```

instead of 21. Next, we set the vertical extent of the destination rectangle. Since the bottom row of pixels of the sprite must be drawn at row `y` of the destination, we set `rectDest.bottom` to `y+1`. Then, we set `rectDest.top` to whatever it will take to give the rectangle height `m_nHeight`.

```
rectDest.top=y-m_nHeight+1;
rectDest.bottom=y+1;
```

Did we get it right?

```
rectDest.bottom-rectDest.top=(y+1)-(y-m_nHeight+1)=m_nHeight,
```

as required. Now we can blit the image using the destination surface's `Blt` function. The first four parameters of this function are the destination rectangle, the source surface, the source rectangle, and a flags word (set the same—although the names of the flags have changed slightly—as for the `BltFast` function in Chapter 5). The last parameter, which we will leave `NULL`, would allow us to set some special blit effects if we used it.

```
dest->Blt(&rectDest,m_lpDDImage[frame],&m_rectSource,
  DDBLT_KEYSRC|DDBLT_WAIT,NULL);
}
```

Changes to the Object Class

Since Demo 4 has more sophisticated objects than Demo 3 did, we need to add some functionality to the object class CObject.

Declarations

The first change to Objects.h involves the declaration of an enumerated type for the different kinds of objects in our game:

```
enum ObjectType{CROW_OBJECT=0,PLANE_OBJECT,NUM_SPRITES};
```

Enumerated types are very useful; we use them here to give human-readable names to things like crows and planes while at the same time allowing us to index them easily. We could do the same thing with a collection of #defines or const ints, but enumerated types are easier because the compiler takes care of assigning numbers to the names. Notice that the last declaration is NUM_SPRITES. We'll leave that at the end when we insert new object names into the list, giving us a handy way of knowing how many object types there are without the overhead of having to increment a counter by hand whenever a new object type is introduced.

CObject needs some new private member variables. Now our objects can move both horizontally and vertically, so we add a new member variable m_nLastYMoveTime to go along with the m_nLastXMoveTime declared in Demo 3.

```
int m_nLastYMoveTime; //last time moved vertically
```

Our objects need a minimum and maximum allowed speed to prevent the user (or any new code) from making them move faster or slower than they are allowed to:

```
int m_nMinXSpeed,m_nMaxXSpeed; //min, max horizontal speeds
int m_nMinYSpeed,m_nMaxYSpeed; //min, max vertical speeds
```

The crows have multiple frames of animation (wings flapping), so we'll record the current frame index, the total number of frames, the last time the frame was changed, and the *frame interval*, that is, the number of milliseconds between frame changes. We'll make the crows' wings flap faster by decreasing the frame interval when they fly faster.

```
int m_nCurrentFrame; //frame to be displayed
int m_nFrameCount; //number of frames in animation
int m_nLastFrameTime; //last time the frame was changed
int m_nFrameInterval; //interval between frames
```

Some of our animations will repeat in cyclic order. For example, if there are four frames of animation, they will be displayed in the following order: 0, 1, 2, 3, 0, 1, 2, 3,... Others, for example the crow wing beats, will repeat forward to the last frame, then repeat backward, as follows: 0, 1, 2, 3, 2, 1, 0, 1, 2,... We will keep a Boolean variable m_bForwardAnimation, which is TRUE when the animation sequence is going forward and FALSE when it is going backward.

```
BOOL m_bForwardAnimation; //is animation going forwards?
```

The CObject public member function create gets its parameters changed from Demo 3. Instead of getting a pointer to the sprite image for the object, it gets a parameter of type ObjectType and must locate the sprite corresponding to that object type itself.

```
void create(ObjectType object,int x,int y,
  int xspeed,int yspeed); //create object
```

Some Code Changes

The first noteworthy change to the CObject code in Objects.cpp is the extern declaration of an array of sprite pointers. This array will be declared and initialized in Main.cpp, and will be indexed using an index of type ObjectType. This will let us easily locate a pointer to the shared sprite for any object.

```
extern CClippedSprite *g_pSprite[]; //sprites
```

The CObject constructor gets some new code to set the new private member variables to sensible initial values. Notice that a frame interval of 30 milliseconds gets us a frame rate of about 33 frames a second.

```
m_nLastXMoveTime=m_nLastYMoveTime=0;
m_nCurrentFrame=m_nFrameCount=m_nLastFrameTime=0;
m_bForwardAnimation=TRUE;
m_nFrameInterval=30;
```

The Draw Function

The CObject draw function first draws the current frame, using the frame number recorded in the private member variable m_nCurrentFrame:

```
void CObject::draw(LPDIRECTDRAWSURFACE surface){ //draw
  //draw the current frame
  m_pSprite->draw(m_nCurrentFrame,m_nX,m_nY,surface);
```

After having drawn the current frame, we have to figure out which frame is next. We want the crow's wings to beat faster when it flies faster in the x direction, so we compute a frame interval t that is inversely proportional to m-nXspeed. As m_nXspeed increases, the frame interval gets smaller, which makes the animation move faster. Notice the use of the C standard library function abs to ensure that the frame interval is always positive, and the addition of 1 to the denominator to prevent a divide-by-zero error.

```
int t=m_nFrameInterval/(1+abs(m_nXspeed)); //frame interval
```

We use the timer to make sure that the frame number is only updated when sufficient time has passed, and we make use of the way that Boolean expressions are evaluated in C and C++ to ensure that the question never even arises unless the sprite has more than one frame:

```
if(m_nFrameCount>1&&Timer.elapsed(m_nLastFrameTime,t))
```

We check that the animation is going forward:

```
if(m_bForwardAnimation){ //forward animation
```

If it is going forward, we increment the frame number and check to see whether we have just displayed the last frame. Notice that we use pre-incrementing so that the value is tested after it has been incremented.

```
if(++m_nCurrentFrame>=m_nFrameCount){ //wrap
```

If we have just displayed the last frame, m_nCurrentFrame needs to be wound back to the second-from-last frame, which is frame m_nFrameCount-2 (the last frame is frame m_nFrameCount-1). We then set m_bForwardAnimation to FALSE so that the animation now goes backward.

```
        m_nCurrentFrame=m_nFrameCount-2;
        m_bForwardAnimation=FALSE;
      }
    }
```

Otherwise, the animation is already going backward:

```
else{ //backward animation
```

We decrement the current frame and check to see whether we just displayed the first frame, frame 0. If so, we set the current frame to the second frame, frame 1, and set m_bForwardAnimation to TRUE so the animation now goes forward.

```
        if(--m_nCurrentFrame<0){ //wrap
          m_nCurrentFrame=1;
          m_bForwardAnimation=TRUE;
        }
      }
    }
```

The Create Function

The `CObject create` function has some small changes; it now initializes `m_nLastYMoveTime` along with `m_nLastXMoveTime` to the current time so that the first move will be a reasonable one:

```
m_nLastXMoveTime=m_nLastYMoveTime=Timer.time(); //time
```

Instead of being given a pointer to the shared sprite that stores the image of this object, the `create` function was given an `ObjectType` parameter called `object`. We use this to index into the global sprite array `g_pSprite` to get that pointer.

```
m_pSprite=g_pSprite[object]; //sprite
```

Next, we interrogate the sprite object for its frame count so that we can manage the animation of this particular object. Note that although many objects will share the same sprite, they each have their own frame counter, and can therefore potentially be at different points in the sprite animation.

```
m_nFrameCount=m_pSprite->frame_count(); //frame count
```

Finally, the `create` function has a block of code that sets the object properties that are common for all objects of a given type, but are different from one type to another. Ideally, we should place this information into a text file and read it into our game at the appropriate point so that play-testers can tune the values to improve gameplay without the need to recompile the code. However, hard-coding the values like this works fine for a simple game in which the programmer most likely *is* the primary play-tester.

```
//customize properties of each object type
switch(object){
  case PLANE_OBJECT:
    m_nMinXSpeed=-3; m_nMaxXSpeed=-1;
    m_nMinYSpeed=-4; m_nMaxYSpeed=4;
    break;
  case CROW_OBJECT:
    m_nMinXSpeed=-2; m_nMaxXSpeed=-1;
    m_nMinYSpeed=-1; m_nMaxYSpeed=1;
    m_nFrameInterval=250;
    break;
}
```

The Accelerate and Move Functions

The `CObject accelerate` function gets some simple code to enforce maximum and minimum speed limits. After `m_nXspeed` is increased by `xdelta` we enforce the horizontal speed limits.

```
if(m_nXspeed<m_nMinXSpeed)m_nXspeed=m_nMinXSpeed;
if(m_nXspeed>m_nMaxXSpeed)m_nXspeed=m_nMaxXSpeed;
```

After `m_nYspeed` is increased by `ydelta` we enforce the vertical speed limits:

```
if(m_nYspeed<m_nMinYSpeed)m_nYspeed=m_nMinYSpeed;
if(m_nYspeed>m_nMaxYSpeed)m_nYspeed=m_nMaxYSpeed;
}
```

The last change to `CObject` code in `Objects.cpp` involves modifying the `move` function to manage vertical movement in addition to the horizontal movement, which was all that was allowed in Demo 3. We change `XSCALE` to `16` (because it looks better) and declare a corresponding constant `YSCALE` for vertical motion.

```
const int XSCALE=16; //to scale back horizontal motion
const int YSCALE=32; //to scale back vertical motion
```

Then, we declare an integer `ydelta` for the change in vertical position, to match the corresponding `xdelta` for the change in horizontal position from Demo 3:

```
int xdelta,ydelta; //change in position
```

Finally, we add code to manage vertical motion. This code looks almost identical to the code for horizontal motion from Demo 3 with all the x's changed to y's.

```
tfactor=time-m_nLastYMoveTime; //time since last move
ydelta=(m_nYspeed*tfactor)/YSCALE; //y distance moved
m_nY+=ydelta; //y motion
if(m_nY<-MARGIN)m_nY=-MARGIN; //wrap top
if(m_nY>SCREEN_HEIGHT+MARGIN)
  m_nY=SCREEN_HEIGHT+MARGIN; //wrap bottom
if(ydelta||m_nYspeed==0) //record time of move
  m_nLastYMoveTime=time;
```

Changes to Main.cpp

The first significant change to `Main.cpp` is the declaration of two crow objects and the sprite array alluded to in the last section. Notice that the sprite array has `NUM_SPRITES` slots, which is the last entry in the `ObjectType` declaration in `Objects.h`, and will therefore (assuming we remember to keep it the last entry) be the number of different object types in the game.

```
CObject crow1,crow2; //crow objects
CClippedSprite *g_pSprite[NUM_SPRITES]; //sprites
```

The LoadCrowSprite Function

Like the `LoadPlaneSprite` function that we've met already, we create a `LoadCrowSprite` function to load the crow sprite images. The crow sprite has four frames, the top left pixels of which can be found at coodinates `(256,183)`, `(320,183)`, `(256,237)`, and `(323,237)`, respectively, in the sprite file `Sprites.bmp`.

```
BOOL LoadCrowSprite(){
  BOOL result=TRUE;
  result=result&&g_pSprite[CROW_OBJECT]->
    load(&g_cSpriteImages,0,256,183); //frame 0
  result=result&&g_pSprite[CROW_OBJECT]->
    load(&g_cSpriteImages,1,320,183); //frame 1
  result=result&&g_pSprite[CROW_OBJECT]->
    load(&g_cSpriteImages,2,256,237); //frame 2
  result=result&&g_pSprite[CROW_OBJECT]->
    load(&g_cSpriteImages,3,323,237); //frame 3
  return result;
} //LoadCrowSprite
```

The LoadImages Function

The code to load the sprites in function LoadImages gets updated as follows, after the background has been loaded and the palette set. The sprite file is loaded into the bmp sprite file reader g_cSpriteImages.

```
if(!g_cSpriteImages.load("sprites.bmp"))return FALSE;
```

A new one-frame, 121x72 clipped sprite object is created and attached to the appropriate place in the global sprite array g_pSprite[PLANE_OBJECT]:

```
g_pSprite[PLANE_OBJECT]=new CClippedSprite(1,121,72);
```

The plane sprite image is loaded to the sprite from the bmp sprite file reader:

```
if(!LoadPlaneSprite())return FALSE; //load plane images
```

A new four-frame, 58x37 clipped sprite object is created and attached to the appropriate place in the global sprite array g_pSprite[CROW_OBJECT]:

```
g_pSprite[CROW_OBJECT]=new CClippedSprite(4,58,37);
```

The crow sprite images are loaded to the sprite from the bmp sprite file reader:

```
if(!LoadCrowSprite())return FALSE; //load crow images
```

The CreateObjects Function

The body of function CreateObjects is replaced by code to create the plane and two crows with the appropriate initial values:

```
void CreateObjects(){
  plane.create(PLANE_OBJECT,320,271,-1,0); //create plane
  crow1.create(CROW_OBJECT,400,100,-2,0); //create a crow
  crow2.create(CROW_OBJECT,300,100,-1,0); //another crow
} //CreateObjects
```

The RestoreSurfaces Function

In the RestoreSurfaces function, in addition to the minor replacement of the now defunct plane sprite pointer planesprite with g_pSprite[PLANE_OBJECT], we need to add code to restore the crow sprite. The code for this looks very similar to the code used to restore the plane sprite; we call the crow sprite's Restore member function, and if the restoration succeeds, we reload the sprite image from the bmp sprite file reader by calling the LoadCrowSprite function described above.

```
if(g_pSprite[CROW_OBJECT]->Restore()) //if crow restored
  result=result&&LoadCrowSprite(); //redraw image
else return FALSE;
```

The ComposeFrame Function

The body of `ComposeFrame` needs to be modified to handle the new objects. First, we use `Blt` instead of `BltFast` to draw the background. In order to do this, we need a local variable `rect` to store the destination rectangle, which we set to the whole screen. Then, we blit the background surface to that rectangle using the secondary surface's `Blt` member function, in much the same way that we blitted the clipped sprites.

```
RECT rect; //drawing rectangle
rect.left=0; rect.right=SCREEN_WIDTH;
rect.top=0; rect.bottom=SCREEN_HEIGHT;
lpSecondary->Blt(&rect,lpBackground,&rect,DDBLT_WAIT,NULL);
```

Then, we move the objects. They can be moved in any order.

```
plane.move();
crow1.move();
crow2.move();
```

Having moved the objects, we draw them. They must be drawn back-to-front, since the more recently drawn objects will overwrite objects previously drawn to the same pixels. We draw one crow first (behind the plane), then the plane, then the other crow (in front of the plane).

```
crow1.draw(lpSecondary);
plane.draw(lpSecondary);
crow2.draw(lpSecondary);
```

The Keyboard Handler

The `keyboard_handler` function has four new `cases` added to its `switch` statement to handle responses to the arrow keys, which are used to accelerate the plane either up, down, left, or right. The virtual key codes for the arrow keys are `VK_UP`, `VK_DOWN`, `VK_LEFT`, and `VK_RIGHT`.

```
case VK_UP: plane.accelerate(0,-1); break;
case VK_DOWN: plane.accelerate(0,1); break;
case VK_LEFT: plane.accelerate(-1,0); break;
case VK_RIGHT: plane.accelerate(1,0); break;
```

The Window Procedure

In function `WindowProc` we need to clean up the sprite surfaces in response to the `WM_DESTROY` message at the end of the game. Notice once again how we enumerate the sprites using the `ObjectType` enumerated type.

```
for(int i=0; i<NUM_SPRITES; i++){ //for each sprite
  if(g_pSprite[i]) //if sprite exists
    g_pSprite[i]->Release(); //release sprite
  delete g_pSprite[i]; //delete sprite
}
```

The "if sprite exists" line is there to ensure that we only try to release sprites that actually exist. Naturally, this will only work if the sprite pointers have been initialized to `NULL` before we try to create the sprites. This is done in `WinMain` as an early part of the initialization before the game begins.

```
for(int i=0; i<NUM_SPRITES; i++) //null out sprites
  g_pSprite[i]=NULL;
```

Demo 4 Files

Code Files

The following files in Demo 4 are used without change from Demo 3:

- Bmp.h
- Bmp.cpp
- Bsprite.h
- Bsprite.cpp
- Defines.h
- Sbmp.h
- Sbmp.cpp
- Timer.h
- Timer.cpp

The following files in Demo 4 have been modified from Demo 3:

- Ddsetup.cpp
- Main.cpp
- Objects.h
- Objects.cpp

The following files are new in Demo 4:

- Csprite.h
- Csprite.cpp

Required Libraries

- Ddraw.lib
- Winmm.lib

Chapter 7

Here's what you'll learn:

- How to manage the player's viewpoint within the virtual universe with a viewpoint manager

- What parallax scrolling is and how to implement it

- How to get subpixel scrolling with integer arithmetic

- How to manage objects with an object manager

- What pseudorandom numbers are, why they are used, and how to generate them

Parallax Scrolling

In Demo 5, we learn how to do parallax scrolling. We manage the objects in a game using an object manager class. Our game now has six crows, and the viewpoint moves horizontally with the plane, displaying it in the middle of the screen at all times (see Figure 7.1). There is a farm drawn in the foreground. The background scrolls horizontally slower than the farm, giving an illusion of depth known as *parallax scrolling*. The plane sprite now has multiple frames of animation. The crow sprites have very few frames of animation—only four frames shown forward and backward for a total of six frames per wingbeat. This relatively low frame count means that the crows' wingbeats can easily become synchronized, which looks unnatural. To combat this problem, the crow sprite animations are desynchronized using a pseudorandom number generator.

Figure 7.1
Screen shot
of Demo 5

Experiment with Demo 5

Take a moment now to run Demo 5.

- You should see a plane and two groups of three crows flying from right to left across the background, one fast and one slow.

- Notice that the plane is at the center of the screen, no matter how you accelerate and decelerate it using the arrow keys.

- Notice that the background moves more slowly than the foreground.

- Notice that the wingbeats of the crows are never in synchrony for more than a few seconds even when the crows are flying at the same speed.

- Notice that as clouds scroll off the right of the screen, they appear immediately on the left of the screen. This is because the background image file Bckgnd.bmp was drawn by the artist so that the left side of the image wraps around to the right side seamlessly.

- Hit the Esc key to exit the program.

The Viewpoint Manager

Ned's Turkey Farm takes place in a two-dimensional virtual universe that is 1,280 pixels wide, twice as wide as the screen. Each object in the game is responsible for recording its position in the virtual universe in its CObject private member variables m_nX and m_nY. The player's viewpoint, to be displayed on the screen, is also free to move arbitrarily within the virtual universe, but we will tie it to the plane so that the plane stays in the center of the screen. The illusion of the plane moving to the left will be provided by having all of the stationary objects in the virtual universe move to the right.

Imagine yourself standing at the side window of a train as it moves, observing stationary objects. As you travel through the countryside, you will notice that things close to you appear to zip speedily across your field of vision, whereas things farther away move less quickly and things on the horizon seem to move hardly at all. This effect of having things cross your field of vision at a speed that is inversely proportional to their distance is called *parallax*. We will create the illusion of depth in our flat two-dimensional virtual universe by having the background scroll at a lower speed than objects in the foreground in a process known as *parallax scrolling*.

We will implement parallax scrolling using a single 640x480 background image. This implies that when part of the background image disappears off one edge of the screen, it must reappear on the other. For this to work properly, the artist must create the background image as if it were rolled into a cylinder, with the right edge of the image merging seamlessly with the left edge. This effect has been achieved in the file Bckgnd.bmp, which you may verify by examining Figure 7.2. At the top of that figure you can see three copies of Bckgnd.bmp that have been laid out side by side to make a long strip. Observe that no seam can be seen. A single copy of Bckgnd.bmp has been placed below the strip for comparison. In practice you should use a virtual universe that is wider than double the screen size, and a background image that is wider than the screen, but we have opted for the simplest example here as a teaching device.

Figure 7.2
Three copies of Bckgnd. bmp (top) pasted side by side to show continuity, with a single copy below

The viewpoint manager CViewPoint is charged with the task of maintaining and manipulating the player viewpoint. It must record and maintain the location of the viewpoint, provide information to objects about where they should be drawn on the screen (which depends on the relative location of the object and the viewpoint in the virtual universe), and implement parallax scrolling.

Viewpoint Manager Overview

The header file for CViewPoint is View.h, which begins with the declaration of the width of the virtual universe:

```
#define WORLD_WIDTH 1280 //width of the world
```

CViewPoint has three private member functions. The first is the x coordinate of the viewpoint in the virtual universe (which will be between 0 and WORLD_WIDTH-1, inclusive), the second is where the right side of the screen hits the background image, and the third is the last time the background was moved and redrawn (which helps the viewpoint manager to compute how far the background has moved since it was last moved).

```
int m_nX; //x coordinate of viewpoint
int m_nBgOffset; //offset of parallax scrolled background
int m_nLastTimeBgDrawn; //last time background was drawn
```

CViewPoint has five public member functions, the first of which is a constructor:

```
CViewPoint(); //constructor
```

The second CViewPoint public member function allows us to set the initial viewpoint to a specific x coordinate in the virtual universe:

```
void set_position(int x); //set current viewpoint
```

The third CViewPoint public member returns the screen-relative x coordinates of a given x coordinate in the virtual universe. This will be used by objects to determine where they should be drawn in the screen.

```
int screen(int x); //screen coords relative to viewpoint
```

The fourth CViewPoint public member function normalizes a given x coordinate in the virtual universe; that is, it rounds it off to a value that is no smaller than 0 and less than WORLD_WIDTH. Notice that the parameter x is a call-by-reference parameter, which means that changes to x in the body of function normalize will affect the calling parameter.

```
void normalize(int &x); //normalize location x
```

The fifth and final CViewPoint public member function draws the background surface pointed to by parameter lpSource to the surface pointed to by lpDestination using parallax scrolling with the background surface moving at the given speed:

```
void draw_background(LPDIRECTDRAWSURFACE lpSource,
    LPDIRECTDRAWSURFACE lpDestination,int speed);
```

Viewpoint Manager Code

The code file for CViewPoint is View.cpp. It begins with the CViewPoint constructor, which initializes the private member variables.

```
CViewPoint::CViewPoint(){ //constructor
  m_nX=0; m_nBgOffset=0; m_nLastTimeBgDrawn=0;
}
```

The CViewPoint set_position function sets the position of the background to a specified x coordinate x, after first calling the public member function normalize to ensure that x falls within the virtual universe:

```
void CViewPoint::set_position(int x){ //set current viewpoint
  normalize(x); m_nX=x;
}
```

The `CViewPoint screen` function returns the screen-relative value of an x coordinate x in the virtual universe. Basically, we want to find out how far x is from the player's viewpoint.

```
int CViewPoint::screen(int x){
```

At first glance, it may seem that all this function needs to do is to compute the difference between the parameter x and the x coordinate of the viewpoint, m_nX, a value that we will call `delta`. We begin by doing this.

```
int delta=x-m_nX;
```

However, in a circular world of width `WORLD_WIDTH`, no two things can be farther away from each other than `WORLD_WIDTH/2`. Think about it for a second—the Earth is about 25,000 miles around, which means that I can never be more than about 12,500 miles away from you as you read this book. Therefore, we need to normalize `delta` so that it is between `-WORLD_WIDTH/2` and `WORLD_WIDTH/2`, inclusive.

```
if(delta>WORLD_WIDTH/2)delta-=WORLD_WIDTH;
if(delta<-WORLD_WIDTH/2)delta+=WORLD_WIDTH;
```

Finally, since m_nX is the x-coordinate of the left side of the screen, we will add `SCREEN_WIDTH/2` to make distances relative to the center of the screen:

```
return SCREEN_WIDTH/2+delta;
}
```

The `CViewPoint normalize` function normalizes the call-by-reference parameter x to be within the virtual universe. Since under normal playing circumstances x will be only slightly outside the virtual universe if at all, we can use additions and subtractions instead of the slightly more costly remainder operator. This is a piece of essentially pointless optimization that dates from the days when multiplication and division hardware was hopelessly slow, but really doesn't make a difference in the performance of this game. Nonetheless, it costs us nothing.

```
void CViewPoint::normalize(int &x){ //nomrmalize to world
  while(x<0)x+=WORLD_WIDTH;
  while(x>=WORLD_WIDTH)x-=WORLD_WIDTH;
}
```

Drawing the Background

The most interesting function in this file is probably the CViewPoint
draw_background function, which has three parameters: a pointer lpSource
to a source surface containing the background image, a pointer lpDestination
to a destination surface to which it is to be drawn using parallax scrolling from the
player's viewpoint, and the speed that the background is to scroll:

```
void CViewPoint::draw_background(LPDIRECTDRAWSURFACE lpSource,
    LPDIRECTDRAWSURFACE lpDestination,int speed){
```

The private member function m_nBgOffset keeps track of where the right side
of the screen hits the source image. A strip of this width must be drawn from the
left side of the source to the right side of the destination, and the remainder of the
source must be drawn to the left side of the destination (see Figure 7.3). This will
be accomplished with two calls to the DirectDraw Blt function. We will start by
drawing the left side of the source to the right side of the destination. First, we
compute the destination rectangle.

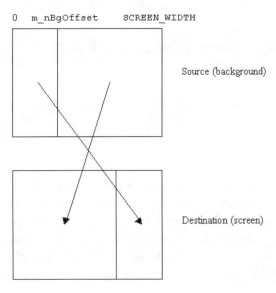

Figure 7.3
Drawing the
background

```
RECT rectDest; //destination rectangle
rectDest.left=SCREEN_WIDTH-m_nBgOffset;
rectDest.right=SCREEN_WIDTH;
rectDest.top=0;
rectDest.bottom=SCREEN_HEIGHT; //vertical extent
```

Then we compute the source rectangle:

```
RECT rectSource; //source rectangle
rectSource.left=0;
rectSource.right=m_nBgOffset;
rectSource.top=0;
rectSource.bottom=SCREEN_HEIGHT;
```

Then, we can do the first blit:

```
lpDestination->
  Blt(&rectDest,lpSource,&rectSource,DDBLT_WAIT,NULL);
```

Now we compute the destination rectangle for the second blit, which is the screen minus the rectangle drawn to by the first blit:

```
rectDest.left=0;
rectDest.right=SCREEN_WIDTH-m_nBgOffset;
rectDest.top=0;
rectDest.bottom=SCREEN_HEIGHT;
```

Then the source rectangle, which is the background image minus the rectangle taken in the first blit, is computed:

```
rectSource.left=m_nBgOffset;
rectSource.right=SCREEN_WIDTH;
rectSource.top=0;
rectSource.bottom=SCREEN_HEIGHT;
```

And we are ready for the second blit:

```
lpDestination->
  Blt(&rectDest,lpSource,&rectSource,DDBLT_WAIT,NULL);
```

Now that drawing has been completed, we are ready to scroll the background sideways to prepare for the next time it is drawn; that is, we need to update m_nBgOffset by the amount that the background is supposed to have moved. This change in m_nBgOffset depends on the parameter speed and the amount of time since the background was last drawn. We compute it in a local variable delta.

```
int delta=(speed*(Timer.time()-m_nLastTimeBgDrawn))/50;
```

If delta is zero, it means that the background is scrolling too slowly for it to have been moved in the current frame. If it has moved, we update m_nBgOffset, check that the new value is within range, and update the private member variable m_nLastTimeBgDrawn to record the last time the background was scrolled. Notice that we *don't* want to update m_nLastTimeBgDrawn when delta is zero. Updating m_nBgOffset when delta is zero would do no harm, but updating m_nLastTimeBgDrawn when delta is zero would make it impossible for us to perform *subpixel scrolling*, that is, to scroll the background at a rate less than one pixel per frame. We can imagine a situation in which the frame rate is so high and the parameter speed is so low that the background scrolls only one pixel every second or third frame. For example, suppose that the game is running at 50 frames per second, that speed is 1, and that the background was scrolled in frame 0. In frame 1, 20 milliseconds later, delta is (1*20)/50, which gets rounded to zero. If m_nLastTimeBgDrawn is not changed, then 20 milliseconds later in frame 2, delta is (1*40)/50, which also gets rounded to zero. In frame 3, however, delta is (1*60)/50, which gets rounded to one, and the background moves by one pixel. If m_nLastTimeBgDrawn is changed when delta is zero, then delta *always* gets assigned (1*20)/50, which gets rounded to zero, and so the background *never* scrolls.

```
if(delta){ //if nonzero
  m_nBgOffset-=delta; //initial offset
  if(m_nBgOffset>SCREEN_WIDTH) //too positive
    m_nBgOffset=0;
  if(m_nBgOffset<0) //too negative
    m_nBgOffset=SCREEN_WIDTH-1;
  m_nLastTimeBgDrawn=Timer.time(); //record time of move
}
} //draw_background
```

The Object Manager

Managing objects is a significant component of any game. We will do this using an object manager class called CObjectManager whose task is to maintain and process a list of all game objects.

Object Manager Overview

The header file for CObjectManager is Objman.h. The object list will be implemented quite simply using a private array of pointers to CObject class instances. Initially we don't know how large that array has to be, so we will declare it as a pointer to a pointer to CObject, and will new enough space for the array later.

```
CObject **m_pObjectList; //list of objects in game
```

We will use the leading entries in the array to hold pointers to the objects in the list, and so we need a count of how many objects are in use:

```
int m_nCount; //how many objects in list
```

We also keep a record of how large the object array is, so that we can check for overflow:

```
int m_nMaxCount; //maximum number of objects
```

Finally, we will distinguish one object from all of the others and call it the *current object*. This object will represent the player.

```
int m_nCurrentObject; //index of the current object
```

All of the above variables are private member variables. The object manager has seven public member functions, including a constructor and a destructor. The constructor has a single parameter max that specifies the size of the object list. This gives us the ability (should we later choose to use it) to use a larger array for more advanced levels of the game that have more objects than earlier levels.

```
CObjectManager(int max); //constructor
~CObjectManager(); //destructor
```

The CObjectManager create function creates a new object, and has five parameters that specify the object type, its initial coordinates, and its initial horizontal and vertical speeds. It returns the index of the newly created object in the object list.

```
int create(ObjectType object,int x,int y,
    int xspeed,int yspeed); //create new object
```

The CObjectManager animate function will animate all of the objects in the object list to a DirectDraw surface (usually the secondary surface) given as the parameter surface:

```
void animate(LPDIRECTDRAWSURFACE surface);
```

The remaining three CObjectManager public member functions operate on the current object. Function accelerate changes the horizontal and vertical components of the current object's speed by specified amounts xdelta and ydelta, respectively, function set_current sets the current object to the object with a given index in the object list, and function speed returns the magnitude of the horizontal speed of the current object.

```
void accelerate(int xdelta,int ydelta=0); //change speed
void set_current(int index); //set current object
int speed(); //return magnitude of speed
```

The Constructor and Destructor

The code file for CObjectManager is Objman.cpp. The first declaration in Objman.cpp is an extern declaration for the viewpoint manager, which was described in the previous section.

```
extern CViewPoint Viewpoint; //player viewpoint
```

The CObjectManager constructor has a single parameter max that specifies the number of entries in the object list:

```
CObjectManager::CObjectManager(int max){ //constructor
```

We start out by recording this value in m_nMaxCount, setting m_nCount to 0 to indicate that the object list is empty, and setting m_nCurrentObject to 0 by default:

```
m_nMaxCount=max; m_nCount=0; m_nCurrentObject=0;
```

The array for the object list is created by allocating an array of max pointers to CObject. Once this has been done, we can address the object list as a normal array. For example, the first entry will be m_pObjectList[0].

```
m_pObjectList=new CObject*[max]; //object list
```

The last thing that the constructor does is to create empty objects for each slot in the object list. These will be initialized and used later.

```
for(int i=0; i<m_nMaxCount; i++) //create objects
  m_pObjectList[i]=new CObject;
}
```

The CObjectManager destructor deletes all of the memory allocated by the constructor. First, it deletes all of the CObject class instances pointed to by the object list.

```
for(int i=0; i<m_nMaxCount; i++) //for each object
  delete m_pObjectList[i]; //delete it
```

Then it deletes the array itself. Notice the use of delete[] to delete the whole array; using delete without the [] would just delete the first entry in the array instead of the whole array. Notice that we must delete the objects first, then the array, which is the reverse of the order in which they were created by the constructor.

```
delete[]m_pObjectList; //delete object list
```

The Create Function

The CObjectManager create function takes five parameters that specify the object's type, location, and speed:

```
int CObjectManager::create(ObjectType object,int x,int y,
                           int xspeed,int yspeed){
```

To avoid array overflow, it checks to see whether there is room in the object array for the new object:

```
if(m_nCount<m_nMaxCount){ //if room, create object
```

If there is room in the array, it uses the next unused object in the array (the one with index m_nCount) for the new object, which it initializes using the CObject create function:

```
m_pObjectList[m_nCount]->
  create(object,x,y,xspeed,yspeed);
```

It then returns the index of the new object, post-incrementing it to indicate that there is one more object in the array:

```
      return m_nCount++; //return index into object list
   }
```

Otherwise, there is no room in the object array for the new object, so it returns −1:

```
      else return -1; //no room
   }
```

The Animate Function

The `CObjectManager animate` function animates each of the objects in the object list to a specified surface. It encapsulates most of the work that was formerly done by the `ComposeFrame` function in `Main.cpp` of Demo 4.

```
   void CObjectManager::animate(LPDIRECTDRAWSURFACE surface){
```

It first moves the objects:

```
      for(int i=0; i<m_nCount; i++)m_pObjectList[i]->move();
```

In Demo 5, we want the viewpoint to move with the plane so that the plane stays in the center of the screen. We do this by calling the viewpoint manager's `set_position` member function and giving it as a parameter the plane's horizontal location within the game world. Note that in order to give the object manager access to `CObject` private member variables such as m_nX, we have chosen to make `CObjectManager` a friend of class `CObject`. We will say more about this in a later section of this chapter in which we describe changes to the `CObject` class.

```
      Viewpoint.set_position(
        m_pObjectList[m_nCurrentObject]->m_nX);
```

Finally, it draws the objects in the object list. Note that the higher-indexed objects in the list are drawn over the lower-indexed objects.

```
      for(i=0; i<m_nCount; i++)m_pObjectList[i]->draw(surface);
   }
```

Other Member Functions

The `CObjectManager accelerate` function is simply a wrapper for the `CObject accelerate` function of the current object:

```
   void CObjectManager::accelerate(int xdelta,int ydelta){
     //change speed of current object
```

```
m_pObjectList[m_nCurrentObject]->
    accelerate(xdelta,ydelta);
}
```

The `CObjectManager set_current` function sets `m_nCurrentObject` to the index provided as a parameter, provided the index is a valid one:

```
void CObjectManager::set_current(int index){
  //set current object
  if(index>=0&&index<m_nCount)m_nCurrentObject=index;
}
```

Finally, the `CObjectManager speed` function returns the absolute value of the horizontal component of the current object's speed. Once again, the fact that `CObjectManager` is a friend of `CObject` allows us to access the private member variable `m_nXspeed` of a `CObject` class instance.

```
int CObjectManager::speed(){
  //return magnitude of current object speed
  return abs(m_pObjectList[m_nCurrentObject]->m_nXspeed);
}
```

Generating Pseudorandom Numbers

A *pseudorandom number generator* is an algorithm for generating a sequence of numbers in which the next number in the sequence is difficult to predict from the previous ones. In a sense, those numbers "look random." They are not truly random—the generation of true random numbers requires specialized hardware not included with the typical PC—but they are good enough for many applications. The most popular pseudorandom number generator is called a *linear congruential random number generator.* If this generator is given an initial random number called a *seed*, it will generate a sequence of numbers that look progressively less random as time goes by. We will compensate for this drift away from randomness by reseeding the random number generator after a certain number of numbers have been generated—we will say that the generator has become *stale* when this happens.

But what will we use for a seed? In practice, a good thing to use is the current time as reported by the `timeGetTime` Windows API function. The linear congruential random number generator provided in the C standard library is encapsulated in the class `CRandom`. The `CRandom` header file is `Random.h`. The first declaration in `Random.h` is for the constant `STALE_RAND`, defined to be the number of expected calls to the linear congruential random number generator before it becomes stale. There is no mathematics for determining how to set this value, but 1,000 will do.

```
#define STALE_RAND 1000 //stale after this many calls
```

CRandom needs to keep track of how many pseudorandom numbers it has generated since it was last reseeded. It uses a private member variable called m_nCount for this purpose.

```
int m_nCount; //count of number of times used
```

Public member functions include a constructor, a function number(i,j) that returns a pseudorandom integer in the range i to j inclusive, and a function sowseed that reseeds the pseudorandom number generator using the current time:

```
CRandom(); //constructor
int number(int i,int j); //return random number in i..j
void sowseed(); //seed the random number generator
```

The code file for CRandom is Random.cpp. It begins with a constructor, which calls the public member function sowseed to seed the linear congruential random number generator.

```
CRandom::CRandom(){ //constructor
  sowseed(); //seed random number generator
}
```

Function sowseed seeds the linear congruential random number generator using the srand function provided in the C standard library. Function srand requires a random number to use as a seed; we will use the value returned by the Windows API function timeGetTime on the assumption that reseeding will take place at unpredictable times. Since the generator is no longer stale, it then resets m_nCount to zero.

```
void CRandom::sowseed(){ //seed random number generator
  srand(timeGetTime()); m_nCount=0;
}
```

Function number(i,j) returns a pseudorandom number in the range i to j inclusive, using the C standard library function rand. Unfortunately, rand is a legacy function that returns a positive signed short integer, which is only 15 bits long. This lets us generate pseudorandom numbers up to 32,767, which is a bit restrictive. We will write code to generate 30-bit random numbers by concatenating two consecutive 15-bit pseudorandom numbers generated by rand. In general, this is *not* a statistically good way to generate pseudorandom numbers, but it is good enough for many purposes. The first thing we do is increment m_nCount and reseed if the generator is stale.

```
if(++m_nCount>STALE_RAND)sowseed(); //reseed if stale
```

If the random number requested is small, we use a single call to rand:

```
int sample; //random sample
//get a random sample
if(j<0x7FFF)sample=rand(); //15-bit
```

Otherwise we take the result from rand, left-shift it 15 bits, then OR a second result from rand into the lower-order 15 bits (which were left zero after the left-shift of the first sample):

```
else sample=((int)rand()<<15)|(int)rand(); //30-bit
```

Now we need to constrain the sample to be in the range i to j inclusive, that is, no smaller than i, and no larger than j. Taking the remainder modulo (j-i+1) makes it no smaller than 0 and no larger than j-i. Adding i to this makes it no smaller than i and no larger than j, as required.

```
return sample%(j-i+1)+i;
```

Changes to the Object Class

Changes to CObject in Demo 5 are fairly minimal. In Objects.h, the only changes are to insert two new entries, FARM_OBJECT and FIELD_OBJECT, in ObjectType for two new objects representing Ned's farm.

```
enum ObjectType{CROW_OBJECT=0,PLANE_OBJECT,FARM_OBJECT,
  FIELD_OBJECT,NUM_SPRITES};
```

As described earlier in this chapter, the following line of code is added to the declaration of CObject. This grants CObjectManager the right to access private and protected member variables of CObject. The friend class construct is a powerful one that can be abused through overuse, though it is legitimate to use it to give a manager class control over the objects that it is managing.

```
friend class CObjectManager;
```

In the CObject draw function in Objects.cpp, we change the first line of code so that it draws the object's sprite image m_pSprite to the correct location on the screen relative to the player's viewpoint instead of its absolute coordinates in the virtual universe, that is, to (Viewpoint.screen(m_nX),m_nY) instead of (m_nX,m_nY):

```
m_pSprite->draw(m_nCurrentFrame,Viewpoint.screen(m_nX),
  m_nY,surface);
```

In the CObject create function, we change the PLANE_OBJECT's frame interval to 250 milliseconds:

```
m_nFrameInterval=250;
```

The CROW_OBJECT wingbeat animations are desynchronized by starting each crow object at a random frame in its animation and setting its frame interval to a random number in the range 220 to 280 milliseconds. Since the random number generator may generate the same frame interval for different crows, some crows *may* remain synchronized. However, this is sufficiently unlikely. The probability of two crows getting the same frame interval is 1/61, which means that the probability of getting two synchronized crows is greater than 1/2 only when there are 30 crows or more, and in such a crowd of crows they are unlikely to be recognized unless the player is particularly looking for them. Crow wingbeats may also appear to be synchronized for short periods of time and then become asynchronous later due to the artificial quantization of time into discrete frames of varying lengths.

```
m_nCurrentFrame=Random.number(0,m_nFrameCount-1);
m_nFrameInterval=250+Random.number(-30,30);
```

We also introduce two new cases into the switch statement for the farm and field objects:

```
case FARM_OBJECT:
case FIELD_OBJECT:
m_nFrameCount=1;
break;
```

Finally, in the CObject move function, we change the definition of the constant YMARGIN:

```
const int YMARGIN=20; //vertical margin;
```

We add the following line of code to normalize the object's x-coordinate to within the virtual universe:

```
Viewpoint.normalize(m_nX); //normalize to world width
```

Finally, we constrain the object's vertical motion so that it remains below the top of the screen and above the bottom of the screen. Since the object's m_nY value is the y-coordinate of its bottom, we will make sure that m_nY is at least YMARGIN so that at least 20 pixels of the object will appear at the top of the screen (which will be large enough to show all of the small objects such as crows), and that m_nY is at most SCREEN_HEIGHT-1 so that it will stay above the bottom of the screen.

```
if(m_nY<YMARGIN)m_nY=YMARGIN;
if(m_nY>=SCREEN_HEIGHT)m_nY=SCREEN_HEIGHT-1;
```

Changes to Main.cpp

The changes to Main.cpp in Demo 5 begin with the declaration of a constant for the maximum number of objects allowed in the game:

```
#define MAX_OBJECTS 32 //max number of objects in game
```

We declare a new bmp sprite file reader to hold the foreground image depicting Ned's farm:

```
CBmpSpriteFileReader g_cFrgndImages; //foreground images
```

We declare an object manager of sufficient size to hold all of the objects:

```
CObjectManager ObjectManager(MAX_OBJECTS); //object manager
```

Then, we declare a viewpoint manager and a random number generator. In Demo 5, we will use the random number generator in the CObject class to desynchronize the crow wingbeats; we will find many other uses for it later.

```
CViewPoint Viewpoint; //player viewpoint
CRandom Random; //random number generator
```

Loading Sprites

The first code change is to the body of LoadPlaneSprite, which now loads six frames of plane animation from locations (1,1), (123,1), (245,1), (367,1), (489,1), and (17,74) of the image stored in the bmp sprite file reader g_cSpriteImages:

```
BOOL result=TRUE;
result=result&&g_pSprite[PLANE_OBJECT]->
  load(&g_cSpriteImages,0,1,1);
 result=result&&g_pSprite[PLANE_OBJECT]->
  load(&g_cSpriteImages,1,123,1);
 result=result&&g_pSprite[PLANE_OBJECT]->
  load(&g_cSpriteImages,2,245,1);
 result=result&&g_pSprite[PLANE_OBJECT]->
  load(&g_cSpriteImages,3,367,1);
 result=result&&g_pSprite[PLANE_OBJECT]->
  load(&g_cSpriteImages,4,489,1);
 result=result&&g_pSprite[PLANE_OBJECT]->
  load(&g_cSpriteImages,5,17,74);
return result;
```

A new function, LoadFrgndSprites, loads the foreground images of the farm and the field into two sprites from the bmp sprite file reader g_cFrgndImages:

```
BOOL LoadFrgndSprites(){ //load foreground sprites
  BOOL result=TRUE;
  result=result&&g_pSprite[FARM_OBJECT]->
```

```
   load(&g_cFrgndImages,0,0,0); //load farm sprite
result=result&&g_pSprite[FIELD_OBJECT]->
   load(&g_cFrgndImages,0,640,0); //load field sprite
return result;
} //LoadFrgndSprites
```

We use this function to load the foreground sprites by adding four lines of code to the end of function LoadImages. We load the new bmp file Farm.bmp (see Figure 7.4) into the bmp sprite file reader g_cFrgndImages.

```
if(!g_cFrgndImages.load("farm.bmp"))return FALSE;
```

Figure 7.4 The foreground image Farm.bmp

We then create two clipped sprites for the farm and the field, and call function LoadFrgndSprites to load the images into the sprites from the bmp sprite file reader g_cFrgndImages:

```
g_pSprite[FARM_OBJECT]=new CClippedSprite(1,640,162);
g_pSprite[FIELD_OBJECT]=new CClippedSprite(1,640,162);
if(!LoadFrgndSprites())return FALSE; //load foreground
```

The CreateObjects Function

The body of function CreateObjects now requests the object manager to create the objects for us. First, the farm and field objects are placed side by side so as to fill up the virtual universe. The farm object is placed at (0,SCREEN_HEIGHT-1), and the field object is placed at (SCREEN_WIDTH,SCREEN_HEIGHT-1). The exact x-coordinates are not important provided one is SCREEN_WIDTH larger than the other is. The y-coordinates must be at the bottom of the screen. The farm and field objects have a horizontal and vertical velocity of zero.

```
ObjectManager.create(FARM_OBJECT,0,SCREEN_HEIGHT-1,0,0);
ObjectManager.create(FIELD_OBJECT,SCREEN_WIDTH,
  SCREEN_HEIGHT-1,0,0);
```

Three crow objects are placed, with horizontal speeds of -2 (recall that negative speeds are to the left):

```
ObjectManager.create(CROW_OBJECT,400,100,-2,0);
ObjectManager.create(CROW_OBJECT,420,80,-2,0);
```

```
ObjectManager.create(CROW_OBJECT,430,120,-2,0);
```

Then the plane object, which is made the current object using the ObjectManager set_current function, is created:

```
ObjectManager.set_current(
  ObjectManager.create(PLANE_OBJECT,320,271,-1,0));
```

Lastly, we create three slower crow objects in various places, with horizontal speeds of –1:

```
ObjectManager.create(CROW_OBJECT,320,100,-1,0);
ObjectManager.create(CROW_OBJECT,405,90,-1,0);
ObjectManager.create(CROW_OBJECT,255,125,-1,0);
```

Other Functions

The next function to be changed is RestoreSurfaces, in which we add code to restore the surfaces in the two new sprites:

```
if(g_pSprite[FARM_OBJECT]->Restore()&& //if farm and ...
  g_pSprite[FIELD_OBJECT]->Restore()) //... field restored
  result=result&&LoadFrgndSprites(); //redraw image
else return FALSE;
```

Function ComposeFrame is now a lot simpler than it was in Demo 4. The tasks of drawing the background and animating the objects have been given to the viewpoint manager and the object manager, respectively. ComposeFrame simply asks them to do their jobs, passing to the viewpoint manager the speed of the plane as reported by the object manager so that the background scrolls at a speed proportional to the plane's speed.

```
Viewpoint.draw_background(lpBackground,lpSecondary,
  ObjectManager.speed()); //draw scrolling background
ObjectManager.animate(lpSecondary); //draw objects
```

The last significant change to Main.cpp is that the keyboard_handler function must now request the object manager to accelerate the plane in response to the appropriate keystrokes from the player:

```
case VK_UP: ObjectManager.accelerate(0,-1); break;
case VK_DOWN: ObjectManager.accelerate(0,1); break;
case VK_LEFT: ObjectManager.accelerate(-1,0); break;
case VK_RIGHT: ObjectManager.accelerate(1,0); break;
```

Demo 5 Files

Code Files

The following files in Demo 5 are used without change from Demo 4:

- Bmp.h
- Bmp.cpp
- Bsprite.h
- Bsprite.cpp
- Csprite.h
- Csprite.cpp
- Defines.h
- Ddsetup.cpp
- Sbmp.h
- Sbmp.cpp
- Timer.h
- Timer.cpp

The following files in Demo 5 have been modified from Demo 4:

- Main.cpp
- Objects.h
- Objects.cpp

The following files are new in Demo 5:

- Objman.h
- Objman.cpp
- Random.h
- Random.cpp
- View.h
- View.cpp

Media Files

The following image files are new in Demo 5:

- Farm.bmp

Required Libraries

- Ddraw.lib
- Winmm.lib

Chapter 8

Here's what you'll learn:

- What a rule-based system is and how to implement it

- How to layer object intelligence on top of the code for dumb objects

- How to prevent intelligent objects from behaving identically using the timer and the pseudorandom number generator

- How to manage objects that are born and die during the course of the game

- How to implement a simple form of collision detection

Artificial Intelligence

In Demo 6, we learn how to create rudimentary artificial intelligence (AI for short) using a simple rule-based system augmented with randomness to make the behavior of the crows less predictable and more chaotic. Suddenly the game becomes more interesting. The crows react to the plane, changing speed and height to get away from it, and dropping behind the plane when the opportunity presents itself. The player can now fire bullets by pressing the Spacebar. When hit, the crows explode and turn into falling corpses (see Figure 8.1). This begins to complicate our object management. The exploding crow and the falling crow are treated as different objects from the flying crow. Whereas the crows and plane, as we have already seen, are animated by playing a single animation sequence forward and backward, the exploding crows have an animation that is played only once. The bullets and falling crows have a single frame of animation and a fixed lifetime.

Figure 8.1
Bullets and an exploding crow

Experiment with Demo 6

Take a moment now to run Demo 6.

- You should see a plane and a flock of crows in random places.
- Use the left and right arrow keys to make the plane accelerate and decelerate.
- Chase the crows that are ahead of you. Notice that they accelerate to get away from you, and change heights chaotically. If you chase one for long enough at maximum speed, it will eventually slow down as if it has become tired.
- Notice that the crows will gradually all fall behind you and drop to minimum speed so that you cannot chase them any more.
- Drop your speed to the minimum. Notice that the crows form two flocks, one ahead of you and one level with or behind you, and keep pace with the plane.
- Chase the flock ahead of you again, and see the crows scatter in alarm.
- Hit the Spacebar to fire a bullet. Hunt down a crow and shoot it. Watch it explode and change into a corpse that falls from the sky, accelerating due to gravity as it falls.
- Hit the Esc key to exit the program.

Intelligent Objects

Some of the objects in our game are intelligent, and some are not. Intelligence comes with a price—it costs in time to compute intelligent actions, and it costs in memory to store information from which to make intelligent choices. There are many different AI designs from which to choose. We will use one of the simplest, a *rule-based system*, which consists of a set of *states* that the intelligent object can be in, and a set of *rules* that determine which state it is in and what actions are to be taken while in those states. The good thing about a rule-based system is that it is easy to program and requires very little computing time to run. The bad thing about it is that it can lead to predictable and, even worse, identical behavior from the objects. This is bad enough when you meet the objects one at a time, but is worse when you have many of them on the screen at the same time. We want our crows to behave like real crows in that they should behave similarly but not identically. We will achieve this by using the pseudorandom number generator to modify their behavior.

Since not all of the objects in our game will be intelligent, we will derive an intelligent object class `CIntelligentObject` from our base object class `CObject`. Intelligent objects will have more private member variables than base objects, and therefore will use more memory. To save memory, we will use both

`CIntelligentObject` and `CObject` in our game, whichever is appropriate for each object.

Intelligent Object Overview

The header file for `CIntelligentObject` is `Ai.h`, which begins with the declaration of an enumerated type for the states that the intelligent objects can be in. `CRUISING_STATE` means that the object is simply cruising around, unaware of the plane. `AVOIDING_STATE` means that it is aware of the plane's nearby location and is trying to avoid it.

```
enum StateType{CRUISING_STATE,AVOIDING_STATE};
```

`CIntelligentObject` is derived from `Cobject`:

```
class CIntelligentObject: public CObject{
```

It has 11 private member variables. The first records the object's current state.

```
StateType m_eState; //state
```

The next three private member variables are associated with height changes. The first of these is the desired height that the object is currently at or moving toward. The second is the last time the object changed height. The third is the desired time between height changes.

```
int m_nDesiredHeight; //desired altitude
int m_nHeightTime; //time between height changes
int m_nHeightDelayTime; //time to next height change
```

The next two private member variables are associated with speed changes. The first of these is the last time the object changed speed. The second is the desired time between speed changes.

```
int m_nSpeedVariationTime; //last time speed varied
int m_nSpeedVariationDuration; //time to next speed variation
```

The next two private member variables are associated with the use of intelligence. Intelligent objects are not intelligent all of the time; they "zone out" for long periods, not paying much attention to what is going on about them. The first of these private member functions is the last time that the object paid attention, and the second is the amount of time that the object is allowed to "zone out."

```
int m_nLastAiTime; //last time AI was used
int m_nAiDelayTime; //time until AI next used
```

The next three private member variables are associated with the plane. The first is the distance to the plane, the second is the vertical distance, and the third is the horizontal distance. All distances are measured in pixels.

```
int m_nDistance; //distance to plane
int m_nVerticalDistance; //vertical distance from plane
int m_nHorizontalDistance; //horizontal distance from plane
```

CIntelligentObject has four private member functions. Function ai is the main artificial intelligence function. It consists of a switch statement based on the object's current state, which then determines which actions are appropriate.

```
void ai(); //artificial intelligence
```

The next two private member functions control the AI for the two possible states that the object can be in.

```
void cruising_ai(); //ai for cruising along
void avoiding_ai(); //ai for avoiding plane
```

The last private member function takes care of the housekeeping that must take place when an object changes state:

```
void set_state(StateType state); //change state
```

CIntelligentObject has three public member functions, starting with a constructor:

```
CIntelligentObject(ObjectType object,int x,int y,
    int xspeed,int yspeed); //constructor
```

The move function is declared virtual void because we are going to take advantage of the fact that, since CIntelligentObject is derived from CObject, a CObject* pointer p can also be used to point to a CIntelligent-Object at run time. The declaration of move as virtual void allows the compiler to tell at run time which move function to call in response to p->move()—the CIntelligentObject one if p is pointing to a CIntelligentObject or the CObject one if p is pointing to a CObject. Leaving out the virtual void would make the compiler call the CObject move function every time.

```
virtual void move(); //move depending on time and speed
```

The plane function is a writer function used to tell the object where the plane is and how far away it is:

```
void plane(int x,int y,int d); //relationship w/plane
};
```

Intelligent Object Code

The code file for `CIntelligentObject` is `Ai.cpp`, which begins with the declaration of some constants. The first two of these constants define when an object is to be considered "close to" and "far from" the plane. It is "close to" the plane when it is at most distance `CLOSE_DISTANCE` from the plane, and "far from" the plane when it is at least `FAR_DISTANCE` from the plane. These constants should be tuned during play testing.

```
const int CLOSE_DISTANCE=200; //close to plane
const int FAR_DISTANCE=300; //far from plane
```

If objects are in front of but much higher or much lower than the plane, they will reduce their speed with the intention of falling back behind the plane where it is safer. The *fallback distance* is the vertical separation that is considered high enough or low enough to attempt to fall back.

```
const int FALLBACK_DISTANCE=150;
```

Finally, when an object is behind the plane it is safe. When the center of the object is `BEHIND_DISTANCE` away from (in this case slightly in front of) the center of the plane, it considers itself to be behind the plane, and therefore safe from attack.

```
const int BEHIND_DISTANCE=-5;
```

The `CIntelligentObject` constructor passes its parameters on to the `CObject` constructor, then sets the `CIntelligentObject` private member variables to sensible initial values. The alert reader will notice the member variable `m_bIntelligent` that hasn't been discussed yet—it is a new member variable of `CObject` that we will talk about later.

```
CIntelligentObject::CIntelligentObject(ObjectType object,
  int x,int y,int xspeed,int yspeed):
CObject(object,x,y,xspeed,yspeed){ //constructor
  m_bIntelligent=TRUE;
  m_nDesiredHeight=240;
  m_nHeightTime=0;  m_nHeightDelayTime=0;
  m_nSpeedVariationTime=m_nSpeedVariationDuration=0;
  m_nDistance=m_nHorizontalDistance=m_nVerticalDistance=0;
  m_eState=CRUISING_STATE;
  m_nLastAiTime=0; m_nAiDelayTime=0;
}
```

Moving and Thinking

The `CIntelligentObject move` function calls the `CObject move` function to move like a dumb object, then calls the `CIntelligentObject ai` function to act intelligently. The idea is that the `ai` will simply change the private `CObject` member functions in an intelligent way, and leave the `CObject move` function to implement these changes. This division of labor makes sense; otherwise you might end up with both the `CObject` and the `CIntelligentObject` member functions trying to direct the object's actions, with potentially disastrous—or at least hilarious—results.

```
void CIntelligentObject::move(){ //move object
  CObject::move(); //move like a dumb object
  ai(); //act intelligently
}
```

Next, we see the `CIntelligentObject ai` function. If enough time has elapsed since the last time the object acted intelligently, then it calls the AI function corresponding to the object's current state. Notice that this modular design makes it easy to add more states to the state space, which we would definitely want to do if we were to introduce more object types into the game.

```
void CIntelligentObject::ai(){ //main AI function
  //do the following periodically
  if(Timer.elapsed(m_nLastAiTime,m_nAiDelayTime))
    switch(m_eState){ //behavior depends on state
      case CRUISING_STATE: cruising_ai(); break;
      case AVOIDING_STATE: avoiding_ai(); break;
      default: break;
    }
}
```

The Plane and Distance

The `CIntelligentObject plane` function is a method for introducing information about the plane. It has three parameters, the horizontal and vertical coordinates of the plane in the virtual universe, and the Euclidean distance from the plane to the object.

```
void CIntelligentObject::plane(int x, int y,int d){
```

It stores the Euclidean distance and the vertical distance in private member variables:

```
m_nDistance=d;
m_nVerticalDistance=abs(m_nY-y);
```

The horizontal distance requires a little more effort because, as explained in Chapter 7, no two things can be farther away from each other than WORLD_WIDTH/2:

```
m_nHorizontalDistance=m_nX-x;
if(m_nHorizontalDistance>WORLD_WIDTH/2)
  m_nHorizontalDistance-=WORLD_WIDTH;
if(m_nHorizontalDistance<-WORLD_WIDTH/2)
  m_nHorizontalDistance+=WORLD_WIDTH;
}
```

Changing State

The CIntelligentObject set_state function takes a single parameter containing the new state. It begins by changing the state member variable m_eState to the new state.

```
void CIntelligentObject::set_state(StateType state){
  m_eState=state; //change state
```

Most importantly, it takes care of the housekeeping associated with state changes using a switch statement:

```
switch(m_eState){ //change behavior settings
```

It begins with the cruising state:

```
case CRUISING_STATE:
```

In the cruising state, the object is lazy about acting intelligently, so set_state sets the delay time for intelligent acts to a random interval between 300 and 600 milliseconds:

```
m_nAiDelayTime=300+Random.number(0,300);
```

It's feeling pretty relaxed when it starts cruising, so drop the speed to the minimum:

```
m_nXspeed=-1;
```

Change height only every 8 to 13 seconds:

```
m_nHeightDelayTime=8000+Random.number(0,5000);
break;
```

In the avoiding state, things are faster. The AI delay time drops to 200 to 400 milliseconds.

```
case AVOIDING_STATE:
  m_nAiDelayTime=200+Random.number(0,200);
```

Speed increases to the maximum:

```
m_nXspeed=-3;
```

Choose a random height to move to, and change the height delay time to between 3 and 5 seconds:

```
m_nDesiredHeight=Random.number(100,400);
m_nHeightDelayTime=3000+Random.number(0,2000);
```

Change speed every 5 to 7 seconds to make things interesting. What it looks like in practice is that the objects get tired after flying at top speed for a while, then get a "second wind" later.

```
m_nSpeedVariationDuration=5000+Random.number(0,2000);
break;
default: break;
}
}
```

Cruising AI

The `CIntelligentObject cruising_ai` function takes care of AI when the object is cruising:

```
void CIntelligentObject::cruising_ai(){ //just cruising along
```

If the desired height is not too close to the current height, it sets the vertical speed in the correct direction:

```
if(m_nDesiredHeight<m_nY-20)m_nYspeed=-1;
else if(m_nDesiredHeight>m_nY+20)m_nYspeed=1;
else m_nYspeed=0;
```

If enough time has passed since the last height change, it initiates a new height change and sets the time until the next height change to a random number between 15 and 20 seconds:

```
if(Timer.elapsed(m_nHeightTime,m_nHeightDelayTime)){
  m_nDesiredHeight=Random.number(150,400);
  m_nHeightDelayTime=15000+Random.number(0,5000);
}
```

Finally, it looks for the plane. If the plane is close to but not in front of the object, it moves into the avoiding state.

```
if(m_nDistance<CLOSE_DISTANCE&&
m_nHorizontalDistance<BEHIND_DISTANCE)
  set_state(AVOIDING_STATE);
}
```

Avoidance AI

The `CIntelligentObject avoiding_ai` function takes care of AI when the object is avoiding the plane:

```
void CIntelligentObject::avoiding_ai(){ //avoiding plane
```

If enough time has passed since the last height change, it picks a new height, sets the vertical speed to the correct direction, which is a little faster than in the cruising state, then sets the height delay time to a random number between 3 and 5 seconds. Notice that the object will either overshoot the desired height or be reassigned a new height before it gets there, which will make it continually dither from one height to another.

```
if(Timer.elapsed(m_nHeightTime,m_nHeightDelayTime)){
  m_nDesiredHeight=Random.number(100,450);
  if(m_nDesiredHeight<m_nY)m_nYspeed=-2;
  if(m_nDesiredHeight>m_nY)m_nYspeed=2;
  m_nHeightDelayTime=3000+Random.number(0,2000);
}
```

Next, we have the code for the speed variation:

```
if(Timer.elapsed(m_nSpeedVariationTime,
m_nSpeedVariationDuration))
  if(m_nXspeed==-2){
    m_nXspeed=-3;
    m_nSpeedVariationDuration=10000+Random.number(0,3000);
  }
  else{
    m_nXspeed=-2;
    m_nSpeedVariationDuration=5000+Random.number(0,2000);
  }
```

If the object is behind the plane, it slows down:

```
if(m_nHorizontalDistance>BEHIND_DISTANCE) //if behind
  m_nXspeed=-1; //slow down
```

If the plane is far away from the object, or if the plane is close but at a sufficiently different height, then the object drops back to the cruising state. Notice that we will want FAR_DISTANCE to be sufficiently larger than CLOSE_DISTANCE to prevent the object from dithering between the two states (by which I mean swapping between the two states several times a second, resulting in jerky behavior).

```
if(m_nDistance>FAR_DISTANCE|| //if far away, or
(m_nDistance<CLOSE_DISTANCE&& //close and
m_nVerticalDistance>FALLBACK_DISTANCE)) //higher or lower
  set_state(CRUISING_STATE); //then back to cruising
}
```

Changes to the Object Class

Our object class needs substantial changes to handle the new kinds of objects.

Declarations

In `Objects.h`, the `ObjectType` enumerated type is modified by adding the new object types for the bullet, the exploding crow, and the dead crow:

```
enum ObjectType{CROW_OBJECT=0,PLANE_OBJECT,FARM_OBJECT,
    FIELD_OBJECT,BULLET_OBJECT,EXPLODINGCROW_OBJECT,
    DEADCROW_OBJECT,NUM_SPRITES};
```

A new enumerated type `MortalityType` enumerates the different mortality choices for an object. `MORTAL` means having a fixed lifespan, `IMMORTAL` means having no fixed life expectancy (immortal objects can be killed, however; they just don't die of old age), and `ONESHOT_MORTAL` means that they live just long enough to play their animation sequence through once.

```
enum MortalityType{MORTAL,IMMORTAL,ONESHOT_MORTAL};
```

A new enumerated type `LocomotionType` enumerates the different locomotion choices for an object. `FLYING_MOTION` means that they fly, `FALLING_MOTION` means that they fall (accelerating due to gravity), and `NO_MOTION` means they don't move.

```
enum LocomotionType{FLYING_MOTION,FALLING_MOTION,NO_MOTION};
```

The `CObject` private member variables now become `protected` so that they can be inherited by `CIntelligentObject`. `CObject` gains some new protected member variables, starting with two that record the width and height of the sprite.

```
int m_nWidth,m_nHeight; //width and height of sprite
```

The next three protected member variables record the object's mode of locomotion, its object type, and its mortality type:

```
LocomotionType m_eLocomotion; //mode of travel
ObjectType m_eObject; //what kind of object is this?
MortalityType m_eMortality; //whether it dies or not
```

The next three protected member variables relate to the object's mortality: the time that it was born, its life expectancy, and whether it is vulnerable to bullets:

```
int m_nBirthTime; //time of creation
int m_nLifeTime; //time that object lives
BOOL m_bVulnerable; //vulnerable to bullets
```

The last new protected member variable was mentioned in the previous section: `m_bIntelligent` is set to `TRUE` if the object is intelligent, that is, if it is a `CIntelligentObject` class instance rather than a `CObject` class instance. This is because we will use a `CObject*` pointer to point to both `CObject` and `CIntelligentObject` class instances, but C++ provides no facility for telling which is which at run time. So, we will do it ourselves by setting `m_bIntelligent` to `FALSE` in the `CObject` constructor and resetting it to `TRUE` in the `CIntelligentObject` constructor.

```
BOOL m_bIntelligent; //TRUE if object is intelligent
```

Instead of having a constructor and a `create` function, `CObject` will now just have a constructor with the same parameters that function `create` had in Demo 5:

```
CObject(ObjectType object,int x,int y,
   int xspeed,int yspeed); //constructor
```

Finally, function `move` is made a virtual function, as was discussed in the previous section. As far as the compiler is concerned, once we have declared `move` to be a virtual function in `CObject` we don't need to list it as `virtual` again in `CIntelligentObject`, but it is a good idea to do so in both places as a reminder to the programmer.

```
virtual void move(); //move depending on time and speed
```

The Constructor

Changes to `Objects.cpp` begin with the new constructor, which now has the same parameters that function `create` had in Demo 5:

```
CObject::CObject(ObjectType object,int x,int y,
               int xspeed,int yspeed){ //constructor
```

It begins by setting default values for some of the protected member variables including, as mentioned above, setting `m_bIntelligent` to `FALSE`:

```
m_nCurrentFrame=0; m_nLastFrameTime=Timer.time();
m_bForwardAnimation=TRUE; m_nFrameInterval=30;
m_eMortality=IMMORTAL; m_eLocomotion=NO_MOTION;
m_nLifeTime=1000; m_bVulnerable=FALSE;
m_bIntelligent=FALSE;
```

Next, we set the protected member variables that are common to all object types, starting with the object's type and motion characteristics:

```
m_eObject=object; //type of object
m_nLastXMoveTime=m_nLastYMoveTime=Timer.time(); //time
m_nX=x; m_nY=y; //location
m_nXspeed=xspeed; m_nYspeed=yspeed; //speed
```

Then, the object's image characteristics are set:

```
m_pSprite=g_pSprite[object];
m_nFrameCount=m_pSprite->frame_count();
m_nHeight=m_pSprite->height();
m_nWidth=m_pSprite->width();
```

The time that the object was created is recorded in a protected member variable so that we can cull the mortal objects that die of old age:

```
m_nBirthTime=Timer.time(); //time of creation
```

Next, we have the settings that depend on the object type, managed by a switch statement:

```
switch(object){
```

First, the plane object's speed limits and frame interval are set:

```
case PLANE_OBJECT:
   m_nMinXSpeed=-3; m_nMaxXSpeed=-1;
   m_nMinYSpeed=-4; m_nMaxYSpeed=4;
   m_nFrameInterval=250;
```

The plane is immortal, it flies, and it is not vulnerable to bullets:

```
   m_eMortality=IMMORTAL;
   m_eLocomotion=FLYING_MOTION;
   m_bVulnerable=FALSE;
   break;
```

Next, the crow object's speed limits, first frame, and frame interval are set:

```
case CROW_OBJECT:
   m_nMinXSpeed=-2; m_nMaxXSpeed=-1;
   m_nMinYSpeed=-1; m_nMaxYSpeed=1;
   m_nCurrentFrame=Random.number(0,m_nFrameCount-1);
   m_nFrameInterval=250+Random.number(-30,30);
```

The crow is immortal, it flies, and it is vulnerable to bullets:

```
   m_eMortality=IMMORTAL;
   m_eLocomotion=FLYING_MOTION;
   m_bVulnerable=TRUE;
   break;
```

The settings for the farm and field objects are self-explanatory:

```
case FARM_OBJECT:
case FIELD_OBJECT:
   m_nFrameCount=1;
   m_eMortality=IMMORTAL;
   m_eLocomotion=NO_MOTION;
   m_bVulnerable=FALSE;
   break;
```

The bullet object is mortal, it flies, it is not vulnerable, and its lifetime is a random number between 500 and 700 milliseconds. Making each bullet have a different lifetime makes things a little more interesting out at the extreme range of the plane's gun, so that some bullets travel farther than others.

```
case BULLET_OBJECT:
  m_nFrameCount=1;
  m_eMortality=MORTAL;
  m_eLocomotion=FLYING_MOTION;
  m_bVulnerable=FALSE;
  m_nLifeTime=500+Random.number(0,200);
  break;
```

The dead crow is mortal, it falls, it is not vulnerable (it's no use hitting it with bullets since it's already dead), and it has a lifetime of 1 second. It would be cleaner to have the dead crow culled when it hits ground level, and in fact, we will add code to implement this in the next chapter. The finite lifetime set here will act as a backup in case we mess up that code.

```
case DEADCROW_OBJECT:
  m_nCurrentFrame=0;
  m_eMortality=MORTAL;
  m_eLocomotion=FALLING_MOTION;
  m_bVulnerable=FALSE;
  m_nLifeTime=1000;
  break;
```

The exploding crow is mortal and lives for a single run through its animation sequence, it flies, and it is not vulnerable. This is the last `case` statement and ends the new `CObject` constructor.

```
case EXPLODINGCROW_OBJECT:
  m_nCurrentFrame=0;
  m_nFrameInterval=100;
  m_eMortality=ONESHOT_MORTAL;
  m_eLocomotion=FLYING_MOTION;
  m_bVulnerable=FALSE;
  break;
  }
}
```

Drawing and Moving

The `CObject draw` function changes slightly because the next frame of the new `ONESHOT_MORTAL` objects is computed differently from the others. Right after the call to the `m_pSprite->draw` function, we insert the following code. If the object is `ONESHOT_MORTAL`, then we increment the frame counter without wrapping it around the ends; this is so we can detect when the animation is over by checking whether `m_nCurrentFrame` is at least as large as `m_nFrameCount`.

```
if(m_eMortality==ONESHOT_MORTAL){ //animation plays once
  if(Timer.elapsed(m_nLastFrameTime,m_nFrameInterval))
    ++m_nCurrentFrame;
}
else{ //repeating animation
```

Otherwise, we perform the animation as in Demo 5.

The `CObject move` function is changed slightly because we now have different modes of locomotion. A switch statement is placed around the entire body of the function under the `case FLYING_MOTION`.

```
switch(m_eLocomotion){
  case FLYING_MOTION:
```

Then, a new case is created for falling objects:

```
    break;
  case FALLING_MOTION:
```

Horizontal speed is set to zero:

```
    m_nXspeed=0;
```

We compute the time since the object was born since the acceleration due to gravity means that vertical distance traveled is proportional to the amount of time that it has been falling:

```
    tfactor=time-m_nBirthTime;
```

The vertical distance traveled is scaled, recorded, and timed:

```
    ydelta=tfactor/YSCALE; m_nY+=ydelta;
    if(m_nY<YMARGIN)m_nY=YMARGIN;
    if(ydelta||m_nYspeed==0) //record time of move
      m_nLastYMoveTime=time;
    break;
```

Objects with other modes of locomotion (such as `NO_MOTION`) don't move at all:

```
    default: break;
}
```

Changes to the Object Manager Class

Our object manager also needs substantial changes to handle the interactions between the new kinds of objects. The way we handle the object list will be substantially different. In Demo 5, we created a `CObject` class instance for every slot in the object list. Now, we will keep unused slots empty, `new` ourselves a `CObject` or `CIntelligentObject` class instance when an object is born, and `delete` it when it dies. Some purists will object to this reliance on the C++ operators `new` and `delete`, which can be slow. However, in defense of this approach, it should be observed that the birth and death of objects is a relatively infrequent occurrence, and therefore any attempt to optimize this code is probably a waste of time and effort.

Secondly, a reader who has taken a course on algorithm analysis may object to our naïve implementation of the object list as a simple array. While such an implementation is efficient for most of the operations used in our game, the insertion of a new object in the object list will in the worst case take time proportional to the number of objects already in the list. It is tempting to propose the use of more sophisticated data structures with a faster insertion time. For example, with a linked list, insertions could take place almost instantaneously. However, the extra overhead inherent in more sophisticated data structures will actually make them slower for the small number of objects that we have in our game. Remember, most data structures have the caveat that they are what is called *asymptotically faster*, that is, faster when the amount of data gets large. For small tasks, simpler is better. If your game has thousands of objects in it, however, you might want to review this decision.

Declarations

In `Objman.h`, the class `CObjectManager` gets a new private variable `m_nLastGunFireTime`, which records the last time that the gun fired. We will use this to make sure that the gun doesn't fire too often, to foil (for instance) a sophisticated user who increases the autorepeat rate to get a machine-gun effect by holding down the Spacebar.

```
int m_nLastGunFireTime; //time gun was last fired
```

`CObjectManager` has seven new private member functions, the first two of which compute distances in the virtual universe. One of these distance functions takes two sets of coordinates, `(x1,y1)` and `(x2,y2)`, and computes the Euclidean distance between them. The other function takes two indices, and returns the distance between the centers of the objects at those indices in the object list.

```
int distance(int x1,int y1,int x2,int y2); //in universe
int distance(int first,int second); //between objects
```

The next pair of functions handles collision detection. The first of these computes collisions between all objects, and the second computes collisions between a particular object at a given `index` in the object list with all other objects.

```
void collision_detection(); //all collisions
void collision_detection(int index); //with this object
```

The remaining three functions deal with dead objects. The `cull` function goes through the object list and removes those objects that have exceeded their allotted lifetimes (the Grim Reaper of the object list). The `kill` function takes an index as a parameter and removes the object at that index from the object list. The `replace` function takes an index as a parameter and replaces the object at that index with the next object in the sequence, if that object is part of a sequence (for example, crow, exploding crow, dead crow).

```
void cull(); //cull dead objects
void kill(int index); //remove object from list
void replace(int index); //replace by next in series
```

The Constructor

The changes to `Objman.cpp` begin with the `CObjectManager` constructor. The private member variable that records the last time the gun fired is set to zero, so that the gun is ready for immediate firing.

```
m_nLastGunFireTime=0;
```

Each pointer in the object list is set to `NULL` inside the `for` loop instead of being initialized with a `CObject` class instance the way it was in Demo 5. This is because some of them will be `CIntelligentObject` class instances instead. We'll create them later as needed.

```
m_pObjectList[i]=NULL;
```

In the `CObjectManager` `create` function, after testing to see if there is room for the new object, the following code is used. A local variable `i` is used to find the first unused slot in the object list, indicated by a `NULL` pointer.

```
int i=0; //index into object list
while(m_pObjectList[i]!=NULL)i++; //find first free slot
```

An intelligent object is created for a crow, and a base object is created for the other object types (such as the plane and the bullets):

```
if(object==CROW_OBJECT) //intelligent object
  m_pObjectList[i]=
    new CIntelligentObject(object,x,y,xspeed,yspeed);
else //dumb object
  m_pObjectList[i]=new CObject(object,x,y,xspeed,yspeed);
```

We then increment the object count and return the index of the new object:

```
m_nCount++;
return i;
```

The Animate Function

In the `CObjectManager animate` function, we begin by protecting the calls to `m_pObjectList[i]->move()` and `m_pObjectList[i]->draw(sur-face)` with an `if(m_pObjectList[i]!=NULL)` conditional. Failure to do this would obviously result in a nasty crash.

After the call to `m_pObjectList[i]->move()`, we insert the following code to notify intelligent objects about the plane's current position. Notice that we must cast the `CObject*` pointer `m_pObjectList[i]` to `CIntelligentObject*` before the compiler will let us call its `plane` member function. If `m_pObject-List[i]` points to `CObject` class instance, doing this will result in a crash, which is why we use the `CObject` private member variable `m_bIntelligent` to distinguish `CObject` class instances from `CIntelligentObject` class instances.

```
if(m_pObjectList[i]->m_bIntelligent) //if intelligent
  //tell object about plane current position
  ((CIntelligentObject*)m_pObjectList[i])->plane(
    m_pObjectList[m_nCurrentObject]->m_nX,
    m_pObjectList[m_nCurrentObject]->m_nY,
    distance(i,m_nCurrentObject));
```

Immediately before the objects are drawn, we do collision detection and cull the old objects (that is, remove the ones that have lived out their allotted lifespan):

```
collision_detection();
cull();
```

The Distance Functions

Now we have the new object manager functions. The first of the two `CObjectManager distance` functions takes two sets of coordinates, `(x1,y1)` and `(x2,y2)`, and computes the Euclidean distance between them.

```
int CObjectManager::distance(int x1,int y1,int x2,int y2){
```

It begins by computing the x and y components of the distance:

```
int x=abs(x1-x2),y=abs(y1-y2);//x and y distance
```

Then it adjusts the horizontal component of the distance, remembering that in a circular world, no two objects can be farther apart than `WORLD_WIDTH/2`:

```
if(x>WORLD_WIDTH/2)x-=WORLD_WIDTH;
```

Finally, it returns the distance according to the well-known formula of Euclid:

```
return (int)sqrt((double)x*x+(double)y*y);
}
```

The second of the two `CObjectManager distance` functions takes two indices, `first` and `second`, and computes the distance between the objects at those indices in the object list:

```
int CObjectManager::distance(int first,int second){
```

First, it checks that the indices are within range. (Actually, in retrospect I should have checked that the object pointers at those indices are not NULL instead.)

```
if(first<0||first>=m_nMaxCount)return -1;
if(second<0||second>=m_nMaxCount)return -1;
```

Then it computes the coordinates of the centers of the objects in local variables `x1,y1` and `x2,y2`. Notice that we adjust the vertical coordinates by subtracting half of the height of the object so that the coordinates are those of the center of the object.

```
int x1,y1,x2,y2; //coordinates of objects
x1=m_pObjectList[first]->m_nX;
y1=m_pObjectList[first]->m_nY-
  m_pObjectList[first]->m_nHeight/2;
x2=m_pObjectList[second]->m_nX;
y2=m_pObjectList[second]->m_nY-
  m_pObjectList[second]->m_nHeight/2;
```

Finally, it calls the first `distance` function to do the hard work:

```
return distance(x1,y1,x2,y2);
}
```

Killing and Firing the Gun

The `CObjectManager kill` function takes a single parameter `index`, and removes the object at that index in the object list by decrementing the counter, deleting the object, and setting its pointer to NULL:

```
void CObjectManager::kill(int index){ //remove object
  m_nCount--;
  delete m_pObjectList[index];
  m_pObjectList[index]=NULL;
}
```

The CObjectManager fire_gun function creates a bullet object 60 pixels to the left and 50 pixels above the bottom center of the plane, moving to the left at speed 5. This makes it appear to have been fired from the plane's gun. Note that if the artist decides to change the position of the gun, we would have to change this code. The timer's elapsed function is used to ensure that bullets can only be fired every 200 milliseconds.

```
void CObjectManager::fire_gun(){ //fire current object's gun
  CObject *plane= m_pObjectList[m_nCurrentObject];
  if(Timer.elapsed(m_nLastGunFireTime,200))
    create(BULLET_OBJECT,plane->m_nX-60,plane->m_nY-50,-5,0);
}
```

Culling Objects

The CObjectManager cull function kills all old objects. It declares a local variable object, which will be used to point to the current object.

```
void CObjectManager::cull(){ //cull old objects
  CObject *object;
```

Then, in a for loop that addresses each place in the object list, it sets object to point to the current object:

```
for(int i=0; i<m_nMaxCount; i++){ //for each object
  object=m_pObjectList[i]; //current object
```

It checks to see whether there is an object at that place in the object list. If not, it continues on to the next object in the list.

```
if(object!=NULL){
```

If there is an object there, it checks to see whether it should die of old age, that is, whether it is mortal and has lived long enough. By "lived long enough," we mean that the amount of time that it has been alive, which is the difference between the current time and its birth time Timer.time()-object->m_nBirthTime, is greater than its life expectancy, which is object->m_nLifeTime. If so, then it calls the kill member function to remove it from the object list.

```
if(object->m_eMortality==MORTAL&& //if mortal and ...
(Timer.time()-object->m_nBirthTime>object->m_nLifeTime))
  kill(i); //...then kill it
```

Otherwise, we check to see if it is a one-shot animation object that has been played through completely, that is, its current frame object->m_nCurrent-Frame is greater than or equal to its frame count object->m_nFrameCount. If so, then it calls the replace member function to replace the object with the next object in the appropriate sequence (which for now is limited to the sequence crow, exploding crow, dead crow), if there is one.

```
        else //one-shot animation
          if(object->m_eMortality==ONESHOT_MORTAL&&
          object->m_nCurrentFrame>=object->m_nFrameCount)
            replace(i); //...then replace the object
      }
    }
  }
```

The Replace Function

The CObjectManager replace function takes an index as a parameter and replaces the object at that index in the object list with the next object in the sequence associated with that object type:

```
void CObjectManager::replace(int index){
```

It begins with three local variables, object to point to the current object as we scan the object list, newtype to record the type of the new object, and a Boolean successor, which is TRUE if the object has a successor in the object sequence (set TRUE initially until we learn otherwise):

```
CObject *object=m_pObjectList[index]; //current object
ObjectType newtype;
BOOL successor=TRUE; //assume it has a successor
```

A switch statement sets newtype to the next object type in the sequence, setting successor to FALSE if it doesn't have one. The only object sequence available in Demo 6 is CROW_OBJECT, EXPLODINGCROW_OBJECT, DEADCROW_OBJECT.

```
switch(object->m_eObject){
  case CROW_OBJECT: newtype=EXPLODINGCROW_OBJECT; break;
  case EXPLODINGCROW_OBJECT: newtype=DEADCROW_OBJECT; break;
  default: successor=FALSE; break; //has no successor
}
```

We then read the location and speed of the old object into local variables x, y, xspeed, and yspeed:

```
int x=object->m_nX,y=object->m_nY; //location
int xspeed=object->m_nXspeed;
int yspeed=object->m_nYspeed;
```

We then kill the old object, and if it has a successor, create a new one of type newtype with the same location and speed as the old object. Notice that the new object won't necessarily have the same index in the object list as the old object, but then that isn't a requirement.

```
      kill(index); //kill old object
      if(successor) //if it has a successor
        create(newtype,x,y,xspeed,yspeed); //create new one
    }
```

Collision Detection

The last pair of functions in the object manager deals with collision detection, which at this stage simply means bullets colliding with crows. The first instance of this function has no parameters; it collides all objects with all other objects. It runs through the object list with a `for` loop. For each non-NULL entry, if the object there is a bullet, then it passes its index to the second `collision_detection` function which does the real work.

```
void CObjectManager::collision_detection(){
//check for all collisions
  for(int i=0; i<m_nMaxCount; i++) //for each object slot
    if(m_pObjectList[i]!=NULL) //if object exists
      if(m_pObjectList[i]->m_eObject==BULLET_OBJECT)
        collision_detection(i); //check for collisions
}
```

The second `CObjectManager collision_detection` function has a single parameter `index`, and takes care of collisions between the (bullet) object at that place in the object list with every other object in the list:

```
void CObjectManager::collision_detection(int index){
```

It has two local variables, an index `i` for the object that is checked for collision with object `index` and a Boolean variable `finished` that will be set to TRUE when a collision has been detected. We will design the code so that each object can collide with only one other object at a time, so when `finished` is TRUE we can exit the function.

```
  int i=0; //index of object collided with
  BOOL finished=FALSE; //finished when collision detected
```

We use a `while` loop to run `i` through the object list, allowing premature exit if `finished` ever becomes TRUE:

```
  while(i<m_nMaxCount&&!finished){
```

We check to see that there is an object at index `i` of the object list, that this object is vulnerable, and that it is "close enough" to the object at `index` (where "close enough" was defined after some experimentation to be 15). This is very naïve collision detection that doesn't depend on the size of the object being hit. If you want to get more sophisticated, you can replace 15 by some function of the sprite size, thus creating an invisible bounding box or bounding circle around the vulnerable parts of the object.

```
if(m_pObjectList[i]!=NULL) //if i is a valid object index
  if(m_pObjectList[i]->m_bVulnerable&& //if vulnerable
    distance(index,i)<15){ //and close enough, then
```

If there is a collision, then we record a hit by setting `finished` to `TRUE`, calling member function `replace` to replace the object that was hit, and killing the object doing the hitting (in this case, a bullet). Notice that if we were to remove the statement `kill(index)`, bullets could continue through the crows to potentially kill other crows. We have coded it in such a way that bullets remain lodged in crow corpses. This is a design decision that makes the game different, though not necessarily better.

```
finished=TRUE; //hit found, so exit loop
replace(i); //replace object that is hit
kill(index); //kill object doing the hitting
}
```

We then move on to the next object in the while loop, and exit the function after its termination:

```
    ++i; //next object
  }
}
```

Changes to Main.cpp

Changes to `Main.cpp` in Demo 6 mainly involve the processing of the new objects and their sprites.

Loading Sprites

Function `LoadDeadCrowSprite` loads the single frame of the dead crow sprite from location (453,230) of the image in the bmp sprite file reader `g_cSpriteImages`:

```
BOOL LoadDeadCrowSprite(){ //load dead crow
  return g_pSprite[DEADCROW_OBJECT]->
    load(&g_cSpriteImages,0,453,230);
} //LoadDeadCrowSprite
```

Function `LoadExplodingCrowSprite` loads six frames of exploding crow animation from locations (257,294), (321,294), (386,162), (453,162), (386,230), and (453,230) of the image in the bmp sprite file reader `g_cSpriteImages`:

```
BOOL LoadExplodingCrowSprite(){ //load exploding crow
  BOOL result=TRUE;
  result=result&&g_pSprite[EXPLODINGCROW_OBJECT]->
    load(&g_cSpriteImages,0,257,294);
  result=result&&g_pSprite[EXPLODINGCROW_OBJECT]->
    load(&g_cSpriteImages,1,321,294);
  result=result&&g_pSprite[EXPLODINGCROW_OBJECT]->
    load(&g_cSpriteImages,2,386,162);
  result=result&&g_pSprite[EXPLODINGCROW_OBJECT]->
    load(&g_cSpriteImages,3,453,162);
  result=result&&g_pSprite[EXPLODINGCROW_OBJECT]->
    load(&g_cSpriteImages,4,386,230);
  result=result&&g_pSprite[EXPLODINGCROW_OBJECT]->
    load(&g_cSpriteImages,5,453,230);
  return result;
} //LoadExplodingCrowSprite
```

Function `LoadBulletSprite` loads the single frame of the bullet sprite from location (5,123) of the image in the bmp sprite file reader `g_cSpriteImages`:

```
BOOL LoadBulletSprite(){ //load bullet
  return g_pSprite[BULLET_OBJECT]->
    load(&g_cSpriteImages,0,5,123);
} //LoadBulletSprite
```

Function `LoadImages` has the following new code to load the new sprite images. The dead crow sprite has a single frame of animation and is 62x53 pixels in size.

```
g_pSprite[DEADCROW_OBJECT]=new CClippedSprite(1,62,53);
LoadDeadCrowSprite(); //load dead crow images
```

The exploding crow sprite has six frames of animation and is also 62x53 pixels in size:

```
g_pSprite[EXPLODINGCROW_OBJECT]=new CClippedSprite(6,62,53);
LoadExplodingCrowSprite(); //load exploding crow images
```

The bullet sprite has a single frame of animation and is a tiny 5x3 pixels in size (which is why it is so hard to see in `Sprites.bmp` shown in Figure 5.2):

```
g_pSprite[BULLET_OBJECT]=new CClippedSprite(1,5,3);
LoadBulletSprite(); //load bullet images
```

The CreateObjects Function

Function `CreateObjects` gets its crow creation code replaced. The following code is used to create eight crows before the plane is created, so they are drawn behind the plane. The object manager is asked eight times to create a crow object at a random location, each crow initially moving slowly to the left.

```
for(i=0; i<8; i++)
  ObjectManager.create(CROW_OBJECT,
    Random.number(0,WORLD_WIDTH-1),
    Random.number(100,400),-1,0);
```

The same four lines of code is used again in function CreateObjects *after* the plane has been created, so that eight more crows are drawn in front of the plane.

Other Functions

Function RestoreSurfaces gets nine more lines of code to restore and reload the surfaces in the three new sprites. By now this type of code should be very familiar to you.

```
if(g_pSprite[DEADCROW_OBJECT]->Restore()) //if restored
  result=result&&LoadDeadCrowSprite(); //redraw image
else return FALSE;
if(g_pSprite[EXPLODINGCROW_OBJECT]->Restore()) //if restored
  result=result&&LoadExplodingCrowSprite(); //redraw image
else return FALSE;
if(g_pSprite[BULLET_OBJECT]->Restore()) //if restored
  result=result&&LoadBulletSprite(); //redraw image
else return FALSE;
```

The keyboard_handler function has a new case for the Spacebar added to its switch statement. In response to a space, the keyboard handler asks the object manager to fire the gun.

```
case VK_SPACE: ObjectManager.fire_gun(); break;
```

Demo 6 Files

Code Files

The following files in Demo 6 are used without change from Demo 5:

- Bmp.h
- Bmp.cpp
- Bsprite.h
- Bsprite.cpp
- Csprite.h
- Csprite.cpp
- Defines.h
- Ddsetup.cpp
- Random.h
- Random.cpp
- Sbmp.h
- Sbmp.cpp
- Timer.h
- Timer.cpp
- View.h
- View.cpp

The following files in Demo 6 have been modified from Demo 5:

- Main.cpp
- Objects.h
- Objects.cpp
- Objman.h
- Objman.cpp

The following files are new in Demo 6:

- Ai.h
- Ai.cpp

Required Libraries

- Ddraw.lib
- Winmm.lib

Chapter 9

Here's what you'll learn:

- What a game shell is, and how to wrap one around your game engine

- How to display a logo screen, title screen, and main menu

- How to make your game engine re-entrant

The Game Shell

In Demo 7, we learn how to wrap a game shell around our game. The game shell consists of a logo screen displaying the logo of the company that created the game (in this case, my lab at UNT), a title screen for the game, and a menu screen. The logo and title for *Ned's Turkey Farm* are simply bmp files that are displayed for a few seconds, whereas in a real game you should use fancy animations or a movie clip. However, it is a good idea to keep the title screen low-impact because is a good place to load up resources such as sound and images for use during the game and it gives the player something to look at while they are loading. In our game demo, however, the resource requirements are so low that this is not necessary. Since the player will eventually get tired of seeing the logo and title screens, no matter how entertaining they are, we allow the player to click out of them by hitting any key.

The part of the game that we started in Demos 0-6, where you actually play the game, is called the *game engine*. After the logo screen (Figure 9.1) and the title screen (Figure 9.2) are displayed, the player is dumped into the main menu screen (Figure 9.3). From there, the player has several options, only two of which actually work in Demo 7—entering the game engine for a new game by hitting the "N" key or quitting by using the "Q" key. Which key to hit is indicated by having the artist draw the appropriate letter of each menu item in a different color. Eventually, when we get mouse control, the player will be able to click on the buttons next to the menu items instead. The player can exit the game engine by hitting the Esc key or killing all of the crows, in which case he or she will land in the menu screen again.

Figure 9.1
The logo
screen,
Larc.bmp

Figure 9.2
The title
screen,
Title.bmp

Figure 9.3
The menu
screen,
Menu.bmp

Experiment with Demo 7

Take a moment now to run Demo 7.

- You should see the logo screen displayed for 7 seconds and the title screen displayed for 10 seconds. You will then see the menu screen.
- Hit the "N" key to play a game. Kill all of the crows. When the last corpse hits the ground, you will be sent back to the menu screen.
- Hit the "N" key to play a second game. You will see a new flock of crows to kill. This time quit the game by hitting the Esc key before killing all of the crows. You will end up back at the menu screen again.
- Hit the "Q" key or the Esc key to exit the program.
- Run Demo 7 again. Hit any key to exit the logo screen early. Do the same for the title screen. You may exit the program again by hitting the "Q" key or the Esc key at the menu screen.

Changes to the Object Manager

Changes to the object manager class in Demo 7 involve the insertion of two new public member functions. Since these changes are relatively minor, `Objman.cpp` and `Objman.h` are not listed in the `pdf` supplement on the companion CD with the other changed files.

The first new `CObjectManager` function is a `reset` function, which resets a (possibly used) object manager back to its initial conditions. We need this now because the player may conceivably re-enter the game from the menu screen; up until now the player could only play one game and then quit.

```
void CObjectManager::reset(){ //reset to original conditions
```

We begin by resetting to zero the number of objects, the current object, and the last time the gun fired:

```
m_nCount=0; m_nCurrentObject=0; m_nLastGunFireTime=0;
```

A `for` loop iterates through all of the objects in the object list, calls `delete` to destroy each one, then replaces the corresponding pointer in the object list with `NULL`. This code works even with empty slots in the object list because calling `delete` on a `NULL` pointer does nothing.

```
for(int i=0; i<m_nMaxCount; i++){
  delete m_pObjectList[i];
  m_pObjectList[i]=NULL;
}
}
```

The second new `CObjectManager` function is `won`, which returns `TRUE` if the player has killed all of the enemies in the game. Because the object list may contain friends as well as enemies, we can't use the `m_nCount` member variable. Instead, we search the object list and count the number of crow-related objects. Including the exploding and dead crows in the count means that the game doesn't end until the last corpse has hit the ground.

```
BOOL CObjectManager::won(){ //TRUE if enemies all dead
  int count=0; //how many enemies left
  for(int i=0; i<m_nMaxCount; i++)
    if(m_pObjectList[i]!=NULL)
      switch(m_pObjectList[i]->m_eObject){
        case CROW_OBJECT:
        case EXPLODINGCROW_OBJECT:
        case DEADCROW_OBJECT:
          count++;
```

```
        break;
    }
    return count<=0;
}
```

Phase Management

For want of a better term, we will refer to the various parts of the game—for example, the part where the logo screen is being displayed as opposed to the part where the title screen is being displayed—as *phases*. Defines.h contains a new enumerated type that names the four phases in Demo 7. We will add new phases in later chapters.

```
enum GamePhaseType{
  LOGO_PHASE,TITLE_PHASE,MENU_PHASE,PLAYING_PHASE
};
```

Main.cpp has three new global variables to help manage phase transitions. The first is the current phase GamePhase, and the second a Boolean variable endphase that will be set to TRUE when the current phase should end. We use endphase simply as a convenient way to ensure that phase changes actually take place at only one place in the code, whereas the necessity for a phase change might be discovered in a variety of places. The third new global variable is PhaseTime, which will help us measure the time spent in each phase.

```
GamePhaseType GamePhase; //current phase
BOOL endphase=FALSE; //should we abort current phase?
int PhaseTime=0; //time in phase
```

In function RestoreSurfaces, we need to change the way that the primary and secondary surfaces are restored. Up until now, we have assumed that they should be reloaded immediately after they have been restored. Now things are more complicated, however; the reloading process depends on what phase we are in. Rather than clutter up function RestoreSurfaces, we restore without reloading and deal with it later in the code.

```
    if(FAILED(lpPrimary->Restore()))return FALSE;
    if(FAILED(lpSecondary->Restore()))return FALSE;
```

The Display_screen Function

A new function `display_screen` displays an image from a bmp file. It has a single parameter `filename` that points to the name of the file from which the image should be read. We will use this function to display the logo and title screens.

```
void display_screen(char *filename){ //display bmp file
```

It has a local bmp file reader called `image`:

```
CBmpFileReader image; //file reader
```

We load the image into the file reader, and draw it to the secondary surface:

```
image.load(filename); //load from file
image.draw(lpSecondary); //draw to back buffer
```

The displayed image might have a different palette from the game engine—in fact, I encouraged the artist to do so in order to give him as much creative freedom as possible—so we should set the palette in the primary surface to be the same as the palette in the image:

```
image.setpalette(lpPrimaryPalette); //may have custom palette
```

Function `display_screen` ends by page flipping so that the image can be seen:

```
PageFlip(); //display it
} //display_screen
```

The Change_phase Function

There is always some housekeeping to be done when entering a new phase. We will create a function `change_phase` to put all of this code in a common place. Function `change_phase` has a single parameter `new_phase` that tells it which phase to change to.

```
void change_phase(GamePhaseType new_phase){ //start new phase
```

It begins by setting `GamePhase` to the new phase, setting `PhaseTime` to the current time, and setting `endphase` (which we assume triggered the call to `change_phase` by being `TRUE`) to `FALSE`:

```
GamePhase=new_phase; PhaseTime=Timer.time();
endphase=FALSE;
```

A `switch` statement on the current phase helps us write custom phase transition code for each phase. At the start of the logo, title, and menu phases, we need only display the appropriate image.

```
switch(GamePhase){
  case LOGO_PHASE:
    display_screen("larc.bmp");
    break;
  case TITLE_PHASE:
    display_screen("title.bmp");
    break;
  case MENU_PHASE:
    display_screen("menu.bmp");
    break;
```

At the start of the playing phase, we need to set up the game engine to begin play:

```
  case PLAYING_PHASE: //prepare the game engine
```

Now that the player can re-enter the game engine from the menu phase, we must reset the object manager to remove any object left behind from any previous games (the player may have hit the Esc key, leaving any number of crows in the object list). Then we call CreateObjects to create the objects for a new game.

```
    ObjectManager.reset(); //clear object manager
    CreateObjects(); //create new objects
```

Before entering the game engine, we initialize the graphics by setting the palette for the primary surface to the background palette (recall that we are entering the game engine from the menu screen, which has a custom palette), then priming the frame pump by displaying a frame of animation. This ends the switch statement, and ends function change_phase.

```
    background.setpalette(lpPrimaryPalette); //game palette
    ComposeFrame(); PageFlip(); //prime animation pump
    break;
  }
} //change_phase
```

The Redraw Function

Next, we have a function Redraw, which we will use to redraw the screen after surface loss. It consists of a switch statement with a case for each phase. For most of the phases, we simply need to draw the appropriate image to the screen. For the game engine we need do nothing; animation will resume soon enough from the message pump.

```
void Redraw(){ //redraw in response to surface loss
  switch(GamePhase){
    case LOGO_PHASE:
      display_screen("larc.bmp");
      break;
```

```
      case TITLE_PHASE:
        display_screen("title.bmp");
        break;
      case MENU_PHASE:
        display_screen("menu.bmp"); //display main menu
        break;
      case PLAYING_PHASE:
        //do nothing, next frame of animation will catch it
        break;
    }
  }
```

The ProcessFrame Function

The body of function ProcessFrame has become more complicated. It begins
with the declarations of two constants that define how long the logo screen and
title screen should be displayed (7 seconds and 10 seconds, respectively).

```
    const int LOGO_DISPLAY_TIME=7000; //duration of logo
    const int TITLE_DISPLAY_TIME=10000; //duration of title
```

Instead of checking for surface loss as a result of a failed page flip, we will check
explicitly at the next step in ProcessFrame using the primary surface's IsLost
member function. If surface loss is detected, surfaces are restored and then
redrawn using our new Redraw function.

```
    if(lpPrimary->IsLost()){
      RestoreSurfaces(); Redraw();
    }
```

Next, a switch statement is used to determine which phase we are in:

```
    switch(GamePhase){ //what phase are we in?
```

In the logo phase, all we need to do is wait until the phase is over. Rather than
wasting system resources by getting locked into a tight wait loop, we use the API
function Sleep, which makes the game become inactive for a fixed period (100
milliseconds in this case), during which system resources are free for use by other
processes running on the player's computer. Sleeping for a tenth of a second is a
little drastic; a less drastic alternative would be to call Sleep with no parameter,
which forces the scheduler to switch to the next active process without mandating
a sleep period.

```
    case LOGO_PHASE: //displaying logo screen
      Sleep(100); //surrender time to other processes
```

If endphase has been set to TRUE or enough time has elapsed, we change to the title phase. The use of endphase here is to give the player the option of clicking out of the logo screen. With this in place, the keyboard manager need only set endphase to TRUE in response to any keystroke during the logo phase.

```
if(endphase||Timer.elapsed(PhaseTime,LOGO_DISPLAY_TIME))
  change_phase(TITLE_PHASE); //go to title screen
break;
```

The title phase has the same code, but with a different display time and a different next phase (the menu phase this time):

```
case TITLE_PHASE: //displaying title screen
  Sleep(100); //surrender time to other processes
  if(endphase||Timer.elapsed(PhaseTime,TITLE_DISPLAY_TIME))
    change_phase(MENU_PHASE); //go to menu
break;
```

The menu phase is similar, but you can stay in it as long as you want. When the phase ends, we go into the playing phase. None of the other menu items work yet, except for quitting which we handle as a special case in the keyboard handler.

```
case MENU_PHASE: //main menu
  Sleep(100); //surrender time to other processes
  if(endphase)change_phase(PLAYING_PHASE); //play game
break;
```

The code for the playing phase has the ComposeFrame/PageFlip pair of function calls from the old version of ProcessFrame, followed by a new pair of lines that change the phase back to the menu phase if endphase is TRUE (the player hit Esc or "Q"), or the object manager reports that the player has won (by killing all of the crows). This ends the body of ProcessFrame.

```
case PLAYING_PHASE: //game engine
  ComposeFrame(); //compose a frame in back surface
  PageFlip(); //flip video memory surfaces
  if(endphase||ObjectManager.won()) //if end of phase
    change_phase(MENU_PHASE); //go to menu
break;
}
```

The Keyboard Handlers

The keyboard handler code must change, because any given key may have a different effect in different phases. The cleanest way to do this is to make a keyboard handler for different phases, with similar phases sharing a handler. The logo and title phases share a keyboard handler called the `intro_keyboard_handler`, which responds to any keystroke by ending the phase.

```
void intro_keyboard_handler(WPARAM keystroke){
  endphase=TRUE; //any key ends the phase
} //intro_keyboard_handler
```

The keyboard handler for the menu phase is called `menu_keyboard_handler`, which returns `TRUE` if the player wants to exit the game. It has a single parameter that contains the virtual keycode of the key that was pressed.

```
BOOL menu_keyboard_handler(WPARAM keystroke){
```

The function begins with the declaration of a local variable for the return value:

```
BOOL result=FALSE;
```

Then, we have a `switch` statement on the `keystroke` parameter:

```
switch(keystroke){
```

The game exits when the player hits either the Esc key or the "Q" key. When this happens, we want to return `TRUE`. Notice that the virtual keycode for letter keys is identical to the ASCII encoding of the uppercase version of the letter, which we get by using a character in single quotes.

```
case VK_ESCAPE:
case 'Q': //exit game
  result=TRUE;
  break;
```

To play a new game in response to the "N" key, we simply set `endphase` to `TRUE`, which works at the current point in development since the only place to go from the menu phase is the playing phase. In later chapters, we will need to add a facility that lets us go to different phases when the menu phase ends.

```
case 'N': //play new game
  endphase=TRUE;
  break;
default: break; //do nothing
}
```

Finally, we return the result and exit:

```
return result;
} //menu_keyboard_handler
```

The game keyboard handler is identical to the keyboard handler from Demo 6:

```
void game_keyboard_handler(WPARAM keystroke){
  switch(keystroke){
    case VK_ESCAPE: endphase=TRUE; break;
    case VK_UP: ObjectManager.accelerate(0,-1); break;
    case VK_DOWN: ObjectManager.accelerate(0,1); break;
    case VK_LEFT: ObjectManager.accelerate(-1,0); break;
    case VK_RIGHT: ObjectManager.accelerate(1,0); break;
    case VK_SPACE: ObjectManager.fire_gun(); break;
    default: break;
  }
} //game_keyboard_handler
```

The body of the main keyboard handler is replaced by a `switch` statement that calls the appropriate phase keyboard handler to do the real work:

```
BOOL keyboard_handler(WPARAM keystroke){ //keyboard handler
  BOOL result=FALSE; //TRUE if we are to exit game
  switch(GamePhase){ //select handler for phase
    case LOGO_PHASE:
    case TITLE_PHASE:
      intro_keyboard_handler(keystroke);
      break;
    case MENU_PHASE:
      result=menu_keyboard_handler(keystroke);
      break;
    case PLAYING_PHASE:
      game_keyboard_handler(keystroke);
      break;
  }
  return result;
} //keyboard_handler
```

The last change to `Main.cpp` involves setting the initial phase immediately before entering the message loop. This is done with a single-line call to `change_phase`. The first phase is, of course, the logo phase, and the `change_phase` function takes care of the housekeeping that needs to be done on phase entry, such as showing the logo screen and starting to measure the time in phase.

```
change_phase(LOGO_PHASE);
```

Demo 7 Files

Code Files

The following files in Demo 7 are used without change from Demo 6:

- `Ai.h`
- `Ai.cpp`
- `Bmp.h`
- `Bmp.cpp`
- `Bsprite.h`
- `Bsprite.cpp`
- `Csprite.h`
- `Csprite.cpp`
- `Ddsetup.cpp`
- `Objects.h`
- `Objects.cpp`
- `Random.h`
- `Random.cpp`
- `Sbmp.h`
- `Sbmp.cpp`
- `Timer.h`
- `Timer.cpp`
- `View.h`
- `View.cpp`

The following files in Demo 7 have been modified from Demo 6:

- `Defines.h`
- `Main.cpp`
- `Objman.h` (changes minimal; not listed in the pdf supplement)
- `Objman.cpp` (changes minimal; not listed in the pdf supplement)

Media Files

The following image files are new in Demo 7:

- `Larc.bmp`
- `Menu.bmp`
- `Title.bmp`

Required Libraries

- `Ddraw.lib`
- `Winmm.lib`

Chapter 10

Here's what you'll learn:

- What the major issues are in deciding on sound quality
- What the Nyquist frequency is and how it affects the sample rate
- How to set up DirectSound
- What a DirectSound buffer is and how to load sounds into it from WAV files
- How to play and mix sounds with DirectSound
- How to play looping sounds with DirectSound
- How to stop playing sounds in DirectSound
- How to play multiple copies of a sound without duplicating sound data

Sound

In Demo 8, we learn how to play digitally sampled sounds from files in WAV format. DirectSound enables us to play multiple sounds at the same time by digitally mixing the sound for us. Sounds are played asynchronously, which means that gameplay continues while the sound is being played. Although DirectSound only allows us to play one copy of each sound at a time, it gives us the facility to make multiple copies of a sound that share data, thus saving memory. In this chapter, we develop a sound manager that takes care of managing all of these copies. If you ask it to play a sound, it tries to locate a copy of the sound that isn't currently being played, and if it finds one, it begins to play it.

Experiment with Demo 8

Take a moment now to run Demo 8.

- Listen to the sounds! (Assuming that you have a sound card and speakers.)
- The logo and title screens have long sound samples containing music and voice-overs. In the game engine, the crows caw, the exploding crows go "boom," the gun goes "bang," the crow corpses go "thunk" when they hit the ground, and the plane goes "putt-putt."
- Notice that the logo sound stops if you click out of the logo screen. Similarly for the title sound and the game engine sounds.
- Notice that the plane sound is a single short "putt" sample played repeatedly to give a "putt-putt-putt-putt…" effect. Change the plane speed and notice that the sound changes too.
- Chase the crows, and notice that they caw when they enter the avoiding state. Each crow sample contains multiple caws, which makes a pleasant mix of sounds when several crows go into the avoiding state at about the same time.
- Exit the game, then double-click on some of the sound files in the Demo 8 folder, particularly `Caw.wav` and `Putt0.wav`, to see what they sound like outside of *Ned's Turkey Farm*.

The Sound List

Sndlist.h contains a pair of enumerated types for sound lists used during the game. We will use one sound list for the introduction sequence (the logo and title screens) and one sound list for the game engine. Sndlist.h begins with an obscure #define; later we will see a DirectSound function in which a particular parameter must be set to TRUE to make a sound play repeatedly. Instead, we will set it to LOOP_SOUND to make it more readable.

```
#define LOOP_SOUND TRUE
```

The first sound list is GameSoundType, which enumerates the sounds used in the game engine. The sound files will later be read in this order.

```
enum GameSoundType{ //sounds used in game engine
   CAW_SOUND=0, //sound a crow makes
   GUN_SOUND, //sound of gun firing
   BOOM_SOUND, //sound of explosion
   THUMP_SOUND, //sound of object hitting the ground
   //next 3 sounds must be consecutive and in this order
   SLOWPUTT_SOUND, //sound of slow engine
   MEDIUMPUTT_SOUND, //sound of medium engine
   FASTPUTT_SOUND //sound of fast engine
};
```

The second sound list is IntroSoundType, which enumerates the sounds used in the introduction sequence:

```
enum IntroSoundType{ //sounds used during the intro
   TITLE_SOUND=0, //sound used during title screen
   LOGO_SOUND, //signature chord
};
```

Sound Quality

As part of the game design, you have three choices to make regarding the quality of the sound samples in your game. In each of them there is a tradeoff: higher quality of sound means more data, which means more memory devoted to sound samples when your game is playing, more space on your CD to deliver them to the user, more time needed to load your sounds when the game begins, and more of your CPU processing power and bus bandwidth needed to play them. (Forget what I said about processing power and bus bandwidth for that lucky fraction of your customers who have high-end sound cards; they will store the sounds in memory on the sound card and play them directly without much supervision from the CPU.)

The first choice is stereo versus mono sound. Stereo sound takes twice as much memory as mono sound, but of course sounds much better. If you want to use

DirectSound's 3D sound facilities (which are out of the scope of this book), you will need to use mono sound. Is stereo sound overkill for your game? Is halving the amount of space for the sounds more important than stereo sound? For *Ned's Turkey Farm,* we will choose compactness over coolness by opting for mono sound.

The second choice is the number of bits per sample, usually set at either 8 (for low-quality sound) or 16 (for high-quality sound). While 16-bit sound takes twice as much memory as 8-bit sound, it takes a good ear and an excellent sound system to tell the difference between the two. It is most important on parts of the sound sample that have very low volume. The most noticeable difference is usually a higher level of background hiss on the 8-bit sound samples.

The final choice is the sample rate, which is the rate at which the sound is digitally sampled. This is measured in Hertz (Hz for short), which means "samples per second." The most common sample rates in Hertz are 8000, 11025, 12000, 16000, 22050, 24000, 32000, 44100, and 48000 (usually referred to as 8, 11, 12, 16, 22, 24, 32, 44, and 48 kHz, although this is not strictly accurate). The higher the sample rate, the higher the quality of the sound reproduction. With a low sample rate, the high frequency sounds are missed completely. If you have a game in which all of the sounds are fairly low frequency (for example, with no female voices), then 11 kHz is enough. If you have a fairly normal mix of sound frequencies, then 22 kHz is enough. The frequency of sounds that can be reproduced at a given sample rate is called the *Nyquist frequency*. The Nyquist frequency is half the sample rate, so for example, 22 kHz sampling can reproduce sounds that have a frequency of up to 11 kHz. The amount of memory needed to store a sound increases with the sample rate—doubling the sample rate will double the memory requirements.

Take a moment now to compare the sound samples in the folder `Sound Test`. All of the folders referred to below (`mono`, `bits`, `rate`, and `quality`) are subfolders of `Sound Test`. Each folder contains two or more sound files. Double-clicking on each sound file will cause it to play using whatever default player is installed on your computer. The best way to listen for the differences in sound quality is to wear headphones while performing these tests.

- Start in folder `Mono`. First, play file `Stereo.wav`. An overblown panning effect has been used to make it sound truly *stereo*. Then, play `Mono.wav`. It sounds flat and uninteresting compared to the stereo version. Now look at the file sizes: 363 KB for the stereo version, 182 KB for the mono version.

- Go to folder `Bits`. First, play the 16-bit version `16bit.wav`, then the 8-bit version `8bit.wav`. Unless your ear is very good and your sound system is excellent, you may not be able to hear much difference between the files except for a higher level of hiss in `8bit.wav` (you may need to crank the volume a little—but not too much—to hear it). Now look at the file sizes: 363 KB for the 16-bit version, 182 KB for the 8-bit version.

⊚ Go to folder `Rate`. First, play `22KHz.wav`. Then, play `11KHz.wav`, which should sound a little muffled compared to `22KHz.wav`. Finally, play `8KHz.wav`, which should sound even more muffled. The muffled sound quality comes from the suppression of the high frequency part of Mikayla's voice due to the Nyquist frequency. Personally, I think that 22 kHz is acceptable; 11 kHz might be acceptable under certain circumstances but I would rather not use it; and 8 kHz is flat-out unacceptable. You might not agree with me. Now look at the file sizes: 363 KB for the 22 kHz version, 182 KB for the 11 kHz version, and 132 KB for the 8 kHz version.

⊚ Go to folder `Quality`. Compare the sound of `High.wav` (16-bit stereo, 22 kHz) to that of `Low.wav` (8-bit mono, 11 kHz). Which sounds better? Now look at the file sizes: 363 KB for `High.wav`, and 46 KB for `Low.wav`. The low-quality sound sample is under 13% of the size of the high-quality one, smaller by a factor of more than nine.

Which is more important to the sales of your game—sound quality or size? It's up to you to decide. Changing your mind doesn't involve much programming. We will see in a moment that it just means changing a few constants and recompiling.

The Sound Manager

Sound Manager Overview

The header file for the sound manager class `CSoundManager` is `Sound.h`. It begins with a definition for the maximum number of different sound samples that the sound manager can store.

```
#define MAX_SOUNDS 64 //maximum number of different sounds
```

The next definition is the number of channels, which is related to the number of sounds that can be played simultaneously. Mono sound requires one channel per sound, and stereo requires two channels per sound.

```
#define DS_NUMCHANNELS 8 //number of channels
```

The next definition is the number of channels per sound, which is one for mono sound and two for stereo sound. With the settings you have seen so far, we will be able to play eight mono sounds simultaneously.

```
#define DS_CHANSPERSAMPLE 1 //mono sound
```

The next definition is the number of bits per sample, which we will set to 8 for low-quality but compact sound:

```
#define DS_BITSPERSAMPLE 8 //8-bit sound
```

The final definition is the sample rate, which we will set to 22 kHz:

```
#define DS_SAMPLERATE 22050 //22KHz sampling
```

CSoundManager has five private member variables. We start with a counter for the number of distinct sounds loaded so far.

```
int m_nCount; //number of sounds loaded
```

The m_lpDirectSound member variable stores a pointer to the DirectSound object, which is the DirectX object that gives us direct access to the sound hardware on our computer:

```
LPDIRECTSOUND m_lpDirectSound; //DirectSound object
```

Just as the DirectDraw object stores images on surfaces, the DirectSound object stores sounds in *sound buffers*. The best way to think of a sound buffer is that it is like a cassette player. It contains a playback head that tells it where to start playing from, and it contains the media to play from—for a cassette player that's a cassette, and for the sound buffer it's a chunk of memory containing the digital sample. The CSoundManager member variable m_lpBuffer is an array of MAX_SOUNDS pointers, each of which will point to an array containing the appropriate number of pointers to the copies of a sound (see Figure 10.1).

```
LPLPDIRECTSOUNDBUFFER m_lpBuffer[MAX_SOUNDS]; //sound buffers
```

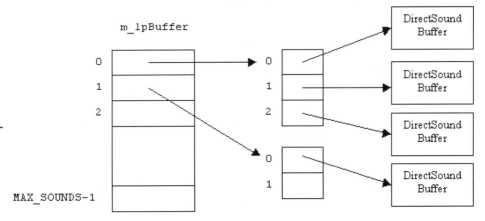

Figure 10.1
The CSound-Manager member variable m_lpBuffer in use

A parallel array m_nCopyCount (parallel to m_lpBuffer) will count the number of copies of each sound. By parallel array we mean that m_nCopyCount[i] will contain the number of copies of the sound number i, so that m_lpBuffer[i] points to an array of m_nCopyCount[i] pointers to sound buffers, each of which will contain a copy of the sound. For example, in Figure 10.1, m_nCopyCount[0] is 3, and m_nCopyCount[1] is 2.

```
int m_nCopyCount[MAX_SOUNDS]; //num copies of each sound
```

We keep a member variable m_bOperational, which will be set to TRUE if DirectSound was initialized correctly. We will use this to bail out of CSoundManager public member functions when DirectSound is not present (for example, if DirectX is not installed, or the computer has no sound card).

```
BOOL m_bOperational; //DirectSound initialized correctly
```

CSoundManager has four private member functions for managing sound buffers. Function CreateBuffer has three integer parameters, index, length, and copies. It creates an array of copies pointers to DirectSound sound buffers, one for each copy of sound number index, and makes m_lpBuffer[index] point to this array. It then creates a DirectSound sound buffer to store a sample of the given length, and sets m_lpBuffer[index][0] to point to the new buffer. The sound buffers for the other copies will be created later by CSoundManager function CopyBuffer (see Figure 10.1).

```
BOOL CreateBuffer(int index,int length,int copies);
```

The next three private member functions LoadBuffer, LoadSound, and CopyBuffer take care of loading sounds into the DirectSound sound buffers. The three-step process is illustrated in Figure 10.2.

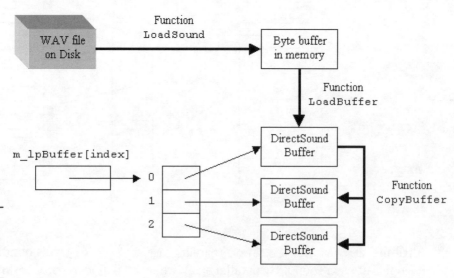

Figure 10.2
The process of loading a sound

Function `LoadBuffer` has three parameters, the integer `index` of a sound, a byte `buffer` containing sound data, and the integer `length` of the byte buffer. It copies the sound data from the `buffer` into the data area of the first copy of the sound in `m_lpBuffer[index]` (that is, to the DirectSound sound buffer pointed to by `*m_lpBuffer[index]`, equivalently, `m_lpBuffer[index][0]`).

```
BOOL LoadBuffer(int index,BYTE *buffer,int length);
```

Function `LoadSound` has two parameters, the name of a file in WAV format as a character string `filename` and the address of a pointer to a byte buffer to receive the sound data, called `sound`. This function queries the file to find the size of the sound data, allocates a large enough buffer to hold it, and loads the sound data from the file into the buffer. It also returns a pointer to the start of the buffer through the parameter `sound` (which is declared as a pointer to a pointer to a byte buffer to facilitate this return) and returns the length of the buffer in the conventional way.

```
int LoadSound(char *filename,BYTE **sound); //load from file
```

Function `CopyBuffer` uses the DirectSound function `DuplicateSound-Buffer` to copy the sound from the DirectSound buffer pointed to by `m_lpBuffer[index][0]` to the DirectSound buffers pointed to by `m_lpBuffer[index][i]` for i ranging from 1 to `copies-1`, inclusive. It does so without duplicating the sound data, which will be shared from the first copy to the other copies. Each copy can independently play from arbitrary points in the same sound data (see Figure 10.3).

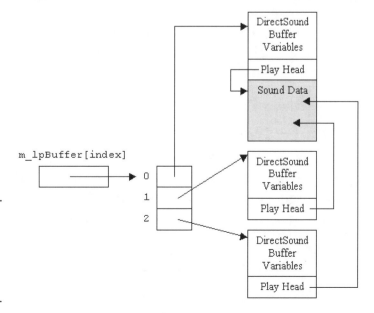

Figure 10.3
CopyBuffer
creates
copies that
share sound
data

```
BOOL CopyBuffer(int index,int copies); //copy sound
```

`CSoundManager` has seven public member functions, including a constructor and a destructor:

```
CSoundManager(HWND hwnd); //constructor
~CSoundManager(); //destructor
```

Function `clear` clears all sounds, reclaiming all of the memory used to store the sound data:

```
void clear(); //clear all sounds
```

Function `load` has two parameters, the name of a file in WAV format as a character string `filename` and an integer number of `copies` of that sound needed (which defaults to 1 if it is not provided). It uses the private member functions to load that many copies of the sound in the file to the next available slot in the sound list `m_lpBuffer`. Slots in the sound list will be filled in numerical order from slot 0 to slot `MAX_SOUNDS-1`.

```
void load(char *filename,int copies=1); //load from file
```

Function `play` has two parameters, the first of which is an integer `index`. It plays the next unused copy of the sound from the copies in the array pointed to by `m_lpBuffer[index]`. If the second parameter (which defaults to `FALSE` if it is not provided) is `TRUE`, the sound is played looping.

```
void play(int index,BOOL looping=FALSE); //play sound
```

There are two versions of the `stop` function. The first has a single parameter, an integer `index`. It stops all copies of the sound `m_lpBuffer[index]` that are currently playing and resets their play heads back to the start of the sample. The second version of the `stop` function has no parameters. It does the same thing to all sounds, that is, to all copies of all currently playing sounds.

```
void stop(int index); //stop playing sound
void stop(void); //stop playing all sounds
```

The Constructor and Destructor

The code file for the sound manager class `CSoundManager` is `Sound.cpp`. It begins with the `CSoundManager` constructor, which has a window handle as a single parameter. It begins by setting the number of loaded sounds to zero.

```
CSoundManager::CSoundManager(HWND hwnd){ //constructor
  m_nCount=0; //no sounds yet
```

Next, it NULLs out the sound buffer copy pointers and zeros the copy counts:

```
//null out sound buffers and flags
for(int i=0; i<MAX_SOUNDS; i++){
  m_lpBuffer[i]=NULL; m_nCopyCount[i]=0;
}
```

Starting DirectSound looks quite a bit like starting DirectDraw. First, we call the DirectSound DirectSoundCreate function, which has three parameters. The first parameter is the GUID of a sound device, which can be set to NULL for the default device. The second parameter is the address of a place to put a pointer to the DirectSound object; we ask DirectSoundCreate to put this pointer into the private member variable m_lpDirectSound. The third parameter must be set to NULL. DirectSoundCreate will return the DirectX defined constant DS_OK if it succeeds. We bail out if it fails.

```
m_bOperational=SUCCEEDED(
  DirectSoundCreate(NULL,&m_lpDirectSound,NULL));
if(!m_bOperational)return;
```

The next thing that must be done is to set the cooperative level by calling the DirectSound object's SetCooperativeLevel member function. The first parameter of this function is the window handle of our application (which is why we specify it as a parameter to the constructor). The second parameter is a cooperative level, which we set to allow the maximum amount of sharing of the sound hardware with other applications.

```
m_bOperational=SUCCEEDED(m_lpDirectSound->
  SetCooperativeLevel(hwnd,DSSCL_NORMAL));
}
```

Next, we have the CSoundManager destructor, which (provided the DirectSound object exists) calls the CSoundManager clear member function to dispose of all of the sound buffers, and then calls the DirectSound object's Release member function to release the DirectSound object:

```
CSoundManager::~CSoundManager(){ //destructor
  if(!m_bOperational)return;
  clear(); //clear all buffers
  (void)m_lpDirectSound->Release(); //release DirectSound
}
```

The Clear Function

The CSoundManager clear function resets the sound manager so that it is ready to load new sounds. It bails out if the sound manager is not operational.

```
void CSoundManager::clear(){ //clear all sounds
  if(!m_bOperational)return;
```

We call the CSoundManager stop function without any parameters to stop all sounds:

```
stop(); //stop all sounds (paranoia)
```

For each sound, we do the following:

```
for(int i=0; i<m_nCount; i++){ //for each sound
```

For each copy of each sound, we call the DirectSound sound buffer's Release function to release the buffer:

```
for(int j=0; j<m_nCopyCount[i]; j++){ //for each copy
  m_lpBuffer[i][j]->Release(); //release the sound
  m_lpBuffer[i][j]=NULL; //probably not needed
}
```

We then delete the array created in the constructor for the pointers to the copies of the current sound:

```
  delete[]m_lpBuffer[i];
}
```

We set the count member variable to zero to indicate that there are no sounds currently loaded, and exit:

```
  m_nCount=0; //no sounds left (hopefully)
}
```

The Load Function

The CSoundManager load function has two parameters, the filename of a file to load and the number of copies of that sound that we want to be able to play simultaneously:

```
void CSoundManager::load(char *filename,int copies){
```

It has two local variables, one for the length of the sound data (which we will get from the file), and a byte pointer that we will use to allocate a byte buffer of that length:

```
int length; //length of sound
BYTE *sound=NULL; //temporary buffer to hold sound data
```

We bail out if there is no DirectSound object, or if there is no space left in the sound list:

```
if(!m_bOperational)return; //bail if not initialized
if(m_nCount>=MAX_SOUNDS)return; //bail if no space left
```

We call the CSoundManager private member function LoadSound to load the sound from the file named filename into a byte buffer of the appropriate size, putting a pointer to the buffer in the local variable sound and the length of the buffer in the local variable length:

```
length=LoadSound(filename,&sound); //load sound from file
```

Next, we call the CSoundManager private member function CreateBuffer to create copies DirectSound sound buffers of length length, pointed to by m_lpBuffer[m_nCount], the next empty slot in the sound list (see Figure 10.1):

```
CreateBuffer(m_nCount,length,copies); //create buffers
```

A call to the CSoundManager private member function LoadBuffer loads the sound from the byte buffer sound of length length into the first of the copy buffers pointed to by m_lpBuffer[m_nCount].

```
LoadBuffer(m_nCount,sound,length); //load into buffer
```

Finally, a call to the CSoundManager private member function CopyBuffer creates duplicates of the sound buffer pointed to by *m_lpBuffer[m_nCount][0] for the remaining copies-1 copies of that sound. (For an overview of the LoadSound—LoadBuffer—CopyBuffer process, refer back to Figure 10.2.)

```
CopyBuffer(m_nCount,copies); //make copies of contents
```

Cleanup consists of deleting the byte buffer created by the call to LoadSound and incrementing the counter so that the next call to the CSoundManager load function will load into the next slot in the sound list. This ends the CSoundManager load function.

```
//clean up and exit
delete[]sound; //delete temporary sound buffer
m_nCount++; //increment counter
}
```

The Play Function

The CSoundManager play function plays the next unused copy of the sound from the copies in the array pointed to by m_lpBuffer[index], looping if looping is TRUE. It bails out if there is no DirectSound object or if the index is out of range.

```
void CSoundManager::play(int index,BOOL looping){ //play sound
  if(!m_bOperational)return; //bail if not initialized
  if(index<0||index>=m_nCount)return; //bail if bad index
```

It has two local variables, an index variable called copy in which we will store the index of the current copy and a status word that we will use to store the playing status of the current copy:

```
int copy=0; //current copy
DWORD status; //status of that copy
```

We begin by getting the status of the first copy of the sound (copy 0). This is done by calling the GetStatus member function of the DirectSound buffer holding the copy. This function takes as a parameter the address of a DWORD variable in which to place a status word and returns DS_OK if it succeeds in getting the status. If it fails, we will assume that the copy is currently playing, so that it is skipped over in the search for a copy to play.

```
if(FAILED(m_lpBuffer[index][copy]->GetStatus(&status)))
  status=DSBSTATUS_PLAYING; //assume playing if failed
```

If the copy is playing, the DSBSTATUS_PLAYING bit of status will be set. As is normal in windows flags, each bit of status corresponds to some property that is either on (if the bit is set) or off (if the bit is unset). The DirectSound constant DSBSTATUS_PLAYING is a power of two (it doesn't matter which one), which means that its binary representation has exactly one bit set, and so the way to check whether that particular bit is set in status is to use the bitwise logical AND operator "&", and check for a nonzero result. So, we use a while loop to march copy from 1 (we did 0 already) to the number of remaining copies m_nCopyCount[index]-1, exiting the loop when either copy goes out of range or we find a copy that is not being currently played.

```
while(copy<m_nCopyCount[index]&&
(status&DSBSTATUS_PLAYING)){ //while current copy in use
```

We increment copy, and check to see that it is still in range (note the pre-increment):

```
if(++copy<m_nCopyCount[index]) //go to next copy
```

We get the status of this new copy and loop back to test the status again:

```
    if(FAILED(m_lpBuffer[index][copy]->GetStatus(&status)))
      status=DSBSTATUS_PLAYING; //assume playing if failed
  }
```

Having exited the `while` loop, we check to see whether `copy` is in range:

```
  if(copy<m_nCopyCount[index]) //if unused copy found
```

If it is, then this copy must not be playing. We play it using the DirectSound buffer's `Play` member function, which has three parameters. The first parameter must be zero. The second parameter is a priority for the sound, which must be set to zero because we are not using prioritized sound in *Ned's Turkey Farm*. The third parameter is a flags word, in which we set the `DSBPLAY_LOOPING` bit if the parameter looping is `TRUE`. This ends the `CSoundManager` play function.

```
  m_lpBuffer[index][copy]->
    Play(0,0,looping?DSBPLAY_LOOPING:0); //play it
}
```

The Stop Functions

The first of two `CSoundManager` `stop` functions has as a parameter the `index` of the sound that we wish to stop playing. As always, it bails out if necessary.

```
void CSoundManager::stop(int index){ //stop playing sound
  if(!m_bOperational)return; //bail if not initialized
  if(index<0||index>=m_nCount)return; //bail if bad index
```

For each copy of the sound, we stop it by calling the DirectSound buffer's `Stop` member function. Calling `Stop` on a nonplaying sound has no effect, so we can go ahead and call it for all copies. Just like a cassette player, the DirectSound `Stop` function stops the tape and leaves the play head somewhere in the middle of the sound. If we were to play this copy again, it would start playing from where it left off. Here we will rewind the sound back to the beginning by calling the DirectSound buffer's `SetCurrentPosition` function to rewind back to `zero`.

```
  for(int i=0; i<m_nCopyCount[index]; i++){ //for each copy
    m_lpBuffer[index][i]->Stop(); //stop playing
    m_lpBuffer[index][i]->SetCurrentPosition(0); //rewind
  }
}
```

The second `CSoundManager` `stop` function stops all sounds by calling the first `stop` function once for each sound:

```
void CSoundManager::stop(void){ //stop playing sound
  if(!m_bOperational)return; //bail if not initialized
  for(int index=0; index<m_nCount; index++) //for each sound
    stop(index); //stop that sound
}
```

The CopyBuffer Function

The `CSoundManager` `CopyBuffer` function makes duplicates of the sound from the first sound buffer for the other copies. It does so without duplicating the sound data (see Figure 10.3). `CopyBuffer` has two parameters containing the index of the sound and the number of copies, respectively. It returns `TRUE` if it succeeds.

```
BOOL CSoundManager::CopyBuffer(int index,int copies){
```

It bails out if DirectSound is not operational:

```
if(!m_bOperational)return FALSE; //bail if not initialized
```

A local variable `result` holds the return result:

```
BOOL result=TRUE; //TRUE if everything went OK
```

The number of copies is recorded in the appropriate place:

```
m_nCopyCount[index]=copies; //record number of copies
```

The copies are made using the DirectSound object's `DuplicateSoundBuffer` function to duplicate the sound buffer from the first copy of the sound to all of the others. The same buffer memory is used for all of the copies; think of them as a collection of cassette players that share a single tape. Each one can be played, stopped, and rewound independently; they just share the same media.

```
for(int i=1; i<copies; i++) //for each copy
  result=result&& //copy the sound
    SUCCEEDED(m_lpDirectSound->
      DuplicateSoundBuffer(*m_lpBuffer[index],
      &(m_lpBuffer[index][i])));
```

If any one or more of the calls to `DuplicateSoundBuffer` returned a value other than `DS_OK`, then `result` was set to `FALSE`. When the copies have been made, the `CSoundManager` `CopyBuffer` function returns `result` and exits.

```
  return result;
}
```

The CreateBuffer Function

Function `CreateBuffer` creates the sound buffers for sound number `index`, of length `length`, with `copies` copies:

```
BOOL CSoundManager::CreateBuffer(int index,int length,
                                 int copies){
  if(!m_bOperational)return FALSE; //bail if not initialized
```

Local variables include a DirectSound buffer descriptor and a PCM wave format structure from the Windows API:

```
DSBUFFERDESC dsbdesc;
PCMWAVEFORMAT pcmwf;
```

This next line of code should probably be moved to the front of the function:

```
if(length<=0)return FALSE; //bail if length info wrong
```

First, we zero out the wave format structure:

```
memset(&pcmwf,0,sizeof(PCMWAVEFORMAT));
```

Then, we start filling out the fields. The `wf` field is a `WAVEFORMAT` structure. The first field in this substructure is `wFormatTag`, the format tag, which must be set to `WAVE_FORMAT_PCM`—there is no other choice.

```
pcmwf.wf.wFormatTag=WAVE_FORMAT_PCM;
```

The `nChannels` field is set to the number of channels, indicating mono or stereo:

```
pcmwf.wf.nChannels=DS_CHANSPERSAMPLE;
```

The `nSamplesPerSec` field is set to the sample rate:

```
pcmwf.wf.nSamplesPerSec=DS_SAMPLERATE;
```

The `nBlockAlign` field is set to the number of bytes per sample:

```
pcmwf.wf.nBlockAlign=
  DS_CHANSPERSAMPLE*DS_BITSPERSAMPLE/8;
```

The `nAvgBytesPerSec` field is set to the sample rate multiplied by bytes per sample:

```
pcmwf.wf.nAvgBytesPerSec=
  pcmwf.wf.nSamplesPerSec*pcmwf.wf.nBlockAlign;
```

This completes the `wf` field of `pcmwf`. The `wBitsPerSample` field of `pcmwf` is set to the number of bits per sample.

```
pcmwf.wBitsPerSample=DS_BITSPERSAMPLE;
```

Next, we fill in the DirectSound buffer descriptor `dsbdesc`, starting by zeroing it out and setting its size field:

```
memset(&dsbdesc,0,sizeof(DSBUFFERDESC));
dsbdesc.dwSize=sizeof(DSBUFFERDESC);
```

The `dwFlags` field must be set to request the capabilities of the requested buffers. We set it to `DSBCAPS_STATIC`, which means that the sound in these buffers will not be edited, and thus that it is a candidate to be loaded to the sound card's memory, if such a thing exists.

```
dsbdesc.dwFlags=DSBCAPS_STATIC;
```

The `dwBufferBytes` field is set to the length of the buffer, which is provided by the parameter `length`:

```
dsbdesc.dwBufferBytes=length;
```

The `lpwfxFormat` is set to the address of the `WAVEFORMAT` structure that we filled in above. This tells it important things like the playback sample rate.

```
dsbdesc.lpwfxFormat=(LPWAVEFORMATEX)&pcmwf;
```

Before actually creating the buffers to these specifications, we create space for the pointers to the buffers for the copies of the current sound (the blocks at the center of Figure 10.1):

```
m_lpBuffer[index]=new LPDIRECTSOUNDBUFFER[copies];
```

We `NULL` out the pointers to indicate that there are no buffers yet:

```
for(int i=0; i<copies; i++)m_lpBuffer[index][i]=NULL;
```

Finally, we ask the DirectSound object to create a sound buffer for the first copy of the sound according to the specifications set in `dsbdesc`. Don't be confused by the second parameter; it is asking that a pointer to the sound buffer be placed in `*m_lpBuffer[index]`, not `m_lpBuffer[index]` itself. The last parameter of `CreateSoundBuffer` is yet another "this must be NULL" parameter. Function `CreateBuffer` then returns `TRUE` if this call to `CreateSoundBuffer` is `DS_OK`.

```
    return SUCCEEDED(m_lpDirectSound->
      CreateSoundBuffer(&dsbdesc,m_lpBuffer[index],NULL));
}
```

The LoadBuffer Function

Function `LoadBuffer` loads sound data from a byte buffer `sound` of length `length` into the DirectSound buffer pointed to by `*m_lpBuffer[index]`.

```
BOOL CSoundManager::LoadBuffer(int index,BYTE *sound,int length){
    if(!m_bOperational)return FALSE; //bail if not initialized
```

Up until now you may have assumed that loading a DirectSound buffer simply involves copying the sound data from the byte buffer to the data field of the DirectSound buffer using either the C standard library function `memcpy` or the Windows API function `CopyMemory`. Unfortunately, it is not quite this easy. The sound data inside the DirectSound buffer may be circularly shifted within the buffer by an arbitrary amount, so we will need to use two calls to the `CopyMemory` function to load the sound data. Before we can load the data, we will need to lock down the DirectSound buffer using its `Lock` function (which is analogous to locking down a DirectDraw surface). This function will return two pointers `w1,w2` and two lengths `l1,l2` (Note: This is *ell-one* and *ell-two*, *not* eleven and twelve), one for each block of data in the DirectSound buffer (see Figure 10.4). We begin by declaring local variables to hold these values.

```
LPVOID w1,w2; //write pointer (use 2 for buffer wraparound)
DWORD l1,l2; //length of sound to be written to write pointers
```

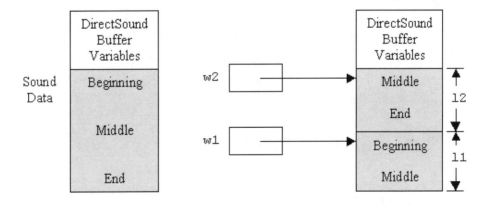

Figure 10.4
How we would like DirectSound buffers to be (left), and how they actually are (right), showing how the DirectSound buffer Lock function sets the local variables w1, w2, l1, and l2 in the CSoundManager LoadBuffer function

We get a pointer directly to the DirectSound buffer into which we're going to be loading data:

```
LPDIRECTSOUNDBUFFER buffer=*m_lpBuffer[index];
```

Just to be paranoid, we make sure that the length information is sensible:

```
if(length<=0)return FALSE; //bail if length info wrong
```

Now, we use the DirectSound buffer's `Lock` function to lock down the buffer so that we can write to it. The first two parameters of this function are the index of the first byte and the length of the area to be locked. We can use this to lock down only a portion of the sound buffer, but here we are locking down the whole thing. The next four parameters are the addresses of two pointers and two lengths as depicted in Figure 10.4. The last parameter is a flags word, which we are ignoring. If the lock fails due to a lost buffer (similar to losing a DirectDraw surface), we try restoring the buffer once and try the lock again. If that fails, then we bail out of the `CSoundManager` `LoadBuffer` function.

```
if(buffer->Lock(0,length,&w1,&l1,&w2,&l2,0)//lock down buffer
==DSERR_BUFFERLOST){ //if buffer lost
  buffer->Restore(); //restore, then try again
  if(FAILED(buffer->Lock(0,length,&w1,&l1,&w2,&l2,0)))
    return FALSE; //abort if failed the second time
}
```

Now that we have the buffer locked down, we can load the first `l1` bytes of `sound` to `w1`:

```
CopyMemory(w1,sound,l1); //load first half
```

Now, things just might look like the left side of Figure 10.4 if we're lucky, in which case `w2` will be NULL. If it is, we are finished already. Otherwise, we need to copy the last `l2` bytes of `sound` to `w2`.

```
if(w2!=NULL)CopyMemory(w2,sound+l1,l2); //load second half
```

Finally, we unlock the buffer and return:

```
if(FAILED(buffer->Unlock(w1,l1,w2,l2)))return FALSE;
return TRUE;
}
```

The LoadSound Function

The last `CSoundManager` function in `Sound.cpp` is `LoadSound`, which loads a sound from a WAV file into a byte buffer. This function uses Windows MMIO functions, which are outside the scope of this book. If you *really* want to know what is going on inside that function, the code is listed in the `pdf` supplement.

Changes to the Object Classes

Now that we have a sound manager, we can use it to play sounds. It can be very tempting to splatter "play sound" code all through your game, which can make it difficult to maintain. To reduce the amount of code clutter, I have adopted the following simple policy: every object in the game is responsible for playing its own sounds. I could have chosen to have the object manager play the sounds, or have them played in `Main.cpp`, but it is easier (and intellectually satisfying) to have the low-level `CObject` and `CIntelligentObject` classes responsible for their own noises.

Changes to the Base Object

Some objects make a sound when they are created. This sound code goes into the `CObject` constructor. In the `switch` statement that separates the code by object type, we add the following to the appropriate `cases`. For the plane, since it starts out moving slowly, we play the slow engine noise sound. Recall that `LOOP_SOUND` was aliased to `TRUE` in `Sound.h`, so that the sound is played looped.

```
SoundManager->play(SLOWPUTT_SOUND,LOOP_SOUND);
```

The creation of a bullet is accompanied by the sound of gunfire:

```
SoundManager->play(GUN_SOUND); //sound of gun firing
```

The creation of an exploding crow is accompanied by the sound of an explosion:

```
SoundManager->play(BOOM_SOUND); //sound of explosion
```

The `CObject accelerate` function must take care of changing the engine sound when the plane changes speed. First, it saves the old horizontal speed in a local variable `old_xspeed`.

```
int old_xspeed=m_nXspeed; //old speed
```

We check that the object is indeed the plane and it has actually changed speed. Why do we check that the speed has actually changed? Because the player may hit the accelerate key when the plane is already at maximum speed, and if we are not careful, our code may restart the engine sound anyway, making the engine seem to stutter. The `old_xspeed!=m_nXspeed` check prevents this from happening.

```
if(m_eObject==PLANE_OBJECT&&old_xspeed!=m_nXspeed){
```

We stop all of the engine sounds (it is faster to stop them all than it is to find out which one is actually playing, and then stop just that one):

```
SoundManager->stop(SLOWPUTT_SOUND);
SoundManager->stop(MEDIUMPUTT_SOUND);
SoundManager->stop(FASTPUTT_SOUND);
```

Now we restart the engine sound. Which one? Well, the comments in `Sndlist.h` indicate that the three engine sound definitions should be consecutive, so that `SLOWPUTT_SOUND+1` is `MEDIUMPUTT_SOUND`, and `MEDIUMPUTT_SOUND+1` is `FASTPUTT_SOUND`. If `m_nXspeed` is -1, we want to play `SLOWPUTT_SOUND`. If `m_nXspeed` is -2, we want to play `MEDIUMPUTT_SOUND`, which is `SLOWPUTT_SOUND+1`. If `m_nXspeed` is -3, we want to play `FASTPUTT_SOUND`, which is `SLOWPUTT_SOUND+2`. Therefore, we play sound `SLOWPUTT_SOUND-1 +abs(m_nXspeed)`. This completes the changes to the `CObject` accelerate function.

```
SoundManager->
  play(SLOWPUTT_SOUND-1+abs(m_nXspeed),LOOP_SOUND);
}
```

The last sound change to the object class involves the `CObject move` function. In `FALLING_MOTION` case, we want things that fall to go "thunk" when they hit the bottom of the screen. This is a good time to force falling objects to be culled then too. If the object's `m_nY` coordinate is greater than `SCREEN_HEIGHT`, we play the sound and force a cull by making the object mortal with a lifespan of zero. This ensures that it will be culled the next time that the object manager's `cull` function is called (see Chapter 8).

```
if(m_nY>SCREEN_HEIGHT){
  SoundManager->play(THUMP_SOUND); //object hitting ground
  m_nLifeTime=0; m_eMortality=MORTAL; //force cull
}
```

Changes to the Intelligent Object

Since the changes to `CIntelligentObject` in Demo 8 are extremely minor—the addition of a single line of code—`Ai.cpp` is not listed in the `pdf` supplement with the other changed files. The change makes the crows caw when they enter the avoiding state. In the `CIntelligentObject set_state` function, under the `AVOIDING_STATE` case, we add a call to `SoundManager->play(CAW_SOUND)`. The entire function is listed below so you can see this line of code in the correct context.

```
void CIntelligentObject::set_state(StateType state){
  m_eState=state; //change state
  switch(m_eState){ //change behavior settings
    case CRUISING_STATE:
      m_nAiDelayTime=300+Random.number(0,300);
      m_nXspeed=-1;
      m_nHeightDelayTime=8000+Random.number(0,5000);
      break;
    case AVOIDING_STATE:
      SoundManager->play(CAW_SOUND); //sound of crow cawing
      m_nAiDelayTime=200+Random.number(0,200);
      m_nXspeed=-3;
      m_nDesiredHeight=Random.number(100,400);
      m_nHeightDelayTime=3000+Random.number(0,2000);
      m_nSpeedVariationDuration=5000+Random.number(0,2000);
      break;
    default: break;
  }
}
```

Changes to Main.cpp

Changes to `Main.cpp` involve creating and setting up the sound manager. Near the top of `Main.cpp`, we add the declaration of a pointer to a sound manager. Why have we declared a pointer to a sound manager instead of declaring a sound manager? Because if we did the latter, the `CSoundManager` constructor would run before `WinMain`. However, the constructor needs a window handle to pass along to DirectSound, and we won't have a window handle until the window is created in `WinMain`. Therefore, we'll actually create the sound manager later, when a window handle is available.

```
CSoundManager* SoundManager; //sound manager
```

Function `LoadSounds` loads the sounds for a particular level. We are not going to use its functionality to have different sounds for different levels, but we will use level 0 for intro sounds and level 1 for all of the other sounds.

```
void LoadSounds(int level=0){ //load sounds for level
```

We'll arbitrarily say that if we keep multiple copies of a sound, we will keep four copies of it. This number was chosen because it just sounded right during play testing. You may want to set this as high as eight.

```
const int copies=4; //copies of repeatable sounds
```

We have the ability to load a different set of sounds for different levels using a `switch` statement on the parameter `level`:

```
switch(level){
```

The intro sounds must be loaded in the same order as the constants in the enumerated type `IntroSoundType` in `Sndlist.h`. This sounds a little clumsy and difficult to maintain, but usually the only changes that are made to the load sequence is to add new sounds to the end of the list. Very rarely is it necessary to reorder the loading order, so why make the code more complicated than necessary?

```
case 0: //intro sounds
  SoundManager->load("intro.wav");
  SoundManager->load("larc.wav");
  break;
```

The game sounds must be loaded in the same order as the constants in the enumerated type `GameSoundType` in `Sndlist.h`. We create multiple copies of the sounds made by the crows, the gun, the exploding crows, and the dead crows.

```
case 1: //game engine sounds
  SoundManager->load("caw.wav",copies);
  SoundManager->load("gun.wav",copies);
  SoundManager->load("boom.wav",copies);
  SoundManager->load("thump.wav",copies);
  SoundManager->load("putt0.wav");
  SoundManager->load("putt1.wav");
  SoundManager->load("putt2.wav");
  break;
  }
}
```

Function `change_phase` must be modified to load the sounds for each phase. To the `LOGO_PHASE` case of the switch statement, we add code to load the intro sounds and begin playing the logo sound.

```
LoadSounds(); //load sounds for intro sequence
SoundManager->play(LOGO_SOUND); //signature chord
```

To the `TITLE_PHASE` case we add code to stop playing all sounds (in case the player clicked out of the logo phase) and begin playing the title sound:

```
SoundManager->stop(); //silence previous phase
SoundManager->play(TITLE_SOUND); //title sound
```

To the `MENU_PHASE` case, we add code to stop playing all sounds (in case the player clicked out of the title phase):

```
SoundManager->stop(); //silence previous phase
```

To the `PLAYING_PHASE` case we add code to stop playing all sounds (out of pure paranoia, since no sounds will be playing), clear the sound manager, and load the game sounds. This ends the changes to function `change_phase`.

```
SoundManager->stop(); //silence previous phase
SoundManager->clear(); //clear out old sounds
LoadSounds(1); //load game sounds
```

In `WindowProc`, we add code to shut down the sound manager in response to the `WM_DESTROY` message:

```
delete SoundManager; //reclaim sound manager memory
```

In `WinMain`, we can create a sound manager at any time after we have a handle to the application window and before the message loop:

```
SoundManager=new CSoundManager(hwnd);
```

Demo 8 Files

Code Files

The following files in Demo 8 are used without change from Demo 7:

- Ai.h
- Bmp.h
- Bmp.cpp
- Bsprite.h
- Bsprite.cpp
- Csprite.h
- Csprite.cpp
- Defines.h
- Ddsetup.cpp
- Objects.h
- Objman.h
- Objman.cpp
- Random.h
- Random.cpp
- Sbmp.h
- Sbmp.cpp
- Timer.h
- Timer.cpp
- View.h
- View.cpp

The following files in Demo 8 have been modified from Demo 7:

- Ai.cpp (changes minimal; not listed in the pdf supplement)
- Main.cpp
- Objects.cpp

The following files are new in Demo 8:

- Sndlist.h
- Sound.h
- Sound.cpp

Media Files

The following sound files are new in Demo 8:

- Boom.wav
- Caw.wav
- Gun.wav
- Intro.wav
- Larc.wav
- Putt0.wav
- Putt1.wav
- Putt2.wav
- Thump.wav

Required Libraries

- Ddraw.lib
- Dsound.lib
- Winmm.lib

Chapter 11

Here's what you'll learn:

- Why you may not see a mouse cursor in DirectDraw and what to do about it
- How to add mouse control to your game using Windows API mouse messages
- How to use the mouse to click on buttons
- How to manage and animate buttons
- How to handle radio buttons
- How to use the mouse as a joystick
- How to manage input with an input manager
- How to implement a device menu

The Mouse

In Demo 9, we learn how to process input from the mouse by responding to Windows API mouse messages. The mouse can be used to navigate the main menu by clicking on the menu buttons for action. You can also play the game using the mouse as a joystick with the invisible cursor position controlling the plane's speed and height and the left mouse button firing the gun. There is now a device menu that lets you choose whether to play using the keyboard, the mouse, or (in the next chapter) the joystick (see Figure 11.1). The buttons on the main menu page are normal buttons, while the top three buttons on the device menu page are radio buttons, meaning that one of the buttons is down while the others are up (in Figure 11.1, however, they are all drawn in the up position). Response to the mouse using mouse messages is fast enough for a game of this type. However, if you need faster response time, you must use DirectInput, which is out of the scope of this book.

Figure 11.1
The device menu screen, Dmenu.bmp

Experiment with Demo 9

Take a moment now to run Demo 9.

- Click out of the intro screens using the left mouse button. You should now see the main menu. Notice that the mouse cursor is visible now.

- Click on the "Saved Game" button a few times; the button seems to get pressed into the screen. Notice the click sound when you press it down and a different click when you release it.

- Click down on the "Devices" button with the left mouse button, then move the mouse cursor off the button without releasing it. The button stays down. Now release it. It pops up, but no action is taken. Try releasing it on the menu screen, and within a different button.

- Now, click down on the "Devices" button and release it. You should now see the device menu, which should look like Figure 11.1 except that the first button is down. Notice that when you click on the "Mouse" button, the "Keyboard" button pops up, and vice versa. Push the "Mouse" button down and then click on the "Done" button. You should now be back at the main menu.

- Start a new game by clicking on the "New Game" button. You will now be able to play using the mouse (provided you followed the previous step of the instructions and selected "Mouse" from the device menu; if not, exit back to the main menu and try again from the previous step). Moving the mouse up moves the plane up, and moving it down moves the plane down. Moving the mouse left accelerates the plane, moving it right decelerates it. Clicking the left mouse button fires the gun. Notice that the keyboard controls for the plane are disabled while playing with the mouse.

- Exit back to the main menu by either hitting the Esc key or killing all of the crows. Notice that the mouse cursor disappeared while you were playing the game and reappears again on the main menu screen.

- Now, click on the "Quit" button to exit the program.

The Elusive DirectDraw Mouse Cursor

DirectDraw does not cooperate with software mouse cursors. This is in part because the API draws the software mouse cursor to what it thinks of as the primary surface and is blithely unaware of page flipping. This means that some of the time it is drawing it to the primary surface and sometimes to the secondary surface, resulting in an essentially useless mouse cursor that pulses dozens of times a second.

Most video cards have a hardware mouse cursor. The Windows Standard mouse cursor is implemented in hardware on most video cards, as is Animated Hourglasses, but not 3D Pointers. If you have trouble with the mouse cursor in Demo 9, go to the Mouse Properties box in the Control Panel and select the Windows Standard mouse cursor on the Pointers tab (see Figure 11.2).

What should you do about this in your game? You really only have three options.

The first option, which is easiest on you but hardest on your customers, is to ignore the problem in your program and add a note in your Help files saying that the player had better not use a software mouse pointer while playing your game. This is essentially what I am doing here.

The second option is to force the mouse cursor to be the Windows Standard cursor while your game is playing. This cursor has the best chance of actually being implemented in hardware. You can do this with the following obscure API function call.

```
SetSystemCursor(LoadCursor(NULL,IDC_ARROW),32512);
```

However, having done that you really should reset the cursor back to its old style when you exit your game. You can find out what the old style was by consulting the `Arrow` value in the `Control Panel\Cursors` subkey of `HKEY_CURRENT_USER` in the Windows registry.

Figure 11.2
Selecting the Windows Standard mouse cursor

The third option is to turn the mouse cursor off and draw it yourself. All you need is a clipped sprite that is drawn last. You must store the mouse position in a global variable, updating it in response to WM_MOUSEMOVE messages. Of course, that means you'll have to animate screens that are currently not animated.

The Button Manager

The button manager maintains a list of buttons on a menu page and takes care of detecting clicks on them, animating them, and making the appropriate sounds. In *Ned's Turkey Farm*, each button is surrounded by a rectangle called a *hotspot*. The player clicks on a button by placing the mouse cursor inside the hotspot and clicking the left mouse button. If we were more sophisticated, we could code an arbitrarily shaped hotspot for each button—in our case, a round hotspot—instead of a bounding rectangle, but rectangles are quicker and easier to code. We will use a different instance of the button manager for each menu page, for instance, one button manager for the main menu and another for the device menu.

Button Manager Overview

The header file for the button manager class CButtonManager is Buttons.h. CButtonManager has 10 private member variables. The first of these is an array of Windows API RECT structures that define the rectangular hotspots for each button on the screen. We don't know how many buttons there will be for any particular instance of the button manager, so we declare the array as a pointer for now, and we'll allocate memory for the array in the CButtonManager constructor.

```
RECT *m_rectHotspot; //hotspot locations
```

A parallel array of Boolean variables records whether each button is currently down. For example, button i will have hotspot m_rectHotspot[i], and m_bDown[i] will be TRUE if it is down.

```
BOOL *m_bDown; //is button held down?
```

The variable m_nMaxCount records the maximum number of hotspots allowed in the button manager:

```
int m_nMaxCount; //number of hotspots allowed
```

The variable m_nCount records how many hotspots have been allocated so far:

```
int m_nCount; //number of current hotspots
```

We assume that all of the buttons will have the same size, and allocate a Windows API SIZE structure to hold it. SIZE has two fields, cx and cy, which record the width and height of a rectangle:

```
SIZE m_sizeButton; //size of buttons, if all the same size
```

Next, we have a pointer to the button sprite for the buttons. The button manager will use the same sprite for each button. We use a base sprite object as opposed to a clipped sprite object because our buttons will always be completely on the screen, and so never need to be clipped. The actual sprite will be created by the constructor.

```
CBaseSprite* m_spriteDefault; //default button sprite
```

We will store the image of the buttons in a bmp sprite file reader in case the button sprite surfaces ever need to be restored and reloaded:

```
CBmpSpriteFileReader m_cImage; //button images
```

The next two private member variables record the indices of the sounds used when the button is pushed down and when it pops up:

```
int m_nButtonDownSound; //sound index for button down
int m_nButtonUpSound; //sound index for button up
```

The last private member variable records whether the buttons are radio buttons (except the last button on the screen, which is assumed to be "Quit" or "Done") or normal buttons:

```
BOOL m_bRadio; //TRUE for radio buttons
```

CButtonManager has five private member functions. The first of these, PointInRect, has two parameters, the first of which is a Windows API RECT structure rect, and the second of which is a Windows API POINT structure point. The POINT structure has two fields x and y which represent the coordinates of a two-dimensional point. PointInRect returns TRUE if point is inside rect.

```
BOOL PointInRect(RECT rect,POINT point); //is point in rect?
```

The CButtonManager addbutton function has a single parameter rect. It adds a new button with hotspot rect to the end of the button list, returning TRUE if it succeeds.

```
BOOL addbutton(RECT rect); //add button to list
```

Function loadsprite loads the button sprite from a file whose name is given as the parameter filename. It creates the CBaseSprite class to hold the sprite, loads the file into the private member variable m_cImage, and calls private member function loadimages to load the images from the bmp sprite file read to the sprite. Function loadimages assumes that the button sprite file image is m_sizeButton.cx pixels wide and 2*m_sizeButton.cy high, large enough to hold two copies of the button image, one above the other. The upper image will be loaded to frame 0 of the button sprite and will be displayed when the button is up. The lower image will be loaded to frame 1 of the button sprite and will be displayed when the button is down. See Figure 11.3 for an example.

```
BOOL loadsprite(char *filename); //load button sprite
void loadimages(); //load button images
```

Figure 11.3
The button
file
Buttons.bmp

Function `display_menu` draws all of the buttons in their current states (up or down) to the secondary surface and flips it to the primary surface, the assumption being that the menu screen will only be redrawn when a button state changes. It assumes that the menu background has already been drawn to both the primary and secondary surfaces.

```
void display_menu(); //display menu page
```

`CButtonManager` has 15 public member functions, including two constructors and a destructor. The first constructor has three parameters, and creates `count` buttons of size `size` with a sprite image from a file named `filename`. The position of these buttons will be specified later. The second constructor has five parameters, including the three already named. The two extra parameters are a point `first` and a distance `ydelta`. These specify that the first button will be placed at point `first` on the screen, and the other buttons (`count` in all) will be placed below it, each at distance `ydelta` below the previous one. Ideally, it would be nice to only use the second version of the constructor. However, since artists (particularly those who, like you, are just learning their trade) are occasionally off by one or two pixels in the positioning of their buttons, the first constructor allows us to place the buttons arbitrarily on the screen. The alternative is going to the trouble and expense of having the artwork redrawn so that the buttons are exactly evenly spaced out, which is a moot point because usually nobody will notice if a button is one or two pixels away from where it should be. If you are lucky enough to have an artist to help you create your first game demo, it might be a good idea not to stress him or her out over a few pixels when it doesn't really make much difference to the game, and you can adapt to it with just a few extra lines of code.

```
CButtonManager(int count,SIZE size,char *filename);
CButtonManager(int count,SIZE size,POINT first,
   int ydelta,char *filename); //constructor
~CButtonManager(); //destructor
```

Function `addbutton` lets you add a button at an arbitrary `point` on the screen. It is designed to be used with the first `CButtonManager` constructor. It returns `TRUE` if it succeeds (it fails if there is not enough room in the button list for a new button). Notice that it is different from the private member function with the same name; the private version of the function takes a `RECT` variable as a parameter.

```
BOOL addbutton(POINT point); //add button of default size
```

If `point` is inside the hotspot of a button, function `hit` returns the index of that button; otherwise it returns -1. We will use this to detect when the left mouse button is pressed down with the mouse cursor inside a button.

```
int hit(POINT point); //return hit, if any
```

If `point` is inside the hotspot of a button that is currently down, function `release` returns the index of that button; otherwise it returns -1. We will use this to detect when the left mouse button is released with the mouse cursor inside the same button that it clicked down on.

```
int release(POINT point); //return hit on down button
```

If `point` is inside the hotspot of a button, the first version of function `buttondown` animates the button going down and returns TRUE; otherwise it returns FALSE:

```
BOOL buttondown(POINT point); //animate button down
```

The second version of function `buttondown` animates a particular button going down, the one with a given `index` in the button list. The second parameter specifies whether a sound is to be played; it defaults to TRUE if it is not provided.

```
BOOL buttondown(int index,BOOL sound=TRUE); //animate
```

The two versions of `buttonup` do the same things for a button going up:

```
BOOL buttonup(POINT point); //animate button up
BOOL buttonup(int index); //animate button up
```

Function `allbuttonsup` animates all of the buttons going up:

```
void allbuttonsup(); //animate all buttons up
```

Function `setsounds` provides the indices (in the sound manager's sound list) of the sounds to be played when a button is pressed down and when it pops up:

```
void setsounds(int down,int up); //set sounds
```

Function `set_radio` can be used to specify radio buttons or normal buttons:

```
void set_radio(BOOL on=TRUE); //set to radio buttons
```

Finally, `CButtonManager` has two public member functions that are required by every class that has private surfaces, a `Restore` and a `Release` function that respectively restore and release those surfaces. (`CButtonManager` has its surfaces contained in the button sprite class.)

```
BOOL Restore(); //restore surfaces
void Release(); //release surfaces
```

The Constructors and the Destructor

The code file for `CButtonManager` is `Buttons.cpp`. It begins with the code for the first of two constructors.

```
CButtonManager::CButtonManager(int count,SIZE size,
                              char *filename){
```

The constructor reserves space for the hotspot list and the button state list and sets all buttons in the down position:

```
m_rectHotspot=new RECT[m_nMaxCount=count]; //hotspot space
m_bDown=new BOOL[m_nMaxCount]; //whether button is down
for(int i=0; i<m_nMaxCount; i++)
  m_bDown[i]=FALSE; //all buttons up
```

It then sets some private member variables and loads the button sprite:

```
m_sizeButton=size; //size of buttons loaded
m_nCount=0; //number of buttons loaded
loadsprite(filename); //load the sprite
m_nButtonDownSound=m_nButtonUpSound=-1; //no sounds yet
m_bRadio=FALSE; //not radio buttons
}
```

The second `CButtonManager` constructor has an additional two parameters that specify the `point` at which the first button is to be drawn and the vertical separation `ydelta` between the buttons:

```
CButtonManager::CButtonManager(int count,SIZE size,
                 POINT point,int ydelta,char *filename){
```

It has the same initial code as the first constructor, plus the addition of the following four lines of code that call the public member function `addbutton` to add the remaining buttons:

```
m_nCount=0; addbutton(point);
for(i=0; i<count-1; i++){
  point.y+=ydelta; addbutton(point);
}
```

The `CButtonManager` destructor `delete`s the things that were `new`ed in the constructors:

```
CButtonManager::~CButtonManager(){ //destructor
  delete[]m_rectHotspot;
  delete m_spriteDefault;
  delete[]m_bDown;
}
```

The Set_radio and Addbutton Functions

The CButtonManager set_radio function is a simple writer function; it writes its parameter to the private member variable m_bRadio:

```
void CButtonManager::set_radio(BOOL on){ //set to radio buttons
  m_bRadio=on;
}
```

The CButtonManager private addbutton function adds a new button to the end of the button list and sets its hotspot to the rectangle rect:

```
BOOL CButtonManager::addbutton(RECT rect){
//add a hotspot in this rectangle
  if(m_nCount>=m_nMaxCount)return FALSE; //bail if no space
  m_rectHotspot[m_nCount++]=rect; //insert hotspot
  return TRUE;
}
```

The CButtonManager public addbutton function adds a new button to the end of the button list and creates a rectangular hotspot for it with the top left corner of the hotspot at point:

```
BOOL CButtonManager::addbutton(POINT point){
```

It first creates the bounding rectangle in a local variable rect:

```
RECT rect; //bounding rectangle
rect.left=point.x; rect.right=point.x+m_sizeButton.cx;
rect.top=point.y; rect.bottom=point.y+m_sizeButton.cy;
```

Then it calls the private addbutton function to do the real work:

```
return addbutton(rect); //add hotspot in this rectangle
}
```

The Hit Function

The CButtonManager hit function has a single parameter point. If point is inside a hotspot, then it returns the index of that hotspot. Otherwise, it returns −1.

```
int CButtonManager::hit(POINT point){
```

It has two local variables, the return result (initially set to −1 indicating "no hit") and an index variable i:

```
int result=-1; //start by assuming no hit
int i=0; //index
```

A `while` loop exits either when we run out of buttons to check or when we detect a hit:

```
while(i<m_nCount&&result<0) //for each button
```

It uses the local member function `PointInRect` to check whether `point` is inside the ith hotspot `m_rectHotspot[i]`.

```
if(PointInRect(m_rectHotspot[i],point)) //check for hit
```

If so, it stores the index of the hit in local variable `result`.

```
result=i; //record hit
```

Otherwise, it moves on to the next button:

```
else i++; //next button
```

When the `while` loop terminates, we return the result:

```
return result;
}
```

The Release and PointInRect Functions

The `CButtonManager release` function is almost exactly the same as the `CButtonManager hit` function, except it looks for hits inside buttons that are currently down. The `if` statement in `hit` is replaced by the following.

```
if(m_bDown[i]&&PointInRect(m_rectHotspot[i],point))
```

The `CButtonManager PointInRect` function returns `TRUE` if `point` is inside `rect`. It simply checks the coordinates of `point` against the boundaries of `rect`.

```
BOOL CButtonManager::PointInRect(RECT rect,POINT point){
//is point in rectangle?
  return point.x>=rect.left&&point.x<=rect.right&&
    point.y>=rect.top&&point.y<=rect.bottom;
}
```

The LoadImages and Loadsprite Functions

The `CButtonManager loadimages` function loads the button sprite images from the private bmp sprite file reader `m_cImage`. The first frame shows the button in the up position, which is located at the top of the image with top left pixel at `(0,0)`. The second frame shows the button in the down position, which is located below the first frame, with the top left pixel at `(0,m_sizeButton.cy)` (see Figure 11.3).

```
void CButtonManager::loadimages(){ //load button images
  m_spriteDefault->load(&m_cImage,0,0,0); //up
```

```
    m_spriteDefault->load(&m_cImage,1,0,m_sizeButton.cy); //down
  }
```

The CButtonManager loadsprite function is given the filename of a file containing the sprite images:

```
BOOL CButtonManager::loadsprite(char *filename){
```

It bails out if the button size member variable hasn't been reset since the constructor ran:

```
if(m_sizeButton.cx==0&&m_sizeButton.cy==0)return FALSE;
```

It asks bmp sprite file reader member variable m_cImage to load the button sprite file, and if it fails, loadimages bails out:

```
if(!m_cImage.load(filename))return FALSE;
```

If the file loaded correctly, it goes ahead and creates a two-frame button sprite of size m_sizeButton in private member variable m_spriteDefault.

```
m_spriteDefault=
  new CClippedSprite(2,m_sizeButton.cx,m_sizeButton.cy);
```

Finally, it calls private member function loadimages to load the sprite images from the bmp file reader to the button sprite, then reports success:

```
loadimages();
return TRUE;
}
```

The Restore and Release Functions

The CButtonManager Restore function restores the sprite surfaces by calling the CBaseSprite Restore function, then reloads the images by calling the CButtonManager private member function loadimages. It returns TRUE if it succeeds.

```
BOOL CButtonManager::Restore(){ //restore surfaces
  if(m_spriteDefault->Restore()){
    loadimages();
    return TRUE;
  }
  else return FALSE;
}
```

The CButtonManager Release function releases the sprite surfaces by calling the CBaseSprite Release function:

```
void CButtonManager::Release(){ //release surfaces
  m_spriteDefault->Release();
}
```

The Buttondown Functions

The CButtonManager public buttondown function returns TRUE if point is within a button hotspot, and if so, takes care of animating the button going down. It calls the CButtonManager member function hit to return the index of the hit hotspot, if there is one, and passes this index to the CButtonManager private buttondown function, which does the real work.

```
BOOL CButtonManager::buttondown(POINT point){
  return buttondown(hit(point));
}
```

The CButtonManager private buttondown function returns TRUE if button index is a valid button index, and if so, that button is not down. The second parameter sound, which defaults to TRUE if it is missing, tells it whether to play a sound. Notice that in the CButtonManager public buttondown function, this function is passed the index returned by the CButtonManager hit function, and so it should expect to occasionally receive an index of −1 indicating a mouse click outside of a button (in which case it should do nothing but return FALSE).

```
BOOL CButtonManager::buttondown(int index,BOOL sound){
```

It first checks that the index is within range, and if so, that the button is up. If either of these fails, it will do nothing.

```
if(index>=0&&index<m_nCount&&!m_bDown[index]){
```

If everything looks kosher, it plays the button down sound if required to do so by parameter sound:

```
if(sound)SoundManager->play(m_nButtonDownSound);
```

If the buttons are radio buttons and the one pressed down is not the last one (which is assumed to be "Done" or "Quit" and hence not strictly part of the radio button set), then it pops up all of the radio buttons and puts down the one that was just clicked on:

```
if(m_bRadio&&index<m_nCount-1) //if radio button (not last)
  for(int i=0; i<m_nCount-1; i++)
    m_bDown[i]=FALSE; //pop up other radio buttons
m_bDown[index]=TRUE; //button is now down
```

It then calls the CButtonManager private display_menu function to draw the buttons in their new positions and returns TRUE. The purist might argue that, since display_menu draws all of the buttons, we are wasting time drawing buttons whose state doesn't change. However, it really isn't worth the effort to recode display_menu to draw only the buttons whose state has changed, since we only call it once every few seconds (whenever the user clicks), and it has very little work to do as it is.

```
display_menu(); //display menu page
return TRUE;
}
```

Otherwise, if there's no action, it returns FALSE:

```
else return FALSE;
}
```

The Buttonup and Allbuttonsup Functions

The two CButtonManager buttonup functions do the same thing for up buttons:

```
BOOL CButtonManager::buttonup(POINT point){
  return buttonup(hit(point));
}
```

Aside from the obvious changes involved in changing "down" to "up," we also want to disable radio buttons from popping up when the mouse button is released. That is, they are allowed to pop up only if they are not radio buttons or they are the last button on a radio button page. This is enforced by adding the condition (!m_bRadio||index==m_nCount-1) to the if statement in the private CButtonManager buttonup function.

```
BOOL CButtonManager::buttonup(int index){
  if((!m_bRadio||index==m_nCount-1)&&
  index>=0&&index<m_nCount&&m_bDown[index]){ //if valid
    SoundManager->play(m_nButtonUpSound);
    m_bDown[index]=FALSE; //button is up
    display_menu(); //display menu page
    return TRUE;
  }
  else return FALSE;
}
```

The CButtonManager allbuttonsup function pops up all buttons and plays the button up sound if anything actually popped up:

```
void CButtonManager::allbuttonsup(){
```

It has a local index variable i:

```
int i; //index
```

If the screen contains radio buttons, it pops up only the last ("Exit" or "Done") button:

```
if(m_bRadio){ //don't pop up radio buttons
  if(m_bDown[m_nCount-1]){ //pop up quit button if down
    m_bDown[m_nCount-1]=FALSE;
```

```
        SoundManager->play(m_nButtonUpSound);
      }
   }
```

Otherwise, it attempts to pop up all of the buttons, playing a sound only if one of them was down:

```
else{ //not radio buttons, so pop up all of them
```

A local variable `found` (initially `FALSE`) is set to `TRUE` if it finds that one of the buttons was down:

```
BOOL found=FALSE; //to make sure sound played only once
```

It loops through each of the button indices `i` with a `for` loop:

```
for(i=0; i<m_nCount; i++) //for each button
```

If button `i` is down, it pops it up and records that it found a down button:

```
if(m_bDown[i]){ //if valid down button
   found=TRUE; //will play sound later
   m_bDown[i]=FALSE; //button is up
}
```

On exit from the `for` loop, it plays the button up sound, provided a button actually popped up:

```
if(found) SoundManager->play(m_nButtonUpSound);
}
```

Finally, it redraws all of the buttons (whether it needs to or not) by calling the `CButtonManager` `display_menu` function:

```
display_menu(); //display menu page
}
```

The Display_menu Function

The `CButtonManager` `display_menu` function draws the buttons to the secondary surface, assuming that the background is already drawn there, and flips it to the primary surface:

```
void CButtonManager::display_menu(){ //display menu page
```

It loops through all of the buttons with a `for` loop:

```
for(int i=0; i<m_nCount; i++) //for each button
```

It checks whether the ith button is down:

```
if(m_bDown[i]) //draw button down
```

If so, it draws frame 1 to the secondary surface, being careful to map from the top left corner of the bounding rectangle to the bottom center pixel of the sprite:

```
m_spriteDefault->
   draw(1,m_rectHotspot[i].left+m_sizeButton.cx/2,
      m_rectHotspot[i].top+m_sizeButton.cy,lpSecondary);
```

If it's down, it draws frame 0 to the secondary surface instead:

```
else //draw button up
   m_spriteDefault->
      draw(0,m_rectHotspot[i].left+m_sizeButton.cx/2,
         m_rectHotspot[i].top+m_sizeButton.cy,lpSecondary);
```

When all the buttons have been drawn, it flips the secondary surface to the primary surface using the `PageFlip` function from `Main.cpp`:

```
PageFlip(); //flip back buffer to front
}
```

The Setsounds Function

The last `CButtonManager` function is `setsounds`, which writes the indices of the button sounds to the appropriate private member variables:

```
void CButtonManager::setsounds(int down,int up){ //set sounds
   m_nButtonDownSound=down; m_nButtonUpSound=up;
}
```

The Input Manager

Processing the input to our game is starting to get a little complicated, so we'll create an input manager `CInputManager` to handle it, and move the input handling functions out of `Main.cpp`. Now that we've got more than one input device, we add a new enumerated type to `Defines.h`.

```
enum InputDeviceType{KEYBOARD_INPUT=0,MOUSE_INPUT=1};
```

Input Manager Overview

The header file for `CInputManager` is `Input.h`. `CInputManager` has two private member functions. The first of these is `InputDevice`, which records the input device that the player currently wishes to use in the game engine. The second is a pointer to a button manager, which will be created and customized when a menu screen is being displayed, and will be disposed of afterward.

```
InputDeviceType InputDevice; //current input device
CButtonManager *ButtonManager; //for managing menu buttons
```

`CInputManager` has 15 private member functions. The first three of these are helper functions. The `is_function_key` function takes a `keystroke` as a parameter and returns `TRUE` if the keystroke is a function key (either Esc, or F1, F2, etc., at the top of the standard keyboard). The `decode` function takes an lparam sent by the operating system in response to a mouse event, and decodes from it the coordinates of the mouse pointer into a parameter point. The set_plane_speed function takes a mouse cursor location point within the screen extent, and uses it like a digital joystick to set the plane's horizontal speed and vertical speed.

```
BOOL is_function_key(WPARAM keystroke); //TRUE if functn key
void decode(LPARAM lparam,POINT &point); //decode mouse click
void set_plane_speed(POINT point,SIZE extent);
```

Each menu screen has its own private member function to set up the button manager pointed to by the private member variable ButtonManager. Since we have two menu screens, we have two of these functions, SetupMainMenuButtons and SetupDeviceMenuButtons.

```
void SetupMainMenuButtons(); //main menu button manager
void SetupDeviceMenuButtons(); //device menu button manager
```

The rest of the CInputManager private member functions are handlers for a particular device event in a particular phase. Devoting one function for each device in each phase makes the code easier to read and maintain. The next four private member functions are keyboard handlers, one for each phase. These are mostly lifted from Main.cpp in Demo 8.

```
void IntroKeyboard(WPARAM keystroke); //keyboard handler
BOOL MainMenuKeyboard(WPARAM keystroke); //keyboard handler
void DeviceMenuKeyboard(WPARAM keystroke); //keyboard handler
void GameKeyboard(WPARAM keystroke); //keyboard handler
```

Analogously, we have handlers for when the left mouse button goes down in the main menu, the device menu, and the game engine. Each of these functions has the mouse cursor location as a parameter.

```
void MainMenuLMouseDown(POINT point); //mouse down handler
void DeviceMenuLMouseDown(POINT point); //mouse down handler
void GameLMouseDown(POINT point); //mouse down handler
```

Then, we have handlers for the left mouse button going up during the intro phases, the main menu phase, and the device menu phase:

```
void IntroLMouseUp(POINT point); //mouse up handler
BOOL MainMenuLMouseUp(POINT point); //mouse up handler
void DeviceMenuLMouseUp(POINT point); //mouse up handler
```

The input manager has nine public member functions, including a constructor and a destructor:

```
CInputManager(); //constructor
~CInputManager(); //destructor
```

Next, we see the mandatory `Restore` and `Release` functions for the surfaces in the input manager. But where *are* the input manager surfaces? In the button manager.

```
BOOL Restore(); //restore surfaces
void Release(); //release surfaces
```

Function `SetupButtons` sets up the button manager for a given `phase`. It will call the appropriate private member function to do the real work.

```
void SetupButtons(GamePhaseType phase); //set up menu buttons
```

The main keyboard handler `Keyboard` parcels out the work to the keyboard manager private member function for the current phase. The keyboard handler will be disabled when the player is playing using the mouse; otherwise, he or she might try to confuse things by pressing the left and right arrow keys while simultaneously using the mouse to control speed. Rather than write code to handle this case, which the user really has no legitimate reason to try (other than jerking your chain, and believe me, some of them will take pleasure in doing exactly that), it is easier just to deactivate the keyboard handler. However, although the *player* has no business using the keyboard handler when playing with the mouse, *you* as programmer may find it convenient to issue fake keystrokes called *virtual keystrokes* (not to be confused with the Windows API virtual key*codes*). These special keystrokes should *not* be disabled. We handle this by giving function `Keyboard` an extra Boolean parameter `virtual_keystroke` that we will set to `TRUE` for virtual keystrokes and default to `FALSE` when it is missing.

```
BOOL Keyboard(WPARAM keystroke,
  BOOL virtual_keystroke=FALSE); //keyboard handler
```

Finally, we have main handlers for the mouse events, including left button down, left button up, and mouse motion:

```
void LMouseDown(LPARAM lparam); //main mouse down handler
BOOL LMouseUp(LPARAM lparam); //main mouse up handler
void MouseMove(LPARAM lparam); //handle mouse motion
```

The Constructor and Destructor

The code file for `CInputManager` is `Input.cpp`. It begins with the constructor, which sets the input device to the keyboard, and sets the button manager pointer to `NULL` so that if the destructor runs before a button manager has been created, the `delete` does not fail. The destructor's only job is to `delete` the button manager.

```
CInputManager::CInputManager(){ //constructor
  InputDevice=KEYBOARD_INPUT; //current input device
  ButtonManager=NULL; //for managing menu buttons
```

```
  }

  CInputManager::~CInputManager(){ //destructor
    delete ButtonManager;
  }
```

The Restore and Release Functions

The `CInputManager` Restore and Release functions respectively call the button manager's Restore and Release member functions:

```
  BOOL CInputManager::Restore(){ //restore surfaces
    return ButtonManager->Restore();
  }

  void CInputManager::Release(){ //release surfaces
    ButtonManager->Release();
  }
```

Setting Up Buttons

The `CInputManager` SetupMainMenuButtons function sets up a button manager for the main menu screen:

```
  void CInputManager::SetupMainMenuButtons(){
```

It begins with two constants, the vertical separation between the buttons and the number of buttons that appear on the main menu:

```
  const int YDELTA=70; //y separation between buttons
  const int BUTTONCOUNT=6; //number of buttons
```

Next, we declare and initialize a `SIZE` structure for the size of the buttons, which are 40 pixels wide and 40 pixels high:

```
  SIZE size; //size of buttons
  size.cx=40; size.cy=40; //size of buttons
```

Similarly, a `POINT` structure holds the location of the top left corner of the first button:

```
  POINT point; //top left corner of first button
  point.x=111; point.y=46; //first button location
```

We delete the old button manager if there is one (as I've mentioned already, calling `delete` on a `NULL` pointer is harmless), and create a new one using the second `CButtonManager` constructor:

```
  delete ButtonManager; //delete any old one
  ButtonManager=new //create new button manager
    CButtonManager(BUTTONCOUNT,size,point,YDELTA,
      "buttons.bmp");
```

Finally, we set the button sounds, which are added to the end of the list of game sounds in `Sndlist.h`.

```
//set button sounds
ButtonManager->
  setsounds(BIGCLICK_SOUND,SMALLCLICK_SOUND);
}
```

The `CInputManager SetupDeviceMenuButtons` function sets up a button manager for the device menu screen:

```
void CInputManager::SetupDeviceMenuButtons(){
```

It begins with a constant declaring the number of buttons that appear on the device menu:

```
const int BUTTONCOUNT=4;
```

It deletes the old button manager and sets up a `SIZE` structure for the buttons:

```
delete ButtonManager; //if there is one already, delete it
SIZE size; //size of buttons
size.cx=40; size.cy=40; //size of buttons
```

Since the locations of the buttons on the device menu are not quite perfect, we use the first `ButtonManager` constructor, the one that does not set up the initial button positions:

```
ButtonManager=new
  CButtonManager(BUTTONCOUNT,size,"buttons.bmp");
```

We set the sounds and make the buttons into radio buttons:

```
ButtonManager->setsounds(BIGCLICK_SOUND,SMALLCLICK_SOUND);
ButtonManager->set_radio(); //radio buttons
```

Then, we add the buttons into the button manager by hand, with their top left pixels at positions (209, 130), (209, 210), (209, 291), and (209, 372). (The first two buttons are separated by 80 pixels, but the rest are separated by 82 pixels. Did you notice that the first time you saw Figure 11.1?)

```
POINT point;
point.x=209; point.y=130;
ButtonManager->addbutton(point);
point.x=209; point.y=210;
ButtonManager->addbutton(point);
point.x=209; point.y=291;
ButtonManager->addbutton(point);
point.x=209; point.y=372;
ButtonManager->addbutton(point);
```

Finally, we push down the radio button corresponding to the current input device using the button manager's `buttondown` function. Naturally, we don't want any sound to be played; that's why we wrote the `buttondown` to play sounds optionally. We want a sound to be played when the player presses down a button, but not when the computer presses it down during initialization.

```
    ButtonManager->buttondown(InputDevice,FALSE); //no sound
}
```

The `CInputManager SetupButtons` public member function consists of a `switch` statement that calls the appropriate `CInputManager` private member function to do the real work:

```
void CInputManager::SetupButtons(GamePhaseType phase){
//set up menu buttons
  switch(phase){
    case MENU_PHASE: SetupMainMenuButtons(); break;
    case DEVICEMENU_PHASE: SetupDeviceMenuButtons(); break;
  }
}
```

Keyboard Handlers

The `CInputManager IntroKeyboard` function is lifted from `Main.cpp` in Demo 8.

```
void CInputManager::IntroKeyboard(WPARAM keystroke){
//keyboard handler for intro
  endphase=TRUE; //any key ends the phase
}
```

There are some changes to the `CInputManager MainMenuKeyboard` from its counterpart in Demo 8's `Main.cpp`. Now that there is more than one phase that we can go to at the end of the main menu phase (either the new device menu phase or the playing phase), we need some method for indicating which phase is next. We do this with a global variable `NextPhase` that, when `endphase` is `TRUE`, indicates the next phase. Purists may object to this use of global variables. I like to use them to avoid getting tangled in a Byzantine return structure. I find that in practice, global variables are fine for unique things (meaning that there can be only one in a program), when they simplify programming, and provided they are not overused. Function `MainMenuKeyboard` also has a new case for the "D" key, which sends the player from the main menu to the device menu.

```
BOOL CInputManager::MainMenuKeyboard(WPARAM keystroke){
//keyboard handler for menu
  BOOL result=FALSE;
  switch(keystroke){
    case VK_ESCAPE:
    case 'Q': //exit the game
```

```
      result=TRUE;
      break;
    case 'N': //play new game
      NextPhase=PLAYING_PHASE; endphase=TRUE;
      break;
    case 'D':
      NextPhase=DEVICEMENU_PHASE; endphase=TRUE;
    default: break; //do nothing
  }
  return result;
}
```

The CInputManager DeviceMenuKeyboard function is the keyboard handler for the device menu:

```
void CInputManager::DeviceMenuKeyboard(WPARAM keystroke){
```

It consists of a switch statement with a case for each legal keystroke.

```
switch(keystroke){
```

The Esc key and the "D" key exit the device menu by setting endphase to TRUE.

```
    case VK_ESCAPE:
    case 'D': //exit menu
      endphase=TRUE;
      break;
```

The second case sets the private member variable InputDevice to indicate keyboard input, then puts the appropriate button down using the private button manager. Since the button manager's m_bRadio private member variable is set, it automatically pops up whichever button was previously down.

```
    case 'K': //play using keyboard
      InputDevice=KEYBOARD_INPUT; //set device
      ButtonManager->buttondown(KEYBOARD_INPUT);
      break;
```

The third case does the same when the player chooses mouse input:

```
    case 'M': //play using mouse
      InputDevice=MOUSE_INPUT; //set device
      ButtonManager->buttondown(MOUSE_INPUT);
      break;
    default: break;
  }
}
```

The CInputManager GameKeyboard function is lifted from Main.cpp in Demo 8:

```
void CInputManager::GameKeyboard(WPARAM keystroke){
//keyboard handler for game play
```

```
switch(keystroke){
  case VK_ESCAPE: endphase=TRUE; break;
  case VK_UP: ObjectManager.accelerate(0,-1); break;
  case VK_DOWN: ObjectManager.accelerate(0,1); break;
  case VK_LEFT: ObjectManager.accelerate(-1,0); break;
  case VK_RIGHT: ObjectManager.accelerate(1,0); break;
  case VK_SPACE: ObjectManager.fire_gun(); break;
  default: break;
}
}
```

The `CInputManager is_function_key` function returns `TRUE` when `keystroke` is a function key. It uses the handy Windows API constants for the function keys, which are fortunately contiguous in the ASCII table. This means that it only has to return `TRUE` when `keystroke` is equal to `VK_ESCAPE`, or `keystroke` is between `VK_F1` and `VK_F12`, inclusive.

```
BOOL CInputManager::is_function_key(WPARAM keystroke){
  return keystroke==VK_ESCAPE||
    (keystroke>=VK_F1&&keystroke<=VK_F12);
}
```

The `CInputManager Keyboard` function is the main keyboard handler. It consists of a `switch` statement that selects the keyboard handler for the current phase using the global variable `GamePhase`. Most `case`s just pass the keystroke to the appropriate private member function without further work.

```
BOOL CInputManager::Keyboard(WPARAM keystroke,
  BOOL virtual_keystroke){ //keyboard handler
  BOOL result=FALSE;
  switch(GamePhase){
    case LOGO_PHASE:
    case TITLE_PHASE:
      IntroKeyboard(keystroke);
      break;
    case MENU_PHASE:
      result=MainMenuKeyboard(keystroke);
      break;
    case DEVICEMENU_PHASE:
      DeviceMenuKeyboard(keystroke);
      break;
```

However, the playing phase is different. We only pass on keystrokes to the private member function `GameKeyboard` if the input device is the keyboard, the key is a function key (for example, we still want the Esc key to work when the player is using the mouse), or the keystroke is a virtual keystroke.

```
    case PLAYING_PHASE:
      if(InputDevice==KEYBOARD_INPUT||
      is_function_key(keystroke)||virtual_keystroke)
```

```
        GameKeyboard(keystroke);
      break;
    }
    return result;
}
```

Mouse Handlers

Next, we have the `CInputManager` mouse left button down handlers. The main menu left button down handler `MainMenuLMouseDown` is relatively simple; if `point` is within a button's hotspot, then that button goes down. No real action is taken; for regular buttons, the action happens when the mouse button is released.

```
void CInputManager::MainMenuLMouseDown(POINT point){
//mouse down handler for menu
  if(ButtonManager->hit(point)>=0) //if a valid hit
    ButtonManager->buttondown(point); //animate a button down
}
```

The `CInputManager` `DeviceMenuLMouseDown` function is different because with radio buttons the action happens when the button goes down:

```
void CInputManager::DeviceMenuLMouseDown(POINT point){
```

It begins by checking whether `point` is inside a hotspot:

```
int hit=ButtonManager->hit(point);
```

Then, a `switch` statement takes different action for each hotspot:

```
switch(hit){
```

Here we come face to face with a design decision. If `hit` is 0, it means that the player clicked in the topmost button on the screen. This means that they want to play using the keyboard instead of the mouse or the joystick. We could insert code here to set `InputDevice` to `KEYBOARD_INPUT`, and animate the button going down, just like in the "K" `case` of the `switch` statement in the device menu keyboard handler. Instead, we are going to pretend that the player hit the "K" key by calling the keyboard manager with parameter "K." Our design philosophy will be that the keyboard handler is in charge of mapping player choices to game actions. Other device handlers will ask the keyboard to take the appropriate action. Why? It means we don't duplicate the code in two places, which would make maintenance a pain; every time we needed to make a change to the code, we'd have to remember to make the changes in two or more places. The obvious alternative would be to create lots of little functions instead, one for each action, but that in itself would make maintenance a bother. This solution is much easier, although it does make the assumption that for every mouse action in the menus, there is a corresponding keyboard command. This, however, is not a bad thing. Although these days everybody has a mouse, not everybody likes to use it all the time.

```
case 0: Keyboard('K'); break; //keyboard
```

Similarly for button 1, which calls for mouse play:

```
case 1: Keyboard('M'); break; //mouse
```

There is no case 2 because that button (joystick play) doesn't work yet. Case 3 is the "Done" button, which exits the menu.

```
case 3:
  ButtonManager->buttondown(hit); //quit button down
  break;
```

The default case is when the player clicked outside an active button, in which case hit is −1. We do nothing.

```
default: break;
    }
  }
```

The CInputManager game left mouse button handler GameLMouseDown sends a Spacebar virtual keystroke to the keyboard handler. Why a virtual keystroke? Because our keyboard handler is disabled during mouse play.

```
void CInputManager::GameLMouseDown(POINT point){
//mouse down handler for game
  Keyboard(VK_SPACE,TRUE);
}
```

The Windows API WM_LBUTTONDOWN message that is delivered to your message handler in Main.cpp when the left mouse button goes down comes with an LPARAM parameter that contains the mouse coordinates encoded as a 32-bit integer. The high 16 bits of this word contain the y coordinate, and the low 16 bits contain the x coordinate. We could shift and mask this integer to extract the fields we want, but the Windows API fortunately contains two macros, LOWORD and HIWORD, that do the job for us. The CInputManager decode helper function decodes lparam into point (note that point is a call-by-reference parameter).

```
void CInputManager::decode(LPARAM lparam,POINT &point){
//decode mouse click lparam to point
  point.x=LOWORD(lparam); point.y=HIWORD(lparam);
}
```

The CInputManager left mouse button down handler LMouseDown takes as a parameter the LPARAM parameter that accompanies the WM_LBUTTONDOWN message:

```
void CInputManager::LMouseDown(LPARAM lparam){
```

It decodes `lparam` into a local variable `point`:

```
POINT point; //mouse location on screen
decode(lparam,point); //decode mouse point
```

The main body of `LMouseDown` is a `switch` statement that passes `point` to the left mouse button down handler for the current phase, which is stored in the global variable `GamePhase`:

```
switch(GamePhase){
  case MENU_PHASE:
    MainMenuLMouseDown(point);
    break;
  case DEVICEMENU_PHASE:
    DeviceMenuLMouseDown(point);
    break;
  case PLAYING_PHASE:
    if(InputDevice==MOUSE_INPUT)
      GameLMouseDown(point);
    break;
  }
}
```

Next, we have the `CInputManager` left mouse button up handlers. There is a left button *up* handler for the intro sequence, but not a left button *down* handler because the action will take place when the left mouse button is released, not when it is pressed down. The `CInputManager IntroLMouseUp` function simply ends the current phase by setting the global `endphase` variable to `TRUE`.

```
void CInputManager::IntroLMouseUp(POINT point){
//mouse left button up handler for intro
  endphase=TRUE;
}
```

The action for the main menu takes place when a button is released. Why not when a button is pressed down? Because the player may mash down on a button and then change his or her mind; they can back out of it by moving the mouse cursor off the button and releasing it elsewhere on the screen. Our code requires that the player mash down on a button *and* release the left mouse button with the cursor on the same screen button to get an action. The `CInputManager MainMenuLMouseUp` function is the left mouse button up handler for the main menu. It returns `TRUE` if the main menu phase is to end because the player clicked on the last button on the screen.

```
BOOL CInputManager::MainMenuLMouseUp(POINT point){
```

It sets local variable `hit` to the index of the button that the cursor was in when the left mouse button was released, provided that button was down:

```
int hit=ButtonManager->release(point); //get button hit
```

It has a local variable `result` for the return result.

```
BOOL result=FALSE;
```

A `switch` statement maps the buttons to keyboard events. The last button is treated differently because it is the "Quit" button.

```
switch(hit){ //depending on which button was hit
  case 0: Keyboard('N'); break; //new game
  case 1: Keyboard('S'); break; //saved game
  case 2: Keyboard('D'); break; //devices
  case 3: Keyboard('L'); break; //high score list
  case 4: Keyboard('H'); break; //help
  case 5: result=Keyboard(VK_ESCAPE); break; //quit
  default: break;
}
```

If there was a legitimate hit, we animate the hit button going up. Otherwise, we animate all the buttons going up, because there may be a down button that the player moved the mouse cursor off prior to releasing the left mouse button. Then, we return the result and exit.

```
//animate button images
if(hit>=0)ButtonManager->buttonup(hit); //hit
else ButtonManager->allbuttonsup(); //nonhit
return result;
}
```

The `CInputManager` device menu left mouse button up function `DeviceMenuLMouseUp` is similar, but it only has to take action for the "Done" button because all of the other buttons on the screen are radio buttons, which means that their actions are handled by the `CInputManager` device menu left mouse button down function `DeviceMenuLMouseDown`:

```
void CInputManager::DeviceMenuLMouseUp(POINT point){
//mouse left button up handler for device menu
  int hit=ButtonManager->release(point);
  switch(hit){
    case 3: //quit button up
      ButtonManager->buttonup(hit); //show quit button up
      Keyboard(VK_ESCAPE);
      break;
  }
  if(hit<0)ButtonManager->allbuttonsup(); //no hit
}
```

The `CInputManager` main left mouse button up function `LMouseUp` is similar to the `CInputManager` main left mouse button down function `LMouseDown`. It decodes `lparam` into a `point`, then uses a `switch` statement to send it to the left mouse button down handler for the current phase.

```
BOOL CInputManager::LMouseUp(LPARAM lparam){
//main mouse left button up handler
  BOOL result=FALSE;
  POINT point; //mouse location on screen
  decode(lparam,point); //decode mouse point
  switch(GamePhase){
    case LOGO_PHASE:
    case TITLE_PHASE:
      IntroLMouseUp(point);
      break;
    case MENU_PHASE:
      result=MainMenuLMouseUp(point);
      break;
    case DEVICEMENU_PHASE:
      DeviceMenuLMouseUp(point);
      break;
  }
  return result;
}
```

The Mouse as Digital Joystick

The last two `CInputManager` functions deal with the use of the mouse as a digital joystick to control the plane's vertical and horizontal speed. We will divide the screen into rectilinear bands, and set the plane's speed according to which band the invisible mouse cursor is in currently. The `CInputManager` `set_plane_speed` function sets the plane's speed using the position of `point` within the screen `extent`.

```
void CInputManager::set_plane_speed(POINT point,SIZE extent){
```

It has four local variables that it sets to the plane's minimum and maximum horizontal and vertical speeds by calling a new `CObjectManager` `speed_limits` function (all four parameters of this function are call-by-reference):

```
int xmin,xmax,ymin,ymax; //plane speed limits
ObjectManager.speed_limits(xmin,xmax,ymin,ymax); //get them
```

The plane has `xmax-xmin+1` different horizontal speeds, and so the screen should be divided into `xmax-xmin+1` different bands, each of width `XBANDWIDTH`, where the constant `XBANDWIDTH` is defined as follows:

```
const int XBANDWIDTH=extent.cx/(xmax-xmin+1);
```

Similarly for the vertical bands:

```
const int YBANDWIDTH=extent.cy/(ymax-ymin+1);
```

Next, we have two local variables for the desired speed of the plane:

```
int xspeed,yspeed; //speed of plane
```

We start by dividing the x coordinate of the point by XBANDWIDTH to get the index of the vertical band containing the mouse pointer, which will be in the range 0 through xmax-xmin, inclusive (see Figure 11.4, in which the band index is listed at the top of each band). The leftmost band, with index 0, corresponds to a speed of xmin (since speeds to the left are negative, xmin is the largest negative speed, corresponding to moving leftward fastest). The rightmost band, with index xmax-xmin, corresponds to a speed of xmax (see Figure 11.4, in which the corresponding speed is listed toward the middle of each band). Therefore, we need to add xmin to the band index point.x/XBANDWIDTH to get the corresponding horizontal speed.

```
xspeed=point.x/XBANDWIDTH+xmin; //horizontal speed
```

Exactly the same argument holds for the vertical speed:

```
yspeed=point.y/YBANDWIDTH+ymin; //vertical speed
```

Finally, having computed the plane's speed, we set it using the new CObjectManager set_speed function:

```
ObjectManager.set_speed(xspeed,yspeed); //pass to plane
}
```

Figure 11.4
Dividing the screen into bands corresponding to horizontal speed

The `CInputManager MouseMove` function is the handler for mouse motion. Its `lparam` parameter carries the mouse cursor's new position on the screen encoded in the same way as for the mouse button handler functions.

```
void CInputManager::MouseMove(LPARAM lparam){
```

If the player isn't using the mouse to play the game, then we bail out; the mouse joystick is not needed:

```
if(InputDevice!=MOUSE_INPUT)return; //bail if not needed
if(GamePhase!=PLAYING_PHASE)return; //bail if not playing
```

We decode the parameter `lparam` into a local variable `point`:

```
POINT point; //mouse location on screen
decode(lparam,point); //decode mouse point
```

We create a local variable to hold the screen extent:

```
SIZE extent; //extent that mouse moves in
extent.cx=SCREEN_WIDTH;
extent.cy=SCREEN_HEIGHT;
```

Then we call the `CInputManager set_plane_speed` function to set the plane's speed using the position of `point` within the screen `extent`:

```
set_plane_speed(point,extent);
}
```

Changes to the Object and Object Manager Classes

There are some small changes to the `CObject` and `CObjectManager` classes —the addition of three new functions (in total) to facilitate the use of the mouse as a digital joystick. Since these changes are so small, we won't list the requisite files—`Objects.h`, `Objects.cpp`, `Objman.h`, and `Objman.cpp`—with the other new and changed files in the `pdf` supplement.

`CObject` has a new public member function `set_speed` to be used by the mouse move handler to transfer the plane's speed from the mouse to the plane. It calls the `CObject accelerate` member function to add `xspeed-m_nXspeed` to `m_nXspeed`, thereby changing it to `xspeed` (similarly for `yspeed` and `m_nYspeed`).

```
void CObject::set_speed(int xspeed,int yspeed){ //set speed
  accelerate(xspeed-m_nXspeed,yspeed-m_nYspeed);
}
```

`CObjectManager` has two new public member functions also for use by the mouse move handler. Function `set_speed` sets the plane's speed by calling the plane object's `set_speed` member function, which was described in the previous paragraph.

```
void CObjectManager::set_speed(int xdelta,int ydelta){
  m_pObjectList[m_nCurrentObject]->set_speed(xdelta,ydelta);
}
```

The `CObjectManager speed_limits` function is a reader function that sets its four call-by-reference parameters to the current object's minimum and maximum horizontal and vertical speeds:

```
void CObjectManager::speed_limits(int &xmin,int &xmax,
                                  int &ymin,int &ymax){
//return speed limits on current object
  CObject *plane=m_pObjectList[m_nCurrentObject];
  xmin=plane->m_nMinXSpeed; xmax=plane->m_nMaxXSpeed;
  ymin=plane->m_nMinYSpeed; ymax=plane->m_nMaxYSpeed;
}
```

Changes to Main.cpp

As we have mentioned already, `Main.cpp` now has a new global variable `NextPhase` that will be used to store the required next phase when the end of the current phase is signaled by setting `endphase` to `TRUE`:

```
GamePhaseType NextPhase; //next phase of game
```

We also need a global input manager:

```
CInputManager InputManager; //device input manager
```

Function `RestoreSurfaces` has the following line of code added to the end to restore the surfaces in the button sprite in the input manager's button manager:

```
if(!InputManager.Restore())return FALSE;
```

Function `LoadSounds` has the following two lines of code added to `case 1` of the `switch` statement. These load the sounds for the buttons going down (a big click) and up (a small click).

```
        SoundManager->load("bgclk.wav",2);
        SoundManager->load("smclk.wav",2);
```

Function `display_screen`, which is used to display the intro screens and the background for the menu screens, also needs a small modification. The code for animating the buttons going up and down assumes that the background screen has been drawn to both the primary and secondary surfaces. In Demo 8, function `display_screen` draws it to the secondary surface, then flips it up to the primary surface, leaving the secondary surface with whatever was in the primary surface before. We add the following extra line of code to the end of `display_screen` to bring it up to spec.

```
image.draw(lpSecondary);
```

The Change_phase Function

Function `change_phase` has been made more complicated by the fact that you can enter more than one phase from the main menu, and of course by the addition of a new phase for the device menu. In Demo 8, it started with the following two lines of code to change the phase. These are now moved to the end of the function because the `switch` statement now needs access to the current phase information to determine what to do.

```
GamePhase=new_phase; PhaseTime=Timer.time();
endphase=FALSE;
```

Because the current phase has not yet been changed to the new phase, the switch statement itself must now look at the new phase, not the current one:

```
switch(new_phase){
```

The case for the `MENU_PHASE` had become much more elaborate:

```
case MENU_PHASE:
```

We begin by setting up the buttons for the main menu phase:

```
InputManager.SetupButtons(MENU_PHASE);
```

What is done to the sound depends on the current phase. If we are leaving the title phase to enter the main menu phase, the title sound needs to be stopped in case the player clicked out of the title screen, and we will load the sounds for level 1 now instead of later because these sounds now include the mouse clicks for the menu pages. If we are leaving the playing phase for the main menu, we need only stop the sounds.

```
switch(GamePhase){ //depending on previous phase
  case TITLE_PHASE: //from intro phase
    SoundManager->stop(); //silence previous phase
    SoundManager->clear(); //clear out old sounds
    LoadSounds(1); //set up game sounds
    break;
  case PLAYING_PHASE: //from game engine
    SoundManager->stop(); //silence game engine
    break;
   case DEVICEMENU_PHASE: //device menu, do nothing
    break;
}
```

We then display the main menu screen from file `Menu.bmp`.

```
display_screen("menu.bmp"); //display main menu
```

The mouse cursor needs to be shown if we are entering the main menu phase (which needs the mouse cursor on) from the playing or title phases (which have the mouse cursor off), but not from the device menu page (which has the mouse cursor on). Some care must be taken with the use of the Windows API function calls `ShowCursor(TRUE)` and `ShowCursor(FALSE)`. Recall from Chapter 2 that instead of setting and unsetting a Boolean value, `ShowCursor(TRUE)` increments a counter and `ShowCursor(FALSE)` decrements it. The counter must be positive for the mouse cursor to be shown. Therefore, if you call `ShowCursor(FALSE)` twice in succession, you must call `ShowCursor(TRUE)` twice before the mouse cursor will reappear (remember these words when your mouse cursor fails to appear when you expect it to). This ends the `case MENU_PHASE` in the main `switch` statement.

```
switch(GamePhase){ //what phase did we come in from?
  case PLAYING_PHASE:
  case TITLE_PHASE:
    ShowCursor(TRUE); //activate the mouse cursor
    break;
}
break;
```

There is a new `case` for the `DEVICEMENU_PHASE`, which displays the device menu screen and sets up the buttons for the device menu:

```
case DEVICEMENU_PHASE:
  //display button background
  display_screen("dmenu.bmp");
  //set up the button manager
  InputManager.SetupButtons(DEVICEMENU_PHASE);
  break;
```

The `case PLAYING_PHASE` has two new lines of code to set up the cursor position and turn off the mouse cursor (which in Demo 8 was turned off at the start of the game and left off; now it will be turned on in the main menu and must be turned off when entering the game engine). The cursor position is set using the Windows API function `SetCursorPos`.

```
SetCursorPos(SCREEN_WIDTH-1,SCREEN_HEIGHT/2); //throttle
ShowCursor(FALSE); //hide the mouse cursor
```

Other Functions

Function `Redraw` has the following case added to its `switch` statement to redraw the device menu screen:

```
case DEVICEMENU_PHASE:
  display_screen("dmenu.bmp");
  InputManager.SetupButtons(DEVICEMENU_PHASE);
  break;
```

The new global variable `NextPhase` gets used in function `ProcessFrame` to set the next phase when exiting the main menu screen. In the `case MENU_PHASE` in its `switch` statement, the call to `change_phase` is changed from `change_phase(PLAYING_PHASE)` in Demo 8 to `change_phase(NextPhase)`. We also add a new `case` for the device menu; when the device menu phase ends, we go to the main menu.

```
case DEVICEMENU_PHASE:
  if(endphase) change_phase(MENU_PHASE); //go to menu phase
  break;
```

There are several changes to the window procedure `WindowProc`. The first is minor; in response to the `WM_KEYDOWN` message, it now uses the input manager's keyboard handler instead of having the keyboard handler functions in `Main.cpp`.

```
case WM_KEYDOWN: //keyboard hit
  if(InputManager.Keyboard(wParam))
    DestroyWindow(hwnd);
  break;
```

There are three new cases for mouse messages, beginning with the left mouse button down message `WM_LBUTTONDOWN`. The `lParam` parameter containing the mouse cursor coordinates is passed on to the input manager's `LMouseDown` function.

```
case WM_LBUTTONDOWN: //left mouse button down
  InputManager.LMouseDown(lParam); //handle it
  break;
```

The response to the left mouse button up handler is similar, with the addition that the input manager's `LMouseUp` function will return `TRUE` if the player wants to exit the program, which, as always, we do with a call to the Windows API function `DestroyWindow`:

```
case WM_LBUTTONUP: //left mouse button up
  if(InputManager.LMouseUp(lParam))
    DestroyWindow(hwnd);
  break;
```

The mouse move message `WM_MOUSEMOVE` is handled similarly:

```
case WM_MOUSEMOVE: //mouse move
  InputManager.MouseMove(lParam);
  break;
```

One line of code is added to the `case WM_DESTROY` to release the input manager's surfaces:

```
InputManager.Release(); //button surfaces
```

Demo 9 Files

Code Files

The following files in Demo 9 are used without change from Demo 8:

- Ai.h
- Ai.cpp
- Bmp.h
- Bmp.cpp
- Bsprite.h
- Bsprite.cpp
- Csprite.h
- Csprite.cpp
- Ddsetup.cpp
- Random.h
- Random.cpp
- Sbmp.h
- Sbmp.cpp
- Sound.h
- Sound.cpp
- Timer.h
- Timer.cpp
- View.h
- View.cpp

The following files in Demo 9 have been modified from Demo 8:

- Defines.h
- Main.cpp
- Objects.h (changes minimal; not listed in the pdf supplement)

- ◎ `Objects.cpp` (changes minimal; not listed in the `pdf` supplement)
- ◎ `Objman.h` (changes minimal; not listed in the `pdf` supplement)
- ◎ `Objman.cpp` (changes minimal; not listed in the `pdf` supplement)
- ◎ `Sndlist.h`

The following files are new in Demo 9:

- ◎ `Buttons.h`
- ◎ `Buttons.cpp`
- ◎ `Input.h`
- ◎ `Input.cpp`

Media Files

The following image files are new in Demo 9:

- ◎ `Buttons.bmp`
- ◎ `Dmenu.bmp`

The following sound files are new in Demo 9:

- ◎ `Bgclk.wav`
- ◎ `Smclk.wav`

Required Libraries

- ◎ `Ddraw.lib`
- ◎ `Dsound.lib`
- ◎ `Winmm.lib`

Here's what you'll learn:

- How the joystick hardware works

- What can go wrong with your joystick handler

- How to access the joystick using the Windows API

- How to get configuration information from the joystick

- How to poll the joystick position

- How to poll the joystick buttons

The Joystick

In Demo 10, we learn how to process input from the joystick. I assume that you do have a joystick attached to your computer. If not, then this chapter is going to be a little boring for you. We will use the joystick position to control the plane's speed, and we will use button 1 on the joystick to fire the gun. The joystick is radically different from any other device attached to your computer—it is analog instead of digital. This introduces some unique programming challenges. Rather than use the Windows API message-passing system, we will poll the joystick hardware directly.

Experiment with Demo 10

Take a moment now to run Demo 10.

◎ If you haven't done so recently, calibrate your joystick. Start by double-clicking on the Game Controllers icon in the Control Panel of your computer. Select a joystick from the list displayed there, and click on the Properties button. You will then see the Game Controller Properties dialog box, which will look similar to Figure 12.1. On the Settings tab, click on the Calibrate button. You will then see the Controller Calibration dialog box, which will look similar to Figure 12.2. Follow the instructions there.

◎ Run Demo 10. Notice that you can click out of the logo and title screens by clicking on button 1 on the joystick.

◎ Go to the device menu and click on the Joystick button. If that button does not depress, it means that something is wrong with your joystick; it is either broken, unplugged, or misconfigured. You should exit Demo 10 before you attempt to rectify this problem.

◎ Now, play a game. Notice that the joystick position controls the plane's speed, and button 1 fires the gun. Notice that the mouse and keyboard controls for the plane are disabled.

◎ Hold the joystick button down for several seconds. Notice that the gun is fired only once. To fire it again, you must first release the button.

◎ Exit from Demo 10, unplug your joystick, and try again. The Joystick button on the device menu should now be inactive.

Figure 12.1
The Game
Controller
Properties
dialog box

Figure 12.2
The
Controller
Calibration
dialog box

How the Joystick Works

Imagine a manager working on a noisy factory floor. He has a bunch of paperwork to do, and he has to oversee his employees at the same time. He's the CPU. He has a bunch of flunkies who constantly tap him on the shoulder and pass him pieces of information. They get his attention for a few seconds, during which time he records their information, then gets back to his paperwork. They are the digital devices on your computer, such as the mouse and the keyboard. The mouse and the keyboard behave exactly in this manner, constantly interrupting the CPU, which must break off from its regular work to service their interrupts.

The joystick is like a roving employee out on the factory floor who needs to report a number to the manager periodically. However, the employee is too far away to be able to send interrupts to the manager. Every so often, the manager calls out to him, and he responds by shouting back his number. However, it's noisy out there on the factory floor, so although the manager can hear when the employee shouts, he can't tell exactly what he's saying. Therefore, they've evolved a system. If the employee wants to communicate the number "5," he waits for 5 seconds after he hears the manager's query, and then answers. If he wants to communicate "10," he waits 10 seconds before responding. The manager notes the time when he sends his request and counts the number of seconds until the employee responds. This gives him the number that the employee wants to shout to him.

The manager has to actively listen for the employee to be able to distinguish his voice over the noise, so, in addition to being taken away from his paperwork, he has to disable all interrupts while he's listening. Otherwise he might miss a response that comes in while he is working or servicing an interrupt. Disabling interrupts is not in general a good idea because it potentially shuts out all sorts of time-sensitive information, but it is acceptable if it is not done too often, or for too long. This means that if for some reason the roving employee doesn't respond at all, the manager needs to time-out after waiting for a period of time that is long enough for any reasonable response, but not long enough to interfere with normal work or important interrupts.

This is how the joystick communicates with the CPU. It doesn't do so because of noise, of course, but because that's the way the analog hardware works. Periodically the CPU must turn off interrupts, send a signal to the joystick, and then wait a reasonable amount of time (measured in milliseconds this time, not seconds) for the joystick to respond. It then decodes the information sent (such as the joystick coordinates) from the amount of time that elapses before a signal returns. This process is called *polling* the joystick.

Turning off interrupts can be *very* dangerous. For example, consider the *RAM refresh interrupt*. The RAM on your computer is volatile and needs to be refreshed periodically by the CPU. A failure to respond to this interrupt in a timely fashion will result in the contents of your computer's memory being sent to the Great Bit-bucket in the Sky. Therefore, you really don't want to poll the joystick too frequently or set the time-out value too high.

Here's an example of the kind of weird thing that can happen when you code for the joystick. The first joystick code that I wrote was under DOS on an old 66MHZ 486. Initially, I had the polling interval and the time-out value a little too high. As a result, the processor spent far too much of its time waiting for the joystick to respond. It also had a cool side effect. The game was playing MIDI music at the time, which involves having the CPU send a signal to the sound card at the beginning and end of every note. The joystick code interfered with the timing of this process by making the CPU too busy to send the MIDI signals on time, and since the amount of time that the CPU must wait for the joystick is longer when the joystick is sending a larger number (for example, more when the joystick is in the back right corner than the forward left corner), the degree of interference was dependent on the joystick's position. The result was that the joystick unintentionally acted as a tempo controller—waggling the joystick made the tempo of the music go up and down in response!

Coding for the joystick in Windows is a lot easier than it was back in the old DOS days. The API provides you with a lot of support. We will use the Windows API to poll the joystick hardware directly. Alternatively, you can (by calling the Windows API `JoySetCapture` function) get Windows to make the joystick appear to send messages. The messages you receive from the joystick have a prefix of "`MM_`", for example, `MM_JOY1MOVE` for joystick motion. The mouse messages that we saw in Chapter 11 are generated by interrupts from the mouse, whereas with the joystick, the Windows API is taking care of polling the joystick behind the scenes and faking the joystick messages for you, just as if the joystick were interrupt driven.

There's one more thing about joysticks that the programmer should know. They contain two variable resistors, one measuring side-to-side motion and the other measuring front-to-back motion. These variable resistors have different physical properties from one joystick to another, even when they are made by the same manufacturer. Even worse, they will behave differently from one day to the next, depending on the ambient temperature and humidity. If you think *that's* bad, listen to this: Electrical resistance is inversely proportional to temperature. Moving the joystick creates friction, which raises the temperature of its components, so it can behave differently during a *single play session* depending on how heavily it is used. The numbers returned by the joystick at the forward left position will almost never be exactly the same each time you poll it. The same for back right, or even the at-rest position in the middle.

The Joystick Manager

The joystick manager class CJoystickManager handles the joystick polling functions for *Ned's Turkey Farm*.

Joystick Manager Overview

The header file for the joystick manager is Joystick.h. It begins with an unusual include that we haven't seen before—the header Mmsystem.h, which we need to access joystick support in the Windows API.

```
#include <mmsystem.h>
```

Then we define the joystick poll interval constant JOYSTICKPOLLINTERVAL, which is the number of milliseconds between polls of the joystick. Setting this to 100 milliseconds means that we poll 10 times per second, which is adequate for a game of this kind.

```
#define JOYSTICKPOLLINTERVAL 100 //time between polls
```

CJoystickManager has 12 private member variables. The first is a Windows API JOYINFOEX structure m_joyInfo. This is the structure that the joystick polling function will use to pass information back to our program.

```
JOYINFOEX m_joyInfo; //current joystick state
```

The next eight private member variables are places into which we will parse the JOYINFOEX information to make it more accessible. The first of these is the joystick identifier; the API allows us to use multiple joysticks if we wish.

```
UINT m_uJoystickid; //joystick id
```

Next are the joystick coordinates stored as percentages, from zero to one hundred percent, inclusive. The joystick manager uses percentages so that the joystick coordinates it delivers to your program are always within the same extent, even though (as we noted already) this cannot be said of the hardware.

```
int m_nX, m_nY; //x and y coordinates as percentages
```

Next, the joystick extents, as reported by the hardware:

```
int m_nXmax, m_nYmax; //maximum x and y from h/w
int m_nXmin, m_nYmin; //minimum x and y from h/w
```

Finally, the positions of up to four joystick buttons are stored in a Boolean array. Note that while we will be indexing these buttons 0 through 3, the joystick indexes them 1 through 4 (joysticks have obviously never heard of C).

```
BOOL m_bButton[4]; //buttons down?
```

A parallel array stores Boolean values that indicate whether a down button has been serviced. We only want to fire a bullet when the button is polled *going down*, that is, it is up on one poll and down on the next. Once it has been serviced, no more bullets will be fired if it remains down on subsequent polls. That is, unless we allow the joystick buttons to *autorepeat*.

```
BOOL m_bServiced[4]; //whether down button was serviced
```

The Boolean variable m_bOperational will be set to TRUE if the joystick was successfully initialized:

```
BOOL m_bOperational; //was init successful?
```

Next, m_nLastPollTime records the last time that the joystick was polled:

```
int m_nLastPollTime; //last time joystick was polled
```

The last private member variable is set to TRUE if we want the joystick buttons to autorepeat when they are held down:

```
BOOL m_bAutoRepeat; //allow autorepeat
```

CJoystickManager has one private member function load_data, which parses information from the JOYINFOEX structure into the private member variables:

```
void load_data(); //process data from m_joyInfo
```

The joystick manager has seven public member functions, including a constructor:

```
CJoystickManager(); //constructor
```

The initialize function initializes the joystick manager by checking whether there is a joystick available, and if so, it gets information about the joystick:

```
BOOL initialize(); //initialize settings
```

The poll function polls the joystick state, returning TRUE if new information was successfully received from the joystick:

```
BOOL poll(); //poll joystick state
```

The button_down function has an integer parameter button in the range 1 through 4, and returns TRUE if that button was down the last time the joystick was polled and has not yet been serviced:

```
BOOL button_down(int button); //is button down?
```

The position function delivers the position of the joystick as a POINT structure provided as a call-by-reference parameter, with the coordinates of that structure expressed as percentages. It returns FALSE if the joystick is not operational.

```
BOOL position(POINT &point); //position as percentage
```

The `autorepeat` function sets and unsets autorepeat on the joystick buttons:

```
void autorepeat(BOOL setting=TRUE); //un/set autorepeat
```

Finally, the `exists` function returns TRUE if the joystick is operational:

```
BOOL exists(); //TRUE if joystick exists
```

Initializing the Joystick Manager

The code file for the joystick manager is `Joystick.cpp`. It begins with the constructor, which simply sets the private member variables to sensible initial values.

```
CJoystickManager::CJoystickManager(){ //constructor
  m_nLastPollTime=0; //not polled yet
  m_bOperational=FALSE; //not initialized yet
  m_uJoystickid=0; m_bAutoRepeat=TRUE;
  m_nX=m_nY=0; m_nXmax=m_nYmax=m_nXmin=m_nYmin=0;
  for(int i=0; i<4; i++) //init button positions
    m_bServiced[i]=m_bButton[i]=FALSE;
}
```

The `CJoystickManager` initialize function gets information about the joystick, setting the private member variable `m_bOperational` to TRUE and returning TRUE if it finds an operational joystick:

```
BOOL CJoystickManager::initialize(){ //init joystick
  m_bOperational=FALSE; //assume failure
```

A call to the Windows API function `joyGetNumDevs` returns the number of joysticks. If this is zero, we bail out.

```
if(!joyGetNumDevs())return FALSE; //bail if no joysticks
```

Next, we set up the JOYINFOEX private member variable `m_joyInfo` by setting all fields to zero, then setting its size field:

```
memset(&m_joyInfo,0,sizeof(JOYINFOEX));
m_joyInfo.dwSize=sizeof(JOYINFOEX);
```

The flags field in `m_joyInfo` is set to indicate that we will be querying the joystick buttons and coordinates:

```
m_joyInfo.dwFlags=JOY_RETURNBUTTONS|JOY_RETURNX|JOY_RETURNY;
```

The API allows us to access at most two joysticks. We next see which, if any, of the two possible joysticks is available. We do this by calling the API function `joyGetPosEx`, which will attempt to get us the joystick position and button states, failing if the joystick is not available. The first parameter of `joyGetPosEx` is the joystick identifier, for which the API kindly provides us two constants, JOYSTICKID1 and JOYSTICKID2. The second parameter is a pointer to a JOYINFOEX structure that receives the joystick information. We try joystick 1 first, and if we get a return of JOYERR_NOERROR, indicating the joystick exists and is operational, we set the private member variable m_uJoystickid to JOYSTICKID1.

```
if(joyGetPosEx(JOYSTICKID1,&m_joyInfo)==JOYERR_NOERROR)
  m_uJoystickid=JOYSTICKID1;
```

Otherwise, we try the same thing with joystick 2:

```
else if(joyGetPosEx(JOYSTICKID2,&m_joyInfo)==JOYERR_NOERROR)
  m_uJoystickid=JOYSTICKID2;
```

If both attempts fail, we bail. Strictly speaking, if we identify two working joysticks, we should ask the player which one they would like to use, but for a simple demo like this, it is good enough to be lazy and just use the first one that works.

```
else return FALSE;
```

Now that we've identified a working joystick, we need to get its minimum and maximum extents. We declare a local structure of type JOYCAPS for the joystick's capabilities.

```
JOYCAPS joycaps;
```

We call the API function joyGetDevCaps to put the joystick capabilities into joycaps, and bail out if it fails to do so:

```
if(joyGetDevCaps(m_uJoystickid,&joycaps,
sizeof(joycaps))!=JOYERR_NOERROR)
    return FALSE; //bail if can't get caps info
```

From joycaps we extract the joystick extents and store them in the appropriate private member variables:

```
m_nXmax=joycaps.wXmax; m_nYmax=joycaps.wYmax; //max extent
m_nXmin=joycaps.wXmin; m_nYmin=joycaps.wYmin; //min extent
```

Now we call the CJoystickManager member function load_data to extract joystick position and button data from the m_joyInfo member variable. This information was placed there by the earlier call to joyGetPosEx, but we couldn't process it until we obtained the joystick extents from which we can compute the joystick coordinates as percentages.

```
load_data();
```

Finally, we record that the joystick is ready for use:

```
return m_bOperational=TRUE;
}
```

Getting Data From the Joystick

The `CJoystickManager load_data` function takes care of processing information from the `JOYINFOEX` information private member variable `m_joyInfo` into the other private member variables:

```
void CJoystickManager::load_data(){ //process joystick data
```

Each button state is recorded in a single bit of the `dwButtons` field of `m_joyInfo`, so we extract each one by performing a bitwise AND of `m_joyInfo.dwButtons` with the appropriate power of two:

```
m_bButton[0]=m_joyInfo.dwButtons&1;
m_bButton[1]=m_joyInfo.dwButtons&2;
m_bButton[2]=m_joyInfo.dwButtons&4;
m_bButton[3]=m_joyInfo.dwButtons&8;
```

After a test to eliminate the possibility of a divide-by-zero error, we normalize the x coordinate of the joystick to between 0 and 100. Notice that if the joystick's x coordinate `m_joyInfo.dwXpos` is at the far left extent, stored in `m_nXmin`, then `m_nX` is set to zero. Similarly, if `m_joyInfo.dwXpos` is at the far right extent, stored in `m_nXmax`, then `m_nX` is set to 100.

```
if(m_nXmax!=m_nXmin)
  m_nX=(100*(m_joyInfo.dwXpos-m_nXmin))/(m_nXmax-m_nXmin);
```

However, the joystick extents were stored in the private member variables `m_nXmax` and `m_nXmin` back when the `CJoystickManager initialize` function was called, which may have been a long time ago. The joystick's temperature may have changed since then, which means that the joystick may report an x coordinate that is larger than `m_nXmax` or smaller than `m_nXmin`. However, it won't be off by much, so we will simply truncate the percentages at 0 and 100.

```
if(m_nX<0)m_nX=0; if(m_nX>100)m_nX=100;
```

The joystick's Y coordinate is handled similarly.

```
if(m_nYmax!=m_nYmin)
  m_nY=(100*(m_joyInfo.dwYpos-m_nYmin))/(m_nYmax-m_nYmin);
if(m_nY<0)m_nY=0; if(m_nY>100)m_nY=100;
}
```

The `CJoystickManager poll` function polls the joystick state using the API function `joyGetPosEx`. It returns `TRUE` if new data was received from the joystick.

```
BOOL CJoystickManager::poll(){ //poll joystick state
```

It bails out if the joystick is not operational:

```
if(!m_bOperational)return FALSE; //bail if not initialized
```

It uses the timer to ensure that the joystick is not polled too often:

```
if(!Timer.elapsed(m_nLastPollTime,JOYSTICKPOLLINTERVAL))
    return FALSE;
```

If everything is OK, it calls `joyGetPosEx` to put joystick information in `m_joyInfo`, and bails out if the joystick was unplugged by the player:

```
if(joyGetPosEx(m_uJoystickid,&m_joyInfo)==JOYERR_UNPLUGGED)
    return FALSE; //bail if cannot get data from joystick
```

It parses the `m_joyInfo` information into the other private member variables:

```
load_data();
```

Then it marks all of the up buttons as unserviced, so that they get serviced the next time they are down:

```
for(int i=0; i<4; i++)
    if(!m_bButton[i])m_bServiced[i]=FALSE;
```

Having succeeded, it returns `TRUE`:

```
    return TRUE;
}
```

Other Member Functions

The next two `CJoystickManager` member functions `button_down` and `position` report on the joystick state from the information parsed out of the `JOYINFOEX` structure. The `CJoystickManager button_down` function reports the state of a joystick button. The parameter `button` uses the joystick standard, not the C standard, in that it starts at 1 instead of 0.

```
BOOL CJoystickManager::button_down(int button){
```

We declare a local variable for the returned `result`, decrement `button` so that it can be used as an array index, and then bail out if the joystick is not operational or `button` is out of range:

```
BOOL result;
button--; //adjust for 0-based array
if(!m_bOperational)return FALSE; //bail if not initialized
if(button<0||button>=4)return FALSE; //bail if wrong number
```

We set `result` to `TRUE` if `button` is down:

```
result=m_bButton[button]; //is button down?
```

We pop it up, so that it is not recorded as being down the next time the button is queried even though the joystick may not have been polled in the meantime:

```
m_bButton[button]=FALSE; //pop it up
```

If autorepeat is disabled, and the button was down and has been serviced, then we return FALSE (reporting that the button is up):

```
if(!m_bAutoRepeat&&result&&m_bServiced[button])
  return FALSE; //prevent button bounce
```

Otherwise, if the button is down, then we mark it as serviced. This prevents it from being serviced again until the poll function sees that it has been released and sets m_bServiced[button] to FALSE.

```
if(result) //if button is down
  m_bServiced[button]=TRUE; //mark as serviced
```

Finally, we return the result:

```
  return result;
}
```

The CJoystickManager position function is a simple reader function that reports the joystick coordinates from the private member variables m_nX and m_nY:

```
BOOL CJoystickManager::position(POINT &point){
  if(!m_bOperational)return FALSE; //bail if not initialized
  point.x=m_nX; point.y=m_nY;
  return TRUE;
}
```

The function CJoystickManager autorepeat function changes the autorepeat settings and resets the service flags:

```
void CJoystickManager::autorepeat(BOOL setting){
  m_bAutoRepeat=setting; //allow autorepeat
  for(int i=0; i<4; i++) //reset buttons
    m_bServiced[i]=m_bButton[i]=FALSE;
}
```

The CJoystickManager exists function returns TRUE if an operational joystick exists:

```
BOOL CJoystickManager::exists(){
  //TRUE if joystick apparently exists
  return m_bOperational;
}
```

Changes to the Input Manager

Some changes to the input manager class `CInputManager` are needed to incorporate the joystick code.

Declarations

In `Defines.h`, we add a new entry `JOYSTICK_INPUT` to the enumerated type `InputDeviceType`:

```
enum InputDeviceType{KEYBOARD_INPUT=0,MOUSE_INPUT,
  JOYSTICK_INPUT};
```

The changes to `Input.h` begin with the declaration of a joystick manager as a private member variable:

```
CJoystickManager JoystickManager; //joystick manager
```

Two new private member functions `IntroJoystick` and `GameJoystick` act as joystick handlers during the intro and during gameplay, respectively:

```
void IntroJoystick(); //joystick handler
void GameJoystick(); //joystick handler
```

The main joystick handler is a `CInputManager` public member function `Joystick`:

```
void Joystick(); //main joystick handler
```

Changes to the Code

Changes to the `CInputManager` code in `Input.cpp` begin with the constructor, which has two additional lines of code to initialize the joystick manager member variable and set autorepeat on the joystick buttons to `FALSE`:

```
JoystickManager.initialize(); //set up joystick
JoystickManager.autorepeat(FALSE); //disable autorepeat
```

In the `CInputManager` `DeviceMenuKeyboard` function, we add a new `case` to the `switch` statement so that the joystick option is selected when the player hits the "J" key. It checks that the joystick exists by calling the joystick manager's `exists` member function, then sets the input device to `JOYSTICK_INPUT` before drawing the joystick radio button on the screen in the down position.

```
case 'J': //play using joystick
  if(JoystickManager.exists()){ //if joystick exists
    InputDevice=JOYSTICK_INPUT;
    ButtonManager->buttondown(JOYSTICK_INPUT);
  }
  break;
```

Similarly, we add a new `case` to the `switch` statement in the `CInputManager DeviceMenuLMouseDown` function so that the player can click on the "Joystick" button with the mouse. As with the other cases, it relies on the keyboard manager to effect the change by sending it a "J" character.

```
case 2: Keyboard('J'); break; //joystick
```

The remaining three new member functions are the joystick handlers. The `CInputManager GameJoystick` function handles the joystick during gameplay.

```
void CInputManager::GameJoystick(){
```

It bails out if the joystick is not being used:

```
if(InputDevice!=JOYSTICK_INPUT)return; //bail if unneeded
```

If button 1 is down, it fires the gun. Notice that the joystick manager takes care of making sure that the gun is fired once per click.

```
if(JoystickManager.button_down(1)) //button 1...
  Keyboard(VK_SPACE,TRUE); //...fires bullets
```

The next line of code never actually gets used, but it's in there just to provide safety during debugging:

```
if(GamePhase!=PLAYING_PHASE)return; //bail if not playing
```

We declare a local variable `point` to hold the joystick's current coordinates from the joystick manager:

```
POINT point; //coordinates of joystick
JoystickManager.position(point); //get coordinates
```

We set a local variable `extent` for the joystick extent, and pass both `point` and `extent` to the input manager's `set_plane_speed` function to set the plane's speed:

```
SIZE extent; //extent that joystick indicator moves in
extent.cx=100; extent.cy=100; //set extent
set_plane_speed(point,extent); //set plane speed
}
```

The `CInputManager IntroJoystick` function allows the player to click out of the intro screens using the joystick button:

```
void CInputManager::IntroJoystick(){
//joystick handler for intro
  if(JoystickManager.button_down(1)) //click out
    Keyboard(VK_ESCAPE);
}
```

The CInputManager Joystick function is the main joystick handler. As with the other CInputManager device handlers, it consists of a switch statement that selects the private member function for the current phase. First, however, it attempts to poll the joystick by calling the joystick manager's poll function.

Recall that the timer is used in the CJoystickManager poll function to make sure that the joystick is not polled too often.

```
void CInputManager::Joystick(){ //main joystick handler
  JoystickManager.poll(); //poll joystick
  switch(GamePhase){ //call joystick handler for phase
    case PLAYING_PHASE: GameJoystick(); break;
    case LOGO_PHASE:
    case TITLE_PHASE: IntroJoystick(); break;
    case DEVICEMENU_PHASE:
    case MENU_PHASE:
      break; //do nothing
  }
}
```

To ensure that the joystick gets polled regularly, we add a line of code to function ProcessFrame in Main.cpp to process the joystick input:

```
InputManager.Joystick(); //process joystick input
```

Demo 10 Files

Code Files

The following files in Demo 10 are used without change from Demo 9:

- Ai.h
- Ai.cpp
- Bmp.h
- Bmp.cpp
- Bsprite.h
- Bsprite.cpp
- Buttons.h
- Buttons.cpp
- Csprite.h
- Csprite.cpp
- Ddsetup.cpp
- Objects.h
- Objects.cpp

- Objman.h
- Objman.cpp
- Random.h
- Random.cpp
- Sbmp.h
- Sbmp.cpp
- Sndlist.h
- Sound.h
- Sound.cpp
- Timer.h
- Timer.cpp
- View.h
- View.cpp

The following files in Demo 10 have been modified from Demo 9:

- Defines.h
- Input.h
- Input.cpp
- Main.cpp (changes minimal; not listed in the pdf supplement)

The following files are new in Demo 10:

- Joystick.h
- Joystick.cpp

Required Libraries

- Ddraw.lib
- Dsound.lib
- Winmm.lib

Appendix A

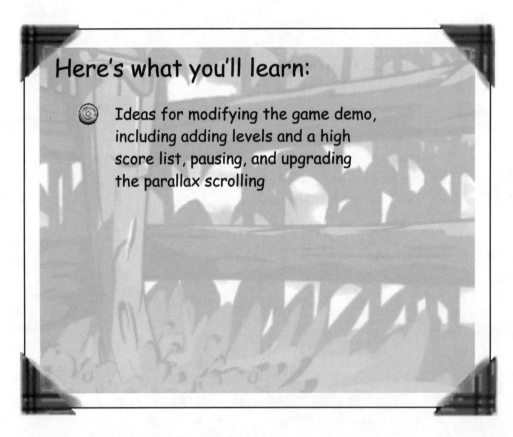

Here's what you'll learn:

- Ideas for modifying the game demo, including adding levels and a high score list, pausing, and upgrading the parallax scrolling

Now What?

So now what do you do? What you *should* do is go write your own game. But if you want to improve your understanding of game programming before you take this major step, I would suggest that you try modifying *Ned's Turkey Farm*. *Ned's Turkey Farm* was chosen to be a simple demo to keep the code small enough to understand while providing enough complexity to illustrate some of the challenges that face the beginning game programmer. There's a lot that can be done to improve it. One thing about a demo is that it is never done. Here are a few suggestions on what to do next.

◎ Add levels to the game, with more crows appearing in each level. Give the player health, score, and lives, and display these statistics on the screen. The player should lose health every time they run into a crow, and lose a life when enough health points are lost. New lives should be awarded when the player score is high enough (say, with each 100 points). Score points should be awarded for killing crows and for completing each level. This material is covered in Chapter 13 of my book *Learn Computer Game Programming with DirectX 7.0*.

◎ Add a high score list containing a small number of names (say 10). Each time the player exits the game engine with a high enough score, he or she should be invited into the high score list. The high score list should be displayed from the main menu. Store the high score list in the Windows registry, and be sure to use some kind of checksum to guard against tampering. While writing registry code, it would be a good idea at this point to also store and retrieve the currently used device (keyboard, mouse, or joystick) so that each time *Ned's Turkey Farm* is played, it starts with the device that the player used last. This material is covered in Chapter 14 of my book *Learn Computer Game Programming with DirectX 7.0*.

◎ Add the facility to pause the game engine. This involves pausing both the timer and the sound manager. Once you can pause, you can also deal with Alt+Tab in a reasonable manner. (Alt+Tab is the Windows method of swapping between running applications.) This material is covered in Chapter 15 of my book *Learn Computer Game Programming with DirectX 7.0*.

◉ Add more objects to the current game scenario. The sprite file `Sprites.bmp` contains images for a few more things including cows, pigs, sheep, and a truck. Write code, including AI, for the cows, pigs, and sheep. You can look at the *Ned's Turkey Farm* screen saver (which is free for downloading from `http://larc.csci.unt.edu/book/ssaver`) for some hints on how you can make them act. I have a version of *Ned's Turkey Farm* in which the truck shadows the plane and extra points are scored if you land each crow carcass into the back of the truck (the truck jumps into the air and a voice says "Yeehaw!" every time a hit is made). This is a reasonable thing to start with provided you've been paying attention to the book up to this point, but I strongly advise that you start by designing and implementing a reasonable sprite manager—sprite management wasn't an issue in *Ned's Turkey Farm* up to this point because there were only a few types of sprites.

◉ Add more levels with different backgrounds and different scenarios. You will want to team up with an artist who can provide the new background art, but the coding is not much more challenging than you have seen already.

◉ Upgrade the parallax scrolling by using backgrounds that consist of more than one 640x480 image, and by increasing the number of layers of parallax scrolling. For example, you could have from back to front: the sky, some hills, some fields, then the current farm foreground. The closer to the foreground, the faster the layers should scroll past. Again, you will need more art but the coding is not particularly challenging if you have been paying attention.

◉ Update the DirectSound sound player by adding the facility to stream sounds from large files, instead of loading them into memory the way we did in Chapter 10. Add 3D sound capability so that crows to the left of the screen make sounds in the left speaker, and crows to the right of the screen make sounds in the right speaker. Add Doppler effects for crows that are moving relative to the plane.

◉ Draw the mouse pointer yourself instead of relying on Windows to draw it for you (see Chapter 11).

◉ Use DirectInput instead of the Windows API to get input from the keyboard, mouse, and joystick. While this is not strictly necessary for a simple game like *Ned's Turkey Farm* (the API calls are fast enough), it is good experience that might help you land your first job in the game industry. This is a challenging proposition because it involves reading the DirectX documentation yourself.

◉ Make *Ned's Turkey Farm* a lot more compliant with Windows: make it run on the desktop in a window, and make it use menu bars and dialog boxes like a normal Windows program. You can't use page flipping when running in a window. Instead use *double buffering*, in which you compose a frame in the secondary surface and blit it to the primary surface. Also, include a page-flipping full-screen mode just like we have done in this book. If you wish to display a dialog box in full-screen mode, you will need to call the DirectDraw function `FlipToGDISurface` before creating the dialog box, and you will need to turn off page flipping while the dialog box is being displayed. This is a challenging proposition because it involves learning to become a real Windows programmer.

◎ Use DirectPlay to make this a two-player game: fly head-to-head with a second plane flying in the opposite direction. A few years ago most game companies were writing their own network-play code using WinSock, but DirectPlay has been steadily improving over the last few releases of DirectX to the point where you might actually want to consider it. It takes care of a lot of the repetitive work for you, including creating a lobby where you can join games in progress. This is a challenging proposition because again it involves reading the DirectX documentation yourself.

The following extensions are covered in supplementary material in the next two appendices:

◎ Upgrade the graphics from 640x480x8 to higher resolutions and color modes. Of course, you will have to find an artist to redo all of the artwork, but the result will be impressive. Appendix B describes a high-color, high-resolution version of Demo 4.

◎ Display an AVI movie during the intro sequence instead of a sequence of still images, and play MIDI music during all of the levels. Of course, you will need to find an artist to create the AVI movie and a musician to write MIDI music. Although there are mechanical means of composing MIDI music, it is inferior to that composed by a talented human musician. AVI movies and MIDI music can be played easily from the Windows API, but MIDI music can be played better using DirectMusic. We will cover AVI movies using the Windows API and MIDI music using DirectMusic in Appendix C, which describes how to add this code to the version of Demo 4 from Appendix B.

Here's what you'll learn:

- How to read in a high-color image

- How to change the resolution and color depth in DirectDraw

- How to do transparent blitting in high-color mode

- How to organize your code so that the player can change the resolution and color depth

High Color and Resolution

One thing that you will probably want to do in your game is to use a higher resolution and a higher color depth than I've shown you in *Ned's Turkey Farm*. Changing the resolution is no problem—at least for the programmer. All you have to do is change the definitions of `SCREEN_WIDTH` and `SCREEN_HEIGHT` in `Defines.h`. High color is less trivial, but happily it is easier than the code we've seen so far for 8-bit color because the Windows API functions that you use to read the image file into the bmp file reader will transform the image in size and color depth if you let it. However, it is lousy at transforming to 8-bit color, so if you want to support multiple color depths, you are better off having your artist make two versions of your artwork, one in 24-bit color, and one in 8-bit color using a custom palette. Fortunately, almost every art tool in existence is better than the Windows API at producing 8-bit color images from high-color ones. You'll have to use the Windows API to transform 24-bit color images to 16-bit color because there is no 16-bit bmp file format, but that's no problem because it is pretty good at it. However, it is possible for an artist to produce an art file that looks great in 24-bit color and awful in 16-bit color—`Test.bmp` is one of them (more about that in a moment).

Demo 4a is a version of Demo 4 that lets you experiment with various resolutions, color modes, and backgrounds. It is based around a new version of `CBmpFileReader` called `CBmpFileReader2`, which is intended to replace both `CBmpFileReader` and `CBmpSpriteFileReader`. One of our biggest problems is setting the transparent color, because DirectDraw requires that the transparent color be expressed as a `DWORD` value in the screen's current color depth. Rather than writing a special piece of code for each possible color depth, I've provided a sneaky piece of code that will map any RGB value to a `DWORD` value by exploiting the eagerness of the Windows API to remap colors for us.

I chose to add high color and resolution code to Demo 4 because I want primarily to illustrate the *process* of adding these features to a game engine. To do the same for *your* game, you only need to borrow my `CBmpFileReader2` and transparency code, and make similar changes to integrate it with the rest of your game engine. Demo 4 was the simplest version of the game engine that it makes sense to add this code to—simple is good in this case because it means that you have the smallest code base to wade through, saving paper, space, and time.

Experiment with Demo 4a

Take a moment now to run Demo 4a.

- You should see the picture shown in Figure B.1. The photograph in the background was taken by the author in November 1999 in the Glasshouse Mountains just north of Brisbane, Australia. It starts out in 640x480 resolution and 16-bit color.

- Hit the Spacebar to change the screen resolution. It should cycle between 640x480, 800x600, and 1024x768 pixels, assuming that your video card supports all three of these resolutions in 16-bit color (if not, it will skip the resolutions that are missing). Notice that the higher the resolution, the better the background looks.

- Hit the Enter key to change the color depth. It should cycle from 16-bit color to 24-bit, 32-bit, and 8-bit color, assuming that your video card supports all of these color modes in the resolution that you have selected (if not, it will skip the color modes that are missing). Note that some video cards support one but not both 24-bit and 32-bit color.

- Notice that we are using a single 1024x768 24-bit background image called Ghouse1.bmp and letting the Windows API functions transform it to the correct resolution and color depth. It does a pretty good job for the higher color modes, but
  - 8-bit color is terrible
  - 16-bit color is good
  - 24-bit color is better than 16-bit color, if you have a good monitor and a good pair of eyes
  - 32-bit color is identical to 24-bit color (take my word for it)

- Although 16-bit color is almost as good as 24-bit or 32-bit color for the background file Ghouse1.bmp, it is alarmingly easy for an artist to produce something that looks great under 24-bit color but terrible under 16-bit color. For example, use the Enter key to enter 24- or 32-bit color mode, then hit the "I" key to change the background image to Test.bmp. In 24- or 32-bit color mode it looks like Figure B.2 or better, but in 16-bit mode it looks like Figure B.3, with a series of concentric circles reminiscent of a "Looney Tunes" cartoon—and 8-bit color looks even worse. Set your monitor to 24- or 32-bit color before viewing Figures B.2 and B.3; otherwise they will look annoyingly the same. They may also look the same on the following page—in which case you are flat out of luck because print technology is way behind monitor technology.

- Notice the changes in frame rate when you change resolution or color depth. The higher the resolution and color depth, the lower the frame rate will be, for the simple reason that we are moving more data to the video card. If you look carefully, you will see that the frame rate decreases in jumps. Sometimes increasing the resolution or color depth won't change the frame rate at all. This is because Demo 4a was originally spending a lot of its time waiting for a page flip to occur (which happens at the vertical retrace), and there was enough slack time there to accommodate an increase in resolution or color depth. However, increasing it again will probably cause the frame rate to drop by a large amount, as we again are spending a lot of time waiting for the next page flip. One way to reduce this quantization of frame rate is to use more than one back buffer.

- Hit the Esc key to exit the program.

Figure B.1
The initial screen for Demo 4a, in 640x480 resolution and 16-bit color

Figure B.2
The background file Test.bmp in 32-bit color

Figure B.3
The background file Test.bmp in 16-bit color. Notice the "Looney Tunes" concentric circles effect.

The New Bmp File Reader Class

New Bmp File Reader Overview

The header file for the high-color version of the bmp file reader class `CBmpFileReader2` is `Bmp2.h`. It has three protected member functions. The first is a handle to a bitmap, which we will use to store the image. The other two member variables are the width and height of the image measured in pixels, which we will read directly from the file:

```
HBITMAP m_hBitmap; //bitmap
int m_nFileWidth,m_nFileHeight; //file height and width
```

It has six public member functions, beginning with a constructor and a destructor:

```
CBmpFileReader2(); //constructor
~CBmpFileReader2(); //destructor
```

The next three functions are variants of the `draw` function. The first variant draws the image to a given `surface`, assuming that the latter is the same size as the screen (designed with the secondary surface in mind), scaling the image if necessary.

```
BOOL draw(LPDIRECTDRAWSURFACE surface); //draw image
```

The second variant draws from a rectangle in the image of a width w and height h with top left pixel at position (x, y) to the `surface`, without scaling. This function replaces the bmp sprite file reader class `CBmpSpriteFileReader`.

```
BOOL draw(LPDIRECTDRAWSURFACE surface,int w,int h,
    int x,int y); //draw image
```

The third variant scales as it draws, drawing to a rectangle of width w1 and height w2 from a rectangle of width w1 and height h1 with top left pixel at position (x, y) in the image. This variant does the actual work, and is called by the other two variants.

```
BOOL draw(LPDIRECTDRAWSURFACE surface,int w1,int h1,
    int w2,int h2,int x,int y); //draw image
```

Finally, the `load` function loads the image from a file with a given `filename`.

```
BOOL load(char *filename); //load from file
```

The Constructor and Destructor

The `CBmpFileReader2` constructor sets the member variables to sensible initial values.

```
CBmpFileReader2::CBmpFileReader2(){ //constructor
  m_hBitmap=NULL; m_nFileWidth=m_nFileHeight=0;
}
```

The destructor reclaims the image bitmap memory by calling the Windows API function `DeleteObject`.

```
CBmpFileReader2::~CBmpFileReader2(){ //destructor
  if(m_hBitmap)DeleteObject(m_hBitmap);
}
```

The Draw Functions

The `draw` functions draw the image from the bitmap to a DirectDraw surface. The first two variants call the third one to do the actual work, and are quite obvious.

```
BOOL CBmpFileReader2::draw(LPDIRECTDRAWSURFACE surface){
//draw whole image scaled from (0,0) to screen-sized surface
  return draw(surface,g_nScreenWidth,g_nScreenHeight,
    m_nFileWidth,m_nFileHeight,0,0);
}

BOOL CBmpFileReader2::draw(LPDIRECTDRAWSURFACE surface,
                          int w,int h,int x,int y){
//draw unscaled rectangle of this width and height from location
  return draw(surface,w,h,w,h,x,y);
}
```

The third variant of `draw` is the important one.

```
BOOL CBmpFileReader2::draw(LPDIRECTDRAWSURFACE surface,
                   int w1,int h1,int w2,int h2,int x,int y){
```

It begins with two device context handles. A *device context* is what the Windows API uses to draw to things. We've avoided using it so far because it is slow and has often-inconvenient side effects. The speed concern is not really an issue here, since we will use this function very infrequently—once when reading in the image, and again when restoring surfaces, changing screen resolution, or changing the screen color depth, all of which are relatively infrequent occurrences.

```
HDC hDCSurface,hDCBitmap; //device contexts for surface, bitmap
```

We get a device context for the DirectDraw `surface` provided as a parameter, and store it in the local variable `hDCSurface`.

```
surface->GetDC(&hDCSurface);
```

Next, we get a compatible device context for our bitmap. What does *compatible* mean? We want a device context that is compatible with the device context for the DirectDraw surface, which we stored in hDCSurface, so that we can use Windows API functions to draw from one to the other correctly. If the device contexts were not compatible, bad things would happen if we were to try. We do this by calling the Windows API function CreateCompatibleDC, storing the result in local variable hDCBitmap.

```
hDCBitmap=CreateCompatibleDC(hDCSurface);
```

Having done this, we set the *mapping mode* of the bitmap's device context to be the same as that of the surface, which of course reflects the video card's current settings. The mapping mode is the relationship between the logical units and the video card's device units—something that the device context needs to know before we can use certain Windows API functions.

```
SetMapMode(hDCBitmap,GetMapMode(hDCSurface));
```

Thus far the bitmap device context knows nothing about the bitmap, so next we attach the bitmap m_hBitmap to the bitmap via the device context handle hDCBitmap using the Windows API function SelectObject.

```
SelectObject(hDCBitmap,m_hBitmap);
```

We use the Windows API function SetStretchBltMode to set the stretch mode to COLORONCOLOR, which allows the scaling of color images by duplicating or deleting rows and columns of pixels.

```
SetStretchBltMode(hDCSurface,COLORONCOLOR);
```

Everything up to this point in the function has been preparation. Now we use the Windows API function StretchBlt to draw the image from its device context hDCBitmap to the device context of the surface, hDCSurface. The final parameter SRCCOPY ensures that it merely copies the source to the destination. The remaining parameters are rectangle origins and sizes.

```
StretchBlt(hDCSurface,0,0,w1,h1,hDCBitmap,x,y,w2,h2,SRCCOPY);
```

Finally, we clean up by deleting the bitmap device context and releasing the surface device context.

```
DeleteDC(hDCBitmap);
surface->ReleaseDC(hDCSurface);
```

This function always returns TRUE; I recommend that you write some error detection code that returns FALSE if one of the above operations fails.

```
return TRUE; //need to write error detection code here
}
```

The Load Function

The load function loads the image from a file with the given filename.

```
BOOL CBmpFileReader2::load(char *filename){ //load from file
```

It begins by unloading any old bitmap that may have been previously loaded.

```
if(m_hBitmap){DeleteObject(m_hBitmap); m_hBitmap=NULL;};
```

We then load the image to the member variable m_hBitmap using the Windows API function LoadImage. This function has six parameters. The first parameter is an instance handle, which can safely be left NULL. The second parameter is the name of the file to be read. The third parameter specifies that a bitmap file is to be read (LoadImage can also be used to load icons and cursors). The fourth and fifth parameters are the desired bitmap width and height, which are set to the actual width and height of the file image if we use zeros. The last parameter is a flag. We use the flags LR_LOADFROMFILE (the alternative is to load from a resource, which is beyond the scope of this book) and LR_CREATEDIBSECTION (DIB stands for *device independent bitmap*, which ensures that the image is not remapped to the screen size and color depth—we want to do so when the image is drawn, not when it is loaded).

```
m_hBitmap=(HBITMAP)LoadImage(NULL,filename,IMAGE_BITMAP,0,0,
  LR_LOADFROMFILE|LR_CREATEDIBSECTION);
```

If the LoadImage fails, we bail out.

```
if(m_hBitmap==NULL)return FALSE;
```

Finally we get the image width and height and store them in the member variables m_nFileWidth and m_nFileHeight. This is done by using the Windows API function GetObject to get information about the image into a local BITMAP structure bm.

```
BITMAP bm; //bitmap info
GetObject(m_hBitmap,sizeof(bm),&bm); //get info
m_nFileWidth=bm.bmWidth; m_nFileHeight=bm.bmHeight;
return TRUE;
}
```

Changes to Defines.h

Changes to Defines.h include the deletion of some things that are not needed, the initial color depth setting being changed to 16-bit, and the setting of the transparent color to hot pink. Notice that the transparent color is now an RGB setting, not a palette position. We have yet to translate this to the DWORD value required by DirectDraw.

```
#define COLOR_DEPTH 16 //number of bits to store colors
#define TRANSPARENT_COLOR RGB(254,0,254) //transparent color
```

Changes to the Base Sprite and Object Classes

Changes to the base sprite class `CBaseSprite` in `Bsprite.h` and
`Bsprite.cpp` are minimal. They involve the use of the new bmp file reader
`CBmpFileReader2` in place of `CBmpSpriteFileReader` in the
`CBaseSprite load` function, and the use of a global variable `g_dwTransparentColor` for the transparent color in place of the constant declaration used
in Demo 4.

Changes to the object class `CObject` are likewise minimal, and involve the use
of global variables `g_nScreenWidth` and `g_nScreenHeight` for the screen
width and height in place of the constant declarations used in Demo 4.

You can see these changes for yourself in the code listings.

Changes to Ddsetup.cpp

There are three things that you should take note of in the new version of
`Ddsetup.cpp`. The first is that all of the palette code has been removed—there
is no longer any reference to the primary and secondary palettes, and function
`CreatePalette` has been deleted. The second is that it is now much more complicated to set up the transparent color than it was in Demo 4, because rather than
supplying a transparent palette position, DirectDraw requires that we specify the
transparent color as a `DWORD` value that represents the transparent color in whatever color mode the screen happens to be in. Rather than writing a separate piece
of code for each color mode, I will give you a piece of code that finds out what the
encoding is by using the propensity of the Windows API graphics functions to
remap colors for you while you're not looking. This is done using a new function
`color`, which takes two parameters, the first of which is the RGB value of the
transparent color, and the second of which is a pointer to a surface. It returns a
`DWORD` representing the color in the current color mode:

```
DWORD color(COLORREF rgb,LPDIRECTDRAWSURFACE surface){
```

It begins with the declaration of a `DWORD` value `dw` for the result, a holder `rgbT` to
temporarily hold a color value for us, a device context handle `hdc`, a DirectDraw
surface descriptor `ddsd`, and an `HRESULT` variable `hres`:

```
DWORD dw=CLR_INVALID; //color in DWORD form
COLORREF rgbT; //old color
HDC hdc; //device context
DDSURFACEDESC ddsd; //surface descriptor
HRESULT hres; //result
```

We get a device context for the surface so that we can use Windows API graphics functions on it:

```
if(rgb!=CLR_INVALID&&SUCCEEDED(surface->GetDC(&hdc))){
```

If successful, we use the Windows API function `GetPixel` to get the RGB value of the first pixel (coordinates `(0,0)`) on the surface, which we store temporarily in local variable `rgbT`:

```
rgbT=GetPixel(hdc,0,0); //save current pixel value
```

We use the opposite Windows API function `SetPixel` to set the first pixel on the surface to the transparent color `rgb` that we received as a parameter. `SetPixel` "automagically" remaps the color to the correct value for the current color mode—for example, if the screen is in 16-bit color mode, it remaps it from the 24-bit RGB value to a 16-bit color.

```
SetPixel(hdc,0,0,rgb); //set our value
```

Having successfully modified the first pixel on the surface, we release the device context:

```
surface->ReleaseDC(hdc); //release surface dc
}
```

We then lock down the surface—or rather, we attempt to lock it down until we succeed:

```
ddsd.dwSize=sizeof(ddsd);
while((hres=surface->Lock(NULL,&ddsd,0,NULL))
  ==DDERR_WASSTILLDRAWING); //keep trying
```

We check that we did in fact succeed:

```
if(SUCCEEDED(hres)){ //succeeded at last
```

We set `dw` to the first 32 bits on the surface, utilizing the `lpSurface` pointed to in the DirectDraw surface descriptor `ddsd` that was filled in by the `Lock` function call.

```
dw=*(DWORD *)ddsd.lpSurface; //get DWORD
```

If we are in 32-bit color mode, we are done. Otherwise, `dw` contains more data than we need—for example, if we are in 16-bit color mode, it contains the 16-bit color values for the first two pixels. We need to mask off the pixel that we are interested in.

```
if(ddsd.ddpfPixelFormat.dwRGBBitCount!=32) //no mask
```

This is done by performing a bitwise AND of `dw` with a mask with as many ones in it as our current color depth. The current color depth is contained in

```
ddsd.ddpfPixelFormat.dwRGBBitCount,
```

and the mask is obtained by left-shifting 1 by this amount, and subtracting one from it:

```
(1<ddsd.ddpfPixelFormat.dwRGBBitCount)-1.
```

The mask is then applied like this:

```
dw&=(1<ddsd.ddpfPixelFormat.dwRGBBitCount)-1; //mask
```

It may initially seem confusing that we are using the mask to obtain the least-significant bits of `dw`, when in fact we are interested in the first pixel. This is because of the architecture of the Intel chipset, in which integers are stored least-significant byte first. Now that we have finished reading from the surface, we unlock it.

```
surface->Unlock(NULL);
}
```

Finally, we write back the first pixel, which we temporarily stored in `rgbT`. For this application we needn't bother—it will be overwritten very quickly anyway—but a careful programmer will handle this unimportant detail just in case the code is ever reused in another project.

```
if(rgb!=CLR_INVALID&&SUCCEEDED(surface->GetDC(&hdc))){
  SetPixel(hdc,0,0,rgbT); //replace old value
  surface->ReleaseDC(hdc); //release surface dc
}
```

Having tidied up the surface, we return `dw`.

```
return dw;
}
```

The third thing to notice in `Ddsetup.cpp` is that the new version of `InitDirectDraw`, called `InitDirectDraw2`, is a lot shorter than the old version. This is because all of the code after the call to `SetDisplayMode` has been moved to a new function `InitSurfaces` so that it can also be called after the screen resolution or color depth is changed by the user, since changing either will create the need for new, differently sized or differently colored surfaces. Other, more minor changes involve the use of global variables for the screen height, width, and color depth (as previously mentioned), and the call to the new function `color` while setting the transparent color.

Changes to Main.cpp

The first changes that you may notice in Main.cpp are relatively minor; these include the modified header file inclusion and declarations for the use of the new CBmpFileReader2 class instead of CBmpFileReader and CBmpSprite-FileReader, and the addition of frame rate measuring code. There is a new function PutText which uses the Windows API function DrawText to draw text to the screen. It is used in ComposeFrame to draw the screen resolution, color depth, and frame rate to the top right corner of the screen, along with a reminder of which keys to hit. There are also three new cases to the switch statement in the keyboard handler for the Enter key, the Spacebar, and the "I" key.

The most visible change to Main.cpp involves a fairly intricate reorganization of the code for managing surfaces. Figure B.4 shows the new pattern of function calls associated with the care and feeding of DirectDraw surfaces in Main.cpp and Ddsetup.cpp, with a box corresponding to each function, and an arrow drawn from box A to box B whenever function A calls function B. The two gray boxes are for functions ResetColorDepth and ResetResolution which are called whenever the user hits the appropriate key to change the color depth and resolution, respectively—these functions are the primary reason for the reorganization of function calls in Demo 4a. The two heavily outlined boxes at top left correspond to WinMain and WindowProc, which are the two entry points from the operating system into our application. The boxes with drop shadows (for example, ReleaseSurfaces at the top right of the figure) correspond to terminal functions, that is, functions that don't call any other function.

Functions ResetColorDepth and ResetResolution both follow a simple pattern. After doing their respective things, they must release all of the DirectDraw surfaces currently in use, create new surfaces with the correct color depth or resolution, and redraw the images from the CBmpFileReader2 class instances to the new surfaces. The code for releasing the DirectDraw surfaces was in the WM_DESTROY case in WindowProc in Demo 4. We move this code to a new function ReleaseSurfaces which is called from a new function (created for enhanced readability) named ShutDownDirectDraw, a call to which replaces the corresponding code in WindowProc. The code for creating new surfaces was in function InitDirectDraw in Ddsetup.cpp; as noted at the end of the previous section, it was moved to a new function InitSurfaces, now called from InitDirectDraw2. In Demo 4, the code for drawing images from the file readers to the surfaces was interleaved with the code for reading it from files into the file readers. In Demo 4a, however, we need only redraw it from the file readers to the new surfaces when changing the color depth and screen resolution—there is no need to reread them from the files.

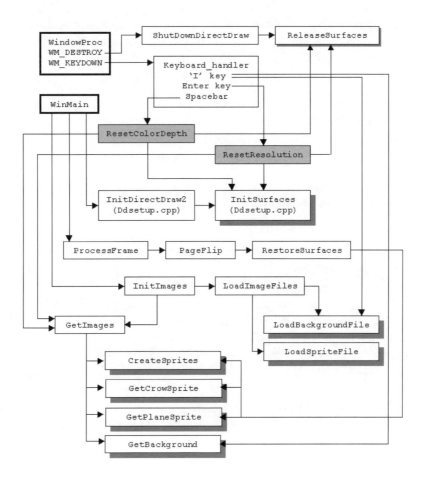

Figure B.4
Function calls
from Main.cpp
and
Ddsetup.cpp
in Demo 4a

Therefore, the following reorganization took place. The process of reading images from the files into the file readers is handled by function `LoadImageFiles` which calls functions `LoadBackgroundFile` and `LoadSpriteFile`, the former of which is also called from the keyboard handler when the user hits the "I" key to change the background image. The process of drawing images from the file readers into the surfaces is handled by function `GetImages` which calls `CreateSprites` to create new sprite surfaces, and `GetCrowSprite`, `GetPlaneSprite`, and `GetBackground` to draw the corresponding images to their respective surfaces. Of these four functions, the former three are also called from `RestoreSurfaces`, and the latter one is also called from the keyboard handler when the user hits the "I" key.

Once this reorganization has taken place, function `ResetColorDepth` is defined as follows:

```
BOOL ResetColorDepth(){
```

It has two local variables, nNewColorDepth which stores the new color depth, and succeeded which will be TRUE if the color depth was changed successfully:

```
int nNewColorDepth;
BOOL succeeded=FALSE;
```

We start with the new color depth nNewColorDepth set to the current color depth from the global variable g_nColorDepth, and we will attempt to increment it to the next legal color depth:

```
nNewColorDepth=g_nColorDepth;
```

A while loop keeps attempting new color depths until we have successfully found one that is supported by the video card:

```
while(!succeeded){
```

Within the while loop we use a switch statement to increment the color depth to the next candidate:

```
switch(nNewColorDepth){
  case 8:  nNewColorDepth=16; break;
  case 16: nNewColorDepth=24; break;
  case 24: nNewColorDepth=32; break;
  case 32: nNewColorDepth=8; break;
  default: nNewColorDepth=16; break;
}
```

We then attempt to set the display mode. If this fails (for example, some video cards support 32-bit but not 24-bit color), we take another iteration of the while loop and try the next color depth:

```
  succeeded=
    SUCCEEDED(lpDirectDrawObject->SetDisplayMode(
      g_nScreenWidth,g_nScreenHeight,nNewColorDepth));
}
```

We exit the loop with a new color depth in place, update the global color depth variable g_nColorDepth, and go through the procedure described above: releasing all surfaces with ReleaseSurfaces, creating new surfaces with InitSurfaces, and drawing images from the file readers to the surfaces with GetImages:

```
  g_nColorDepth=nNewColorDepth;
  ReleaseSurfaces();
  InitSurfaces(g_hwnd);
  GetImages(); //reload the images from file reader
  return TRUE;
}
```

Function `ResetResolution` performs the corresponding sequence of operations to change the screen resolution, with local variables `nNewWidth` and `nNewHeight` playing the role of `nNewColorDepth`. It tries the following sequence of resolutions in turn: 640x480, 800x600, and 1024x768: the higher resolutions may not be supported at higher color depths due to lack of video memory. Demo 4a starts at 640x480x16 because most video cards support this mode.

Demo 4a Files

Code Files

The following files in Demo 4a are used without change from Demo 4:

- Csprite.h
- Csprite.cpp
- Objects.h
- Timer.h
- Timer.cpp

The following files in Demo 4a have been modified from Demo 4:

- Bsprite.h
- Bsprite.cpp
- Ddsetup.cpp
- Defines.h
- Main.cpp
- Objects.cpp

The following files are new in Demo 4a:

- Bmp2.h
- Bmp2.cpp

Media Files

The following image files are new in Demo 4a:

- Test.bmp
- Ghouse1.bmp

Required Libraries

- Ddraw.lib
- Winmm.lib

Here's what you'll learn:

- How to play AVI movies using MCI function calls

- Why choose MIDI music

- How to play MIDI music using DirectMusic

AVI Movies and MIDI Music

Once you have a simple game prototype up and running you should try adding some more sophisticated multimedia to it. It is relatively easy to use MCI function calls from the Windows API to play an AVI movie during the intro sequence instead of a sequence of still images. MIDI music can also be played easily using the Windows API, but it can be played better using DirectMusic. What do I mean by "better"? Better in two ways. Firstly, when you play MIDI music from the API you will typically get a hiccup in your game when the MIDI player starts and stops. The DirectMusic MIDI player that we will see in this appendix will not share this fault. Secondly, the API MIDI player will sound different from one wave table sound card to another, because different sound cards and different media players will load different instrument sounds. DirectMusic will load a default instrument set that will enable your music to sound the same (or as close to it as the hardware will allow) on any computer.

This appendix will add code for AVI movies and MIDI music to Demo 4a from Appendix B to create Demo 4b.

Experiment with Demo 4b

Take a moment now to run Demo 4b.

- Observe the intro animation that runs at the start of the game. It is not hard-coded—it is a movie in AVI format that is played before the game engine. Notice that it has a sound track that plays along with the animation.
- Listen to the MIDI music that starts when the intro movie ends.
- Hit the "I" key and hear the music change to a second composition when the background image changes. This is what you will do when changing levels in your game.
- Hit the "M" key to stop and restart the MIDI music.
- Hit the Esc key to exit the program.

- Restart Demo 4b and hit a key while the intro movie is running. What happens?
- After exiting Demo 4b, in the Windows Explorer double-click on the file `Intro.avi` to watch the intro movie using the default media player in your Windows installation.
- After exiting Demo 4b, in the Windows Explorer double-click on the file `Music1.mid` to listen to the music using the default MIDI player in your Windows installation. Repeat with `Music2.mid`. Notice that they sound different than when they are played in Demo 4b.
- If you can, run Demo 4b on two computers with different wave table sound cards. Notice that the music will sound almost identical, even though it may sound radically different from one machine to the other when played from the Explorer using the default MIDI player.

Playing AVI Movies

One of the first changes you will notice in `Main.cpp` is a new global variable `g_hInstance` to hold the instance handle. We'll need this to play AVI movies. It is set during the first few lines of `WinMain`.

```
HINSTANCE g_hInstance; //instance handle
```

Other new global variables needed for movie playing are the following. The first is `g_bPlayingMovie`, which we will set to TRUE while a movie is playing. This is required because we will be using the Windows API to play the movie and must disable page flipping while the movie is running.

```
BOOL g_bPlayingMovie=TRUE; //TRUE if playing a movie
```

The second new global variable is a handle to an MCI window, which is the window in which the movie will be played. MCI stands for *Media Control Interface*, a part of the Windows multimedia platform SDK.

```
HWND g_MCIHand;  // handle to MCI window (for AVI movie)
```

Function `PlayMovie` takes one parameter, a filename, and plays a movie from that file. It plays the movie asynchronously, that is, the function returns before the movie is finished.

```
void PlayMovie(char *filename){ //play the movie
```

We begin by blackening the primary surface. I've noticed that on older, slower machines, AVI movies are slow to fire up, and the player is left looking for a significant fraction of a second at a primary surface that occasionally contains some graphical garbage that looks ugly. Blackening the primary surface first will reduce the ugliness. We start by creating a blit effects data structure ddBltFx, initializing it, and setting its dwFillColor field to zero (the color black).

```
DDBLTFX ddBltFx; //blit fx structure
ZeroMemory(&ddBltFx,sizeof(DDBLTFX)); //zero it
ddBltFx.dwSize=sizeof(DDBLTFX); //set size
ddBltFx.dwFillColor=0; //black fill
```

We then call the primary surface's Blt function with a DDBLT_COLORFILL flag to fill the primary surface using the settings in ddBltFx.

```
lpPrimary->Blt(NULL,NULL,NULL,DDBLT_COLORFILL,&ddBltFx); //fill
```

That done, we create a movie window and load the movie file into it using the MCI function MCIWndCreate. The MCIWNDF_NOTIFYMODE and MCIWNDF_NOTIFYMEDIA flags specify that it should send our app messages whenever a device changes modes or a data file is opened or closed. The MCIWNDF_NOMENU and MCIWNDF_NOPLAYBAR flags indicate that we don't want a menu bar or a playbar, that is, we just want the movie playing on an otherwise blank screen.

```
g_MCIHand=MCIWndCreate(g_hwnd,g_hInstance,
  MCIWNDF_NOTIFYMODE|MCIWNDF_NOTIFYMEDIA|
  MCIWNDF_NOMENU|MCIWNDF_NOPLAYBAR,filename);
```

Finally, we start playing the movie by calling the MCI function MCIWndPlay, and then return.

```
  MCIWndPlay(g_MCIHand); // play it
}
```

Function KillMovie will kill the currently playing movie. It checks to see that one is playing, and if so, it kills it by calling the MCI function MCIWndDestroy. We will use this function to let the player click out of the movie early.

```
void KillMovie(){ //stop the movie
  if(g_MCIHand){ //if valid handle
    MCIWndDestroy(g_MCIHand); g_MCIHand=NULL; //kill it
  }
}
```

We will want to delay starting the actual game until after the movie has played. A new function StartLevel handles the starting of the game after the movie has finished, which may happen either when the player clicks out of the movie or when it runs to completion. It begins by calling KillMovie to kill the movie (which will have no effect if it is already over), then setting g_bPlayingMovie to FALSE.

```
void StartLevel(){ //start playing a level
  KillMovie(); //kill movie
  g_bPlayingMovie=FALSE; //movie is off
```

It then does some MIDI stuff that we will return to in a later section.

```
g_cMidiPlayer.Load("music1.mid");
g_cMidiPlayer.Play();
}
```

A small change to the keyboard handler function is needed to let the player click out of the movie. The following `if` statement is inserted in front of the main `switch` statement in function `keyboard_handler`.

```
if(g_bPlayingMovie)StartLevel(); else
```

We also want to call `StartLevel` when the movie is over. This is done by adding a handler for the `MCIWNDM_NOTIFYMODE` message to the `switch` statement in `WindowProc`. This message is sent by the MCI movie player whenever the movie player changes mode. The message's `lParam` contains information on the mode change that we are being notified of: here, we are interested in `MCI_MODE_STOP`. If we get it, we call `StartLevel`:

```
case MCIWNDM_NOTIFYMODE:
  if((int)lParam==MCI_MODE_STOP) //if movie over
    StartLevel(); //start game engine
  break;
```

To start the movie playing, we insert the following line of code in `WinMain` immediately before the message loop:

```
PlayMovie("intro.avi");
```

Finally, to prevent page flipping while the movie is playing, we change the call to `ProcessFrame` in the message loop from:

```
if(ActiveApp)ProcessFrame();
```

to:

```
if(ActiveApp&&!g_bPlayingMovie)ProcessFrame();
```

AVI Movies and DirectX

If you want to get more sophisticated with AVI movies than we have done in this appendix, try using the DirectDraw video ports in the DirectDraw 7 object. Stunning effects can be obtained by using Direct3D to map a movie onto a texture map on a polygon that rotates and moves in 3D space. For more control over the movie player, the MCI commands described in the previous section have been replaced with an API called DirectShow.

One last note on movies before we move on to MIDI music: Demo 4b is perhaps a little too simplistic in that it doesn't use DirectSound. You may be tempted to use the technique outlined in this section to play movies between levels of your game (these are called *cut-scenes* in the game industry). If so, be aware that DirectSound and MCI do not get along well. If you play a movie when DirectSound is active, the movie will not have any sound. If you attempt to initialize DirectSound while playing a movie, the initialization will fail. So, for playing cut-scenes you will need to shut down DirectSound, play the movie, then restart DirectSound.

The MIDI Music Player

The MIDI music player is encapsulated in a new class called `CDirectMidi`. This class encapsulates the code in Tutorial 1 in the DirectMusic documentation and corrects several typos found there. Before looking at the code, however, let's consider why we should play MIDI music in the first place.

The Pros and Cons of MIDI Music

Why are we even considering using MIDI music? DirectSound gave us the ability to play wave format sound files in Chapter 10, so why don't we just sample our music in wave format and play it from there? The biggest drawback to doing that is the size of the sampled music. Recall that digitally sampled sounds are typically played at 22KHz or above—that's 22,000 samples per second that have to be sent to the sound card. This slows the processor and clogs the bus, as well as taking up a lot of space in memory. You can alleviate the memory problem by streaming the sound from a file instead of loading it to memory the way we did in Chapter 10, but the load on the processor and the bus remains high.

Fortunately, modern sound cards have the hardware capability to play MIDI music. MIDI music is much more compact than sampled music because it merely records things analogous to the keys on a piano keyboard going up and down. You basically send "start note" and "stop note" messages to the sound card, and it takes care of making the appropriate noises. It can do this in one of two ways. With *FM synthesis*, oscillators on the sound card are used to generate what is essentially a set of sophisticated beeps that supposedly mimic the sound of real instruments playing. A *wave table* sound card is much more sophisticated: it contains a hardware table of digitally sampled sounds in wave format, one for the piano, one for the guitar, etc. Instead of using DirectSound to ship the sound of a guitar playing high C, for example, with MIDI music you simply tell the sound card to look up the sample in its table and play it, a massive savings in data transfer. Needless to say, a wave table sound card sounds immensely better than one that uses FM synthesis. These days, even cheap sound cards have a wave table. FM synthesis is mostly found on laptops, and even then, it is rapidly disappearing from that market.

So the pros to playing MIDI music are associated with data—less load on processor, bus, memory, and the CD that you use to ship your game. The obvious con is that MIDI music doesn't sound as good as digitally sampled music—not every guitar sounds alike, for example. Another possible drawback is that MIDI music can sound different on different wave table sound cards. DirectMusic helps us out here by allowing us to load a default set of instrument sounds into the wave table on the sound card (fortunately, a large number of wave table sound cards have this functionality), thus ensuring a large degree of conformity in sound from one computer to another.

Multithreading

DirectMusic will play MIDI music by spawning a separate thread that will run concurrently with your game. Although DirectMusic will take care of most of the details of multithreading for you, you will need to direct your compiler to use the multithreaded runtime libraries. To do this in Visual C++ 6.0, begin by selecting Settings from the Project menu as shown in Figure C.1.

Figure C.1
Selecting Settings from the Project menu

This will pop up the Project Settings dialog box. Select the C/C++ tab. Select Code Generation from the Category pull-down edit box, then select Multithreaded from the Use Run-time Library pull-down edit box, shown highlighted to the far right of Figure C.2. Be sure to do this for all configurations (Debug or Release) that you intend to use.

Figure C.2
The Project Settings dialog box

MIDI Music Player Overview

The header file for CDirectMidi is DirectMidi.h. The declaration of CDirectMidi begins with five private member variables. The first of these, m_bInitialized, will be set to TRUE if DirectMusic has been initialized correctly.

```
class CDirectMidi{ //DirectMusic MIDI class
private:
  BOOL m_bInitialized; //TRUE if initialized correctly
```

The next four private member variables are related to how DirectMusic views the performance of a piece of MIDI music. The DirectMusic music manager is called a *performance*. The first CDirectMidi private member variable is a pointer to a performance:

```
  IDirectMusicPerformance* m_pPerf; //performance
```

DirectMusic includes loaders for various music formats. The second CDirectMidi private member variable is a pointer to a loader:

```
  IDirectMusicLoader* m_pLoader; //loader
```

The DirectMusic analog of a surface for storing music is called a *segment*. The third CDirectMidi private member variable is a pointer to a MIDI segment, and the fourth is a pointer to a state variable that will report the playing state of that segment:

```
  IDirectMusicSegment* m_pMIDIseg; //midi segment
  IDirectMusicSegmentState* m_pSegState; //segment state
```

Next, we have three private member functions that will take care of setting up DirectMusic. Function CreatePerformance creates a performance and leaves a pointer to it in the private member variable m_pPerf. Function CreateLoader creates a MIDI loader and leaves a pointer to it in the private member variable m_pLoader. Function LoadMIDI Segment loads a MIDI file from the file named wszMidiFileName into a MIDI segment pointed to by the private member variable m_pMIDIseg.

```
  BOOL CreatePerformance(void); //create performance
  BOOL CreateLoader(void); //create MIDI loader
  BOOL LoadMIDISegment(char* wszMidiFileName); //create segment
```

The CDirectMidi public member functions begin with a constructor and a destructor:

```
public:
  CDirectMidi(); //constructor
  virtual ~CDirectMidi(); //destructor
```

Function `Load` loads a piece of MIDI music from a given `filename`:

```
void Load(char* filename); //load MIDI from file
```

Functions `Play` and `Stop` respectively play and stop the loaded MIDI music.

```
void Play(); //play loaded MIDI
void Stop(); //stop playing MIDI
```

Function `IsPlaying` returns TRUE if there is MIDI music currently playing.

```
BOOL IsPlaying(); //TRUE if playing
```

Finally, function `Toggle` toggles the playing state of the music: if it is playing, then it stops it; if it is not playing, then it starts it:

```
void Toggle(); //toggle stop/play
};
```

The Constructor and Destructor

The code file for `CDirectMidi` is `DirectMidi.cpp`. It begins with the definition of a macro to convert standard characters to wide characters. Wide characters are used in foreign language versions of apps, and DirectMusic functions are set up to require wide characters. This macro is taken verbatim from the DirectMusic documentation:

```
#define MULTI_TO_WIDE( x,y )  MultiByteToWideChar(CP_ACP,\
      MB_PRECOMPOSED,y,-1,x,_MAX_PATH);
```

The `CDirectMidi` constructor first sets default values for the private member variables:

```
CDirectMidi::CDirectMidi(){ //constructor
  //default values for member variables
  m_bInitialized=FALSE; //uninitialized
  m_pPerf=NULL; //performance
  m_pLoader=NULL; //loader
  m_pMIDIseg=NULL; //midi segment
  m_pSegState=NULL; //segment state
```

Next, it attempts to fire up DirectMusic. DirectMusic requires a more sophisticated approach to COM than we have so far used in this book. To initialize COM, we first need to call the `CoInitialize` COM function. As with all of the function calls in this constructor, we will bail out if it fails:

```
if(FAILED(CoInitialize(NULL)))return; //init COM
```

We create a default DirectMusic performance (which, recall, is the music manager):

```
if(FAILED(CreatePerformance()))return; //create performance
```

We then initialize the performance, and add the default port to it. A DirectMusic port corresponds to the hardware port on the sound card for the MIDI hardware.

```
if(FAILED(m_pPerf->Init(NULL,NULL,NULL)))return; //init it
if(FAILED(m_pPerf->AddPort(NULL)))return; //add default port
```

Finally, we create a MIDI loader.

```
if(FAILED(CreateLoader()))return; //create MIDIloader
```

If all of this succeeds, we record the fact in private member variable m_bInitialized and return.

```
    m_bInitialized=TRUE;
  }
```

The CDirectMidi destructor undoes all of this, in the reverse order of course.

```
CDirectMidi::~CDirectMidi(){ //destructor
```

It bails out if DirectMusic was not correctly initialized. Otherwise, it begins by stopping any music that is playing. This is not strictly necessary, since the music will stop anyway when DirectMusic is shut down.

```
if(!m_bInitialized)return; //bail if not ready
Stop(); //stop music (paranoia)
```

It unloads any instruments that were loaded:

```
m_pMIDIseg->SetParam(GUID_Unload,-1,0,0,(void*)m_pPerf);
```

Then, it releases the MIDI segment.

```
m_pMIDIseg->Release();
```

The performance is then shut down and released:

```
m_pPerf->CloseDown(); m_pPerf->Release();
```

The loader is released:

```
m_pLoader->Release();
```

Finally, we release COM and return.

```
  CoUninitialize();
}
```

Creating a Performance

The `CDirectMidi CreatePerformance` function creates a performance and stores a pointer to it in the private member variable `m_pPerf`. It does this by calling the COM function `CoCreateInstance`:

```
BOOL CDirectMidi::CreatePerformance(void){ //create performance
  return SUCCEEDED(CoCreateInstance(
    CLSID_DirectMusicPerformance,NULL,CLSCTX_INPROC,
    IID_IDirectMusicPerformance2,(void**)&m_pPerf));
}
```

Creating a Loader

The `CDirectMidi CreateLoader` function creates a loader and stores a pointer to it in the private member variable `m_pLoader`. Like `Create-Performance` above, it does this by calling the COM function `CoCreateInstance`:

```
BOOL CDirectMidi::CreateLoader(void){
  return SUCCEEDED(CoCreateInstance(CLSID_DirectMusicLoader,
    NULL,CLSCTX_INPROC,IID_IDirectMusicLoader,
    (void**)&m_pLoader));
}
```

The `CDirectMidi LoadMIDISegment` function loads a MIDI file. It has one parameter, a filename `szMidiFileName`.

```
BOOL CDirectMidi::LoadMIDISegment(char* szMidiFileName){
```

It has three local variables, the first of which is a DirectMusic object descriptor `ObjDesc`.

```
DMUS_OBJECTDESC ObjDesc;
```

The DirectMusic loader must be pointed to a directory from which it loads the music. We will use the current directory. The local variable `szDir` will be used to store the name of the current directory as a string.

```
char szDir[_MAX_PATH];
```

A call to the Windows API function `_getcwd` gets the name of the current directory into `szDir`; the second parameter is the size of the string buffer `szDir`.

```
if(_getcwd(szDir,_MAX_PATH)==NULL)return FALSE;
```

Next, we convert the name of the current directory from a normal character string in `szDir` to a wide character string in a new local variable `wszDir`, using the macro `MULTI_TO_WIDE` mentioned previously:

```
WCHAR wszDir[_MAX_PATH];
MULTI_TO_WIDE(wszDir,szDir);
```

Similarly, we convert the MIDI filename in parameter `szMidiFileName` to a wide character string in a new local variable `wszMidiFileName`:

```
WCHAR wszMidiFileName[_MAX_PATH];
MULTI_TO_WIDE(wszMidiFileName,szMidiFileName);
```

We set the loader pointed to by private member variable `m_pLoader` to the current directory:

```
HRESULT hr=m_pLoader->SetSearchDirectory(
  GUID_DirectMusicAllTypes,wszDir,FALSE);
if(FAILED(hr))return FALSE; //bail if failed
```

The DirectMusic object descriptor is used to describe a DirectMusic segment to be read from the file with wide filename `wszMidiFileName`:

```
ObjDesc.guidClass=CLSID_DirectMusicSegment;
ObjDesc.dwSize=sizeof(DMUS_OBJECTDESC);
wcscpy(ObjDesc.wszFileName,wszMidiFileName);
ObjDesc.dwValidData=DMUS_OBJ_CLASS|DMUS_OBJ_FILENAME;
```

We direct the loader to load that file to the MIDI segment pointed to by private member variable `m_pMIDIseg`:

```
m_pLoader->GetObject(&ObjDesc,
  IID_IDirectMusicSegment2,(void**)&m_pMIDIseg);
```

We set the segment to play as a standard MIDI file:

```
m_pMIDIseg->SetParam(GUID_StandardMIDIFile,
  -1,0,0,(void*)m_pPerf);
```

Finally, we load the default instrument set to the MIDI segment. This will load a standard set of instruments that sound the same on all wave table sound cards.

```
m_pMIDIseg->SetParam(GUID_Download,-1,0,0,(void*)m_pPerf);
return TRUE;
}
```

Loading, Playing, and Stopping

The `CDirectMidi Load` function is a public member function used to load a piece of MIDI music from a file. It starts by checking that DirectMusic was initialized correctly, bailing out if it wasn't:

```
void CDirectMidi::Load(char* filename){ //load file
  if(!m_bInitialized)return; //bail if not ready
```

There may already be MIDI music loaded; if so, it is unloaded:

```
//release old music
if(m_pMIDIseg){ //if there is old music, flush it
  m_pMIDIseg->Release(); m_pMIDIseg=NULL;
}
```

Finally, we are ready to call the private member function `LoadMIDISegment` to load the new MIDI music.

```
    LoadMIDISegment(filename);
}
```

The `CDirectMidi Play` function is a public member function that starts playing the loaded MIDI music at the beginning. Once again, it bails out if DirectMusic was not initialized correctly:

```
void CDirectMidi::Play(){ //play loaded music
  if(!m_bInitialized)return; //bail if not ready
```

Being completely paranoid, it checks that there is a MIDI segment and a performance:

```
    if(m_pMIDIseg&&m_pPerf){ //no bad pointers
```

If so, it sets the number of repeats of the MIDI segment to a very high number. You should expect to be playing a piece of MIDI music that is three to five minutes long. Even if it is only one minute long, setting the number of repeats to the maximum possible 32-bit unsigned integer, which in hexadecimal is `0xFFFFFFFF`, assures you of 4,294,967,295 minutes of playing time—more than 8,000 years:

```
    m_pMIDIseg->SetRepeats(0xFFFFFFFF); //repeat lotsa times
```

We then call the MIDI segment's `PlaySegment` function to begin playing:

```
    m_pPerf->PlaySegment(m_pMIDIseg,0,0,&m_pSegState); //play
    }
}
```

The `CDirectMidi Stop` function is a public member function that stops playing the current MIDI music. After checking for failure, it calls the performance object's `Stop` member function.

```
void CDirectMidi::Stop(){ //stop playing music
  if(!m_bInitialized)return; //bail if not ready
  if(m_pPerf)m_pPerf->Stop(NULL,NULL,0,0); //stop
}
```

Other Functions

Other `CDirectMidi` public member functions include `IsPlaying`, which interrogates the performance object to see whether music is currently playing:

```
BOOL CDirectMidi::IsPlaying(){ //TRUE if playing
  if(!m_bInitialized)return FALSE; //bail if not ready
  if(m_pPerf) //if loaded
    return m_pPerf->IsPlaying(m_pMIDIseg,NULL)==S_OK;
  else return FALSE;
}
```

Finally, the CDirectMidi Toggle function toggles the current music—if it is playing, then it stops it; otherwise, it starts it:

```
void CDirectMidi::Toggle(){ //toggle stop/play
  if(!m_bInitialized)return; //bail if not ready
  if(m_pPerf) //if loaded
    if(IsPlaying())Stop(); else Play(); //toggle
}
```

Changes to Main.cpp

The primary changes to Main.cpp include the declaration of a MIDI music player:

```
CDirectMidi g_cMidiPlayer; //midi player
```

As mentioned already, the StartLevel function has the following two lines of code which load the initial MIDI music file and begin playing it:

```
g_cMidiPlayer.Load("music1.mid");
g_cMidiPlayer.Play();
```

The keyboard handler keyboard_handler has new code added to case 'I' of its switch statement. Recall that this case changes the background image. When this happens, we will change the MIDI music to Music1.mid when the photographic background is displayed, and Music2.mid when the abstract background is displayed. First, we stop the old music:

```
g_cMidiPlayer.Stop(); //stop current music
```

Then we load a new piece of music, depending on which background image is displayed:

```
if(g_bGlassHouse) //select music file
  g_cMidiPlayer.Load("music1.mid");
else g_cMidiPlayer.Load("music2.mid");
```

Finally, we play the new music:

```
g_cMidiPlayer.Play(); //and play it
```

A new case is added for the "M" key, which toggles the music on and off:

```
case 'M':
  g_cMidiPlayer.Toggle(); //toggle music on/off
  break;
```

Demo 4b Files

Code Files

The following files in Demo 4b are used without change from Demo 4a:

- ◎ Bmp2.h
- ◎ Bmp2.cpp
- ◎ Bsprite.h
- ◎ Bsprite.cpp
- ◎ Csprite.h
- ◎ Csprite.cpp
- ◎ Defines.h
- ◎ Ddsetup.cpp
- ◎ Objects.h
- ◎ Objects.cpp
- ◎ Timer.h
- ◎ Timer.cpp

The following file in Demo 4b has been modified from Demo 4a:

- ◎ Main.cpp

The following files are new in Demo 4b:

- ◎ Directmidi.h
- ◎ Directmidi.cpp

Media Files

The following media files are new in Demo 4b:

- ◎ Intro.avi
- ◎ Music1.mid
- ◎ Music2.mid

Required Libraries

- ◎ Ddraw.lib
- ◎ Winmm.lib
- ◎ Dxguid.lib
- ◎ Vfw32.lib

Postscript

It's almost 9 P.M. in Denton, Texas. I've been teaching game programming for almost three hours into the evening of a long, long day. The students filter out of the classroom in small groups; some are elated, some subdued, some simply stunned. Tired, I wait for the last one to leave so I can go home and write code. He is very young, unsure of himself. Hesitatingly, he approaches me at the front of the classroom, unwilling to meet my eyes directly. Looking around quickly to make sure we are alone, he haltingly addresses me.

"Ummm, you know, the code you showed us tonight, the overall design... I've been thinking..." Red-faced, he searches for the right words and stumbles on.

"I wouldn't do it that way at all. If you do it *this* way it's much better... "

At the end of his explanation he meets my eyes, his shyness overcome for a moment by the need to show that his way of coding is not just *better*; it's elegant, it's logical, it makes everything fall into place. But he's still not completely sure I won't slap him down for Daring to Criticize The Professor.

But I smile. "Grasshopper," I say, "now it is time for you to leave."

For a moment he is taken aback, but then he smiles as he recognizes the mangled quote from a 1970s-era TV program that he has seen only in reruns.

So, Grasshopper, is it time for *you* to leave?

Index

About the CD

The companion CD-ROM contains the example game *Ned's Turkey Farm*, in addition to the DirectX 8.0 SDK and the code files in pdf format.

To load the game files, simply insert the CD into your CD drive. It should autorun. If it doesn't, open the CD drive with Explorer, double-click the Setup.exe icon, and follow the instructions.

To load the DirectX 8.0 SDK, be sure to check the DirectX check box in the final dialog box of the *Ned's Turkey Farm* setup.

For more information about the CD files, see Chapter 1.

Warning: Opening the CD package makes this book non-returnable.